HEADS OF FAMILIES

AT THE FIRST CENSUS OF THE
UNITED STATES TAKEN
IN THE YEAR
1790

RHODE ISLAND

Originally published: Government Printing Office
Washington, D.C., 1908
Reprinted: Genealogical Publishing Co., Inc.
Baltimore, 1966, 1977, 1992
Library of Congress Catalogue Card Number 66-5873
International Standard Book Number 0-8063-0341-7
Made in the United States of America

HEADS OF FAMILIES AT THE FIRST CENSUS
1790

INTRODUCTION.

The First Census of the United States (1790) comprised an enumeration of the inhabitants of the present states of Connecticut, Delaware, Georgia, Kentucky, Maine, Maryland, Massachusetts, New Hampshire, New Jersey, New York, North Carolina, Pennsylvania, Rhode Island, South Carolina, Tennessee, Vermont, and Virginia.

A complete set of the schedules for each state, with a summary for the counties, and in many cases for towns, was filed in the State Department, but unfortunately they are not now complete, the returns for the states of Delaware, Georgia, Kentucky, New Jersey, Tennessee, and Virginia having been destroyed when the British burned the Capitol at Washington during the War of 1812. For several of the states for which schedules are lacking it is probable that the Director of the Census could obtain lists which would present the names of most of the heads of families at the date of the First Census. In Virginia, state enumerations were made in 1782, 1783, 1784, and 1785, but the lists on file in the State Library include the names for only 39 of the 78 counties into which the state was divided.

The schedules of 1790 form a unique inheritance for the Nation, since they represent for each of the states concerned a complete list of the heads of families in the United States at the time of the adoption of the Constitution. The framers were the statesmen and leaders of thought, but those whose names appear upon the schedules of the First Census were in general the plain citizens who by their conduct in war and peace made the Constitution possible and by their intelligence and self-restraint put it into successful operation.

The total population of the United States in 1790, exclusive of slaves, as derived from the schedules was 3,231,533. The only names appearing upon the schedules, however, were those of heads of families, and as at that period the families averaged 6 persons, the total number was approximately 540,000, or slightly more than half a million. The number of names which is now lacking because of the destruction of the schedules is approximately 140,000, thus leaving schedules containing about 400,000 names.

The information contained in the published report of the First Census of the United States, a small volume of 56 pages, was not uniform for the several states and territories. For New England and one or two of the other states the population was presented by counties and towns; that of New Jersey appeared partly by counties and towns and partly by counties only; in other cases the returns were given by counties only. Thus the complete transcript of the names of heads of families, with accompanying information, presents for the first time detailed information as to the number of inhabitants—males, females, etc.—for each minor civil division in all those states for which such information was not originally published.

In response to repeated requests from patriotic societies and persons interested in genealogy, or desirous of studying the early history of the United States, Congress added to the sundry civil appropriation bill for the fiscal year 1907 the following paragraph:

The Director of the Census is hereby authorized and directed to publish, in a permanent form, by counties and minor civil divisions, the names of the heads of families returned at the First Census of the United States in seventeen hundred and ninety; and the Director of the Census is authorized, in his discretion, to sell said publications, the proceeds thereof to be covered into the Treasury of the United States, to be deposited to the credit of miscellaneous receipts on account of "Proceeds of sales of Government property:"

Provided, That no expense shall be incurred hereunder additional to appropriations for the Census Office for printing therefor made for the fiscal year nineteen hundred and seven; and the Director of the Census is hereby directed to report to Congress at its next session the cost incurred hereunder and the price fixed for said publications and the total received therefor.

The amount of money appropriated by Congress for the Census printing for the fiscal year mentioned was unfortunately not sufficient to meet the current requirement of the Office and to publish the transcription of the First Census, and no provision was made in the sundry civil appropriation bill for 1908 for the continuance of authority to publish these important records beyond the present fiscal year. Resources, however, were available for printing a small section of the work, and the schedules of New Hampshire, Vermont, and Maryland have been published.

The urgent deficiency bill, approved February 15, 1908, contained the following provision:

That the Director of the Census is hereby authorized and directed to expend so much of the appropriation for printing for the Department of Commerce and Labor allotted by law to the Census Office for the fiscal year ending June thirtieth, nineteen hundred and eight, as may be necessary to continue and complete the publication of the names of the heads of families returned at the First Census of the United States, as authorized by the sundry civil appropriation act approved June thirtieth, nineteen hundred and six.

In accordance with the authority given in the paragraph quoted above, the names returned at the First Census in the states of Connecticut, Maine, Massachusetts, New York, North Carolina, Pennsylvania, Rhode Island, and South Carolina have been published, thus completing the roster of the heads of families in 1790 so far as they can be shown from the records of the Census Office. As the Federal census schedules of the state of Virginia for 1790 are missing, the lists of the state enumerations made in 1782, 1783, 1784, and 1785 have been substituted and, while not complete, they will, undoubtedly, prove of great value.

THE FIRST CENSUS.

The First Census act was passed at the second session of the First Congress, and was signed by President Washington on March 1, 1790. The task of making the first enumeration of inhabitants was placed upon the President. Under this law the marshals of the several judicial districts were required to ascertain the number of inhabitants within their respective districts, omitting Indians not taxed, and distinguishing free persons (including those bound to service for a term of years) from all others; the sex and color of free persons; and the number of free males 16 years of age and over.

The object of the inquiry last mentioned was, undoubtedly, to obtain definite knowledge as to the military and industrial strength of the country. This fact possesses special interest, because the Constitution directs merely an enumeration of inhabitants. Thus the demand for increasingly extensive information, which has been so marked a characteristic of census legislation, began with the First Congress that dealt with the subject.

The method followed by the President in putting into operation the First Census law, although the object of extended investigation, is not definitely known. It is supposed that the President or the Secretary of State dispatched copies of the law, and perhaps of instructions also, to the marshals. There is, however, some ground for disputing this conclusion. At least one of the reports in the census volume of 1790 was furnished by a governor. This, together with the fact that there is no record of correspondence with the marshals on the subject of the census, but that there is a record of such correspondence with the governors, makes very strong the inference that the marshals re-

ceived their instructions through the governors of the states. This inference is strengthened by the fact that in 1790 the state of Massachusetts furnished the printed blanks, and also by the fact that the law relating to the Second Census specifically charged the Secretary of State to superintend the enumeration and to communicate directly with the marshals.

By the terms of the First Census law nine months were allowed in which to complete the enumeration. The census taking was supervised by the marshals of the several judicial districts, who employed assistant marshals to act as enumerators. There were 17 marshals. The records showing the number of assistant marshals employed in 1790, 1800, and 1810 were destroyed by fire, but the number employed in 1790 has been estimated at 650.

The schedules which these officials prepared consist of lists of names of heads of families; each name appears in a stub, or first column, which is followed by five columns, giving details of the family. These columns are headed as follows:

Free white males of 16 years and upward, including heads of families.
Free white males under 16 years.
Free white females, including heads of families.
All other free persons.
Slaves.

The assistant marshals made two copies of the returns; in accordance with the law one copy was posted in the immediate neighborhood for the information of the public, and the other was transmitted to the marshal in charge, to be forwarded to the President. The schedules were turned over by the President to the Secretary of State. Little or no tabulation was required, and the report of the First Census, as also the reports of the Second, Third, and Fourth, was produced without the employment of any clerical force, the summaries being transmitted directly to the printer. The total population as returned in 1790 was 3,929,214, and the entire cost of the census was $44,377.

A summary of the results of the First Census, not including the returns for South Carolina, was transmitted to Congress by President Washington on October 27, 1791. The legal period for enumeration, nine months, had been extended, the longest time consumed being eighteen months in South Carolina. The report of October 27 was printed in full, and published in what is now a very rare little volume; afterwards the report for South Carolina was "tipped in." To contain the results of the Twelfth Census, ten large quarto volumes, comprising in all 10,400 pages, were required. No illustration of the expansion of census inquiry can be more striking.

The original schedules of the First Census are now contained in 26 bound volumes, preserved in the Census Office. For the most part the headings of the schedules were written in by hand. Indeed, up to and

including 1820, the assistant marshals generally used for the schedules such paper as they happened to have, ruling it, writing in the headings, and binding the sheets together themselves. In some cases merchants' account paper was used, and now and then the schedules were bound in wall paper.

As a consequence of requiring marshals to supply their own blanks, the volumes containing the schedules vary in size from about 7 inches long, 3 inches wide, and ½ inch thick to 21 inches long, 14 inches wide, and 6 inches thick. Some of the sheets in these volumes are only 4 inches long, but a few are 3 feet in length, necessitating several folds. In some cases leaves burned at the edges have been covered with transparent silk to preserve them.

THE UNITED STATES IN 1790.

In March, 1790, the Union consisted of twelve states—Rhode Island, the last of the original thirteen to enter the Union, being admitted May 29 of the same year. Vermont, the first addition, was admitted in the following year, before the results of the First Census were announced. Maine was a part of Massachusetts, Kentucky was a part of Virginia, and the present states of Alabama and Mississippi were parts of Georgia. The present states of Ohio, Indiana, Illinois, Michigan, and Wisconsin, with part of Minnesota, were known as the Northwest Territory, and the present state of Tennessee, then a part of North Carolina, was soon to be organized as the Southwest Territory.

The United States was bounded on the west by the Mississippi river, beyond which stretched that vast and unexplored wilderness belonging to the Spanish King, which was afterwards ceded to the United States by France as the Louisiana Purchase, and now comprises the great and populous states of South Dakota, Iowa, Nebraska, Missouri, Kansas, Arkansas, and Oklahoma, and portions of Minnesota, North Dakota, Montana, Wyoming, Colorado, New Mexico, Texas, and Louisiana. The Louisiana Purchase was not consummated for more than a decade after the First Census was taken. On the south was another Spanish colony known as the Floridas. The greater part of Texas, then a part of the colony of Mexico, belonged to Spain; and California, Nevada, Utah, Arizona, and a portion of New Mexico, also the property of Spain, although penetrated here and there by venturesome explorers and missionaries, were, for the most part, an undiscovered wilderness.

The gross area of the United States was 827,844 square miles, but the settled area was only 239,935 square miles, or about 29 per cent of the total. Though the area covered by the enumeration in 1790 seems very small when compared with the present area of the United States, the difficulties which confronted the census taker were vastly greater than in 1900. In many localities there were no roads, and where these did exist they were poor and frequently impassable; bridges were almost unknown. Transportation was entirely by horseback, stage, or private coach. A journey as long as that from New York to Washington was a serious undertaking, requiring eight days under the most favorable conditions. Western New York was a wilderness, Elmira and Binghamton being but detached hamlets. The territory west of the Allegheny mountains, with the exception of a portion of Kentucky, was unsettled and scarcely penetrated. Detroit and Vincennes were too small and isolated to merit consideration. Philadelphia was the capital of the United States. Washington was a mere Government project, not even named, but known as the Federal City. Indeed, by the spring of 1793, only one wall of the White House had been constructed, and the site for the Capitol had been merely surveyed. New York city in 1790 possessed a population of only 33,131, although it was the largest city in the United States; Philadelphia was second, with 28,522; and Boston third, with 18,320. Mails were transported in very irregular fashion, and correspondence was expensive and uncertain.

There were, moreover, other difficulties which were of serious moment in 1790, but which long ago ceased to be problems in census taking. The inhabitants, having no experience with census taking, imagined that some scheme for increasing taxation was involved, and were inclined to be cautious lest they should reveal too much of their own affairs. There was also opposition to enumeration on religious grounds, a count of inhabitants being regarded by many as a cause for divine displeasure. The boundaries of towns and other minor divisions, and even those of counties, were in many cases unknown or not defined at all. The hitherto semi-independent states had been under the control of the Federal Government for so short a time that the different sections had not yet been welded into an harmonious nationality in which the Federal authority should be unquestioned and instructions promptly and fully obeyed.

AN ACT PROVIDING FOR THE ENUMERATION OF THE INHABITANTS OF THE UNITED STATES

APPROVED MARCH 1, 1790

SECTION 1. Be it enacted by the Senate and House of Representatives of the United States of America in Congress assembled, That the marshals of the several districts of the United States shall be, and they are hereby authorized and required to cause the number of the inhabitants within their respective districts to be taken; omitting in such enumeration Indians not taxed, and distinguishing free persons, including those bound to service for a term of years, from all others; distinguishing also the sexes and colours of free persons, and the free males of sixteen years and upwards from those under that age; for effecting which purpose the marshals shall have power to appoint as many assistants within their respective districts as to them shall appear necessary; assigning to each assistant a certain division of his district, which division shall consist of one or more counties, cities, towns, townships, hundreds or parishes, or of a territory plainly and distinctly bounded by water courses, mountains, or public roads. The marshals and their assistants shall respectively take an oath or affirmation, before some judge or justice of the peace, resident within their respective districts, previous to their entering on the discharge of the duties by this act required. The oath or affirmation of the marshal shall be, "I, A. B., Marshal of the district of ———, do solemnly swear (or affirm) that I will well and truly cause to be made a just and perfect enumeration and description of all persons resident within my district, and return the same to the President of the United States, agreeably to the directions of an act of Congress, intituled 'An act providing for the enumeration of the inhabitants of the United States,' according to the best of my ability." The oath or affirmation of an assistant shall be "I, A. B., do solemnly swear (or affirm) that I will make a just and perfect enumeration and description of all persons resident within the division assigned to me by the marshal of the district of ———, and make due return thereof to the said marshal, agreeably to the directions of an act of Congress, intituled 'An act providing for the enumeration of the inhabitants of the United States,' according to the best of my ability." The enumeration shall commence on the first Monday in August next, and shall close within nine calendar months thereafter. The several assistants shall, within the said nine months, transmit to the marshals by whom they shall be respectively appointed, accurate returns of all persons, except Indians not taxed, within their respective divisions, which returns shall be made in a schedule, distinguishing the several families by the names of their master, mistress, steward, overseer, or other principal person therein, in manner following, that is to say:

The number of persons within my division, consisting of ———, appears in a schedule hereto annexed, subscribed by me this —— day of ———, 179-. A. B. *Assistant to the marshal of* ———.

Schedule of the whole number of persons within the division allotted to A. B.

Names of heads of families.	Free white males of 16 years and upwards, including heads of families.	Free white males under 16 years.	Free white females, including heads of families.	All other free persons.	Slaves.

SECTION 2. And be it further enacted, That every assistant failing to make return, or making a false return of the enumeration to the marshal, within the time by this act limited, shall forfeit the sum of two hundred dollars.

SECTION 3. And be it further enacted, That the marshals shall file the several returns aforesaid, with the clerks of their respective district courts, who are hereby directed to receive and carefully preserve the same: And the marshals respectively shall, on or before the first day of September, one thousand seven hundred and ninety-one, transmit to the President of the United States, the aggregate amount of each description of persons within their respective districts. And every marshal failing to file the returns of his assistants, or any of them, with the clerks of their respective district courts, or failing to return the aggregate amount of each description of persons in their respective districts, as the same shall appear from said returns, to the President of the United States within the time limited by this act, shall, for every such offense, forfeit the sum of eight hundred dollars; all which forfeitures shall be recoverable in the courts of the districts where the offenses shall be committed, or in the circuit courts to be held within the same, by action of debt, information or indictment; the one-half thereof to the use of the United States, and the other half to the informer; but where the prosecution shall be first instituted on the behalf of the United States, the whole shall accrue to their use. And for the more effectual discovery of offenses, the judges of the several district courts, at their next sessions, to be held after the expiration of the time allowed for making the returns of the enumeration hereby directed, to the President of the United States, shall give this act in charge to the grand juries, in their respective courts, and shall cause the returns of the several assistants to be laid before them for their inspection.

SECTION 4. And be it further enacted, That every assistant shall receive at the rate of one dollar for every one hundred and fifty persons by him returned, where such persons reside in the country; and where such persons reside in a city, or town, containing more than five thousand persons, such assistants shall receive at the rate of one dollar for every three hundred persons; but where, from the dispersed situation of the inhabitants in some divisions, one dollar for every one hundred and fifty persons shall be insufficient, the marshals, with the approbation of the judges of their respective districts, may make such further allowance to the assistants in such divisions as shall be deemed an adequate compensation, provided the same does not exceed one dollar for every fifty persons by them returned. The several marshals shall receive as follows: The marshal of the district of Maine, two hundred dollars; the marshal of the district of New Hampshire, two hundred dollars; the marshal of the district of Massachusetts, three hundred dollars; the marshal of the district of Connecticut, two hundred dollars; the marshal of the district of New York, three hundred dollars; the marshal of the district of New Jersey, two hundred dollars; the marshal of the district of Pennsylvania, three hundred dollars; the marshal of the district of Delaware, one hundred dollars; the marshal of the district of Maryland, three hundred dollars; the marshal of the district of Virginia, five hundred dollars; the marshal of the district of Kentucky, two hundred and fifty dollars; the marshal of the district of North Carolina, three hundred and fifty dollars; the marshal of the district of South Carolina, three hundred dollars; the marshal of the district of Georgia, two hundred and fifty dollars. And to

obviate all doubts which may arise respecting the persons to be returned, and the manner of making the returns.

SECTION 5. Be it enacted, That every person whose usual place of abode shall be in any family on the aforesaid first Monday in August next, shall be returned as of such family; the name of every person, who shall be an inhabitant of any district, but without a settled place of residence, shall be inserted in the column of the aforesaid schedule, which is allotted for the heads of families, in that division where he or she shall be on the said first Monday in August next, and every person occasionally absent at the time of the enumeration, as belonging to that place in which he usually resides in the United States.

SECTION 6. And be it further enacted, That each and every person more than 16 years of age, whether heads of families or not, belonging to any family within any division of a district made or established within the United States, shall be, and hereby is, obliged to render to such assistant of the division, a true account, if required, to the best of his or her knowledge, of all and every person belonging to such family, respectively, according to the several descriptions aforesaid, on pain of forfeiting twenty dollars, to be sued for and recovered by such assistant, the one-half for his own use, and the other half for the use of the United States.

SECTION 7. And be it further enacted, That each assistant shall, previous to making his return to the marshal, cause a correct copy, signed by himself, of the schedule containing the number of inhabitants within his division, to be set up at two of the most public places within the same, there to remain for the inspection of all concerned; for each of which copies the said assistant shall be entitled to receive two dollars, provided proof of a copy of the schedule having been so set up and suffered to remain, shall be transmitted to the marshal, with the return of the number of persons; and in case any assistant shall fail to make such proof to the marshal, he shall forfeit the compensation by this act allowed him.

Approved March 1, 1790.

FIRST CENSUS OF THE UNITED STATES.

Population of the United States as returned at the First Census, by states: 1790.

DISTRICT.	Free white males of 16 years and upward, including heads of families.	Free white males under 16 years.	Free white females, including heads of families.	All other free persons.	Slaves.	Total.
Vermont	22,435	22,328	40,505	255	[1] 16	[2] 85,539
New Hampshire	36,086	34,851	70,160	630	158	141,885
Maine	24,384	24,748	46,870	538	None.	96,540
Massachusetts	95,453	87,289	190,582	5,463	None.	378,787
Rhode Island	16,019	15,799	32,652	3,407	948	68,825
Connecticut	60,523	54,403	117,448	2,808	2,764	237,946
New York	83,700	78,122	152,320	4,654	21,324	340,120
New Jersey	45,251	41,416	83,287	2,762	11,423	184,139
Pennsylvania	110,788	106,948	206,363	6,537	3,737	434,373
Delaware	11,783	12,143	22,384	3,899	8,887	[3] 59,094
Maryland	55,915	51,339	101,395	8,043	103,036	319,728
Virginia	110,936	116,135	215,046	12,866	292,627	747,610
Kentucky	15,154	17,057	28,922	114	12,430	73,677
North Carolina	69,988	77,506	140,710	4,975	100,572	393,751
South Carolina	35,576	37,722	66,880	1,801	107,094	249,073
Georgia	13,103	14,044	25,739	398	29,264	82,548
Total number of inhabitants of the United States exclusive of S. Western and N. territory	807,094	791,850	1,541,263	59,150	694,280	3,893,635

	Free white males of 21 years and upward.	Free males under 21 years of age.	Free white females.	All other persons.	Slaves.	Total.
S. W. territory	6,271	10,277	15,365	361	3,417	35,691
N. "						

[1] The census of 1790, published in 1791, reports 16 slaves in Vermont. Subsequently, and up to 1860, the number is given as 17. An examination of the original manuscript returns shows that there never were any slaves in Vermont. The original error occurred in preparing the results for publication, when 16 persons, returned as "Free colored," were classified as "Slave."

[2] Corrected figures are 85,425, or 114 less than figures published in 1790, due to an error of addition in the returns for each of the towns of Fairfield, Milton, Shelburne, and Williston, in the county of Chittenden; Brookfield, Newbury, Randolph, and Strafford, in the county of Orange; Castleton, Clarendon, Hubbardton, Poultney, Rutland, Shrewsbury, and Wallingford, in the county of Rutland; Dummerston, Guilford, Halifax, and Westminster, in the county of Windham; and Woodstock, in the county of Windsor.

[3] Corrected figures are 59,096, or 2 more than figures published in 1790, due to error in addition.

Summary of population, by counties and towns: 1790.

BRISTOL COUNTY.

TOWN.	Number of heads of families.	Free white males of 16 years and upward, including heads of families.	Free white males under 16 years.	Free white females, including heads of families.	All other free persons.	Slaves.	Total.
Barrington	115	165	144	330	32	12	683
Bristol	252	330	291	677	44	64	1,406
Warren	200	286	243	555	16	22	1,122
Total	567	781	678	1,562	92	98	3,211

KENT COUNTY.

TOWN.							
Coventry	395	645	633	1,159	35	5	2,477
East Greenwich	296	426	393	920	72	13	1,824
Warwick	397	566	516	1,152	224	35	2,493
West Greenwich	300	520	586	918	20	10	2,054
Total	1,388	2,157	2,128	4,149	351	63	8,848

NEWPORT COUNTY.

TOWN.							
Jamestown	79	100	91	232	68	16	507
Little Compton	260	365	354	778	22	23	1,542
Middletown	128	214	161	424	26	15	840
New Shoreham	90	155	133	290	57	47	682
Newport	1,242	1,454	1,237	3,385	417	223	6,716
Portsmouth	243	373	346	777	47	17	1,560
Tiverton	407	570	520	1,161	177	25	2,453
Total	2,449	3,231	2,842	7,047	814	366	14,300

PROVIDENCE COUNTY.

TOWN.							
Cranston	315	444	408	942	73	10	1,877
Cumberland	313	501	485	970	8	....	1,964
Foster	363	528	602	1,119	15	4	2,268
Glocester	620	989	999	2,014	22	1	4,025
Johnston	220	333	280	633	71	3	1,320
North Providence	183	270	237	509	50	5	1,071
Providence	1,129	1,709	1,259	2,937	427	48	6,380
Scituate	381	562	548	1,170	29	6	2,315
Smithfield	495	818	682	1,583	83	5	3,171
Total	4,019	6,154	5,500	11,877	778	82	24,391

WASHINGTON COUNTY.

TOWN.							
Charlestown	296	344	445	815	406	12	2,022
Exeter	423	583	613	1,175	87	37	2,495
Hopkinton	404	521	678	1,184	72	7	2,462
North Kingstown	456	602	668	1,342	199	96	2,907
Richmond	290	366	510	815	67	2	1,760
South Kingstown	655	820	1,058	1,605	473	175	4,131
Westerly	359	460	679	1,081	68	10	2,298
Total	2,883	3,696	4,651	8,017	1,372	339	18,075

Return of the Grand Jury of District Court Nov. term 1791, respecting the enumeration of the inhabitants of Rhode I. District.

The Grand Jury for the District Court in and for Rhode Island District at November term 1791—having in charge from the Judge of said Court—an act of the first Congress made and passed at their second session the first of March 1790—entitled "An Act providing for the Enumeration of the Inhabitants of the United States," and having the returns of the several assistants before us for our inspection—have examined into the Manner in which that Business has been transacted—and thereupon do represent to the court that we are fully satisfied, the Marshal and Assistants in making and completing the Enumeration of the Inhabitants of Rhode Island District have conducted agreeably to said Act, and with attention and accuracy, except that the Marshal hath not produced to us any proof, but his own declaration, that he did on or before the first day of September 1791 transmitt to the President of the United States, the aggregate amount of each Description of persons within his district

Nathaniel Dimon Foreman	Samuel Oxx
Benjⁿ Page	Benjᵃ Langford
Wᵐ Burllinggane	William Greene
Amasa Gray	Enos Mowry
Caleb Godfrey	Hezekiah Seumans
Jeremiah Scott Junʳ	James Gardner
Richᵈ Ellssdike	Stephen Evans

BRISTOL COUNTY.[1]

BARRINGTON TOWN.

NAME OF HEAD OF FAMILY.	Free white males of 16 years and upward, including heads of families.	Free white males under 16 years.	Free white females, including heads of families.	All other free persons.	Slaves.
Kelley, Duncan	2		5		1
Kelley, Lydia			3		
Tyler, Mosses	2		2		
Martin, Samuel	2	1	1		
Bowen, James	2		3		
Bowen, James, Jr	1	1	1		
Read, David	2	3	4	1	
Bowen, Jeremiah	2	2	7		
Bowen, Josiah	2	5	2		
Grant, Shubal	3	3	5		
Grant, Rosimond	3	1	4		
Luther, Josiah	1	1	1		
Luther, Margaret	1		2		
Horton, Simeon	2	4	2		
Martin, Rufus	1				
Martin, Mary			2		
Martin, Edward	1	3	2		
Barney, Peleg	1		3		
Kent, Samuel	1		3		
Kent, John	1	1	4		
Kent, Joseph	1		2		
Martin, James	1	2	5		
Martin, John	1		1		
Drowne, Philip	1	2	1		
Drowne, Jonathan	1	1	4		
Hewes, Spicers	1	1	2		
Wilson, Samuel	1	1	2		
Bishop, Ebenezar	1		1		
Carey, Micheal	1	2	1		
Drowne, Benjamin	1		4		
Drowne, Daniel	1	1	4		
Grant, Joseph	3	6	4		
Short, John	2		2		
Martin, John	2	1	3	2	
Drown, Benjamin J	1	3	5		
Elliot, Nathaniel	1	2	5		
Allen, Joseph	2	2	3		
Salsbury, George	4	1			
Richmond, Cyprian					2
Viol, Sylvester	1		1		
Harding, Abigail	1	1	1		
Humphry, John	1		4		
Allen, Mathew	1	2	6	2	
Allen, Pero				6	
Hill, Tower				3	
Brown, Prince				8	
Allin, Thomas	2	5	9	1	
Tiffany, Ebenezar	1	1	8	1	1
Pain, Peleg	1	1	7		
Watson, Mathew	1	2	1		
Watson, Mathew, Jun	2	2	3	1	
Smith, Hannah			1		
Bicknall, James	3		1		1
Short, John	3	4	5		
Tripp, William	1		1		
Alger, Jonathan	1	2	7		
Smith, Nathaniel	2	4	3		2
Kent, Joshua	1	3	8		
Kinnecutt, Hezekiah	2	1	4		
Allen, John	3		2		
Martin, Anthony	1	2	5		
Martin, Nathaniel	1	1	2		
Martin, Luther	1	4	3		
Martin, Calvin	1		2		
Cole, Ambrose	1	2	1		
Gladding, Joseph	2	2	4		
Ingraham, Joshua	2	1	3		
Bosworth, Edward	1		2		2
Short, Samuel	2		2		
Low, John Wilson	1		2		
Bosworth, Samuel	3	1	4		
Mathewson, Daniel	3	1	1		
Smith, Joseph	1	2	5		
Adams, Newtigate	1	3	3		
Baker, Jeremiah	1	3	3		
Baker, Joseph	1		3		
Tounsend, Solomon, Jur	2	2	3		
Kinnecutt, Daniel	3		5		
Bushee, James	1	3	5		
Mauran, Joseph Carlo	2	3	4		
Brown, William	2	1	4		
Brown, Martin	1	1	1		
Bicknall, Joshua	2	1	4	2	
Viol, Josiah	1	1	5		
Bicknall, Joseph	1		1		
Bicknall, Asa	2	4	4	2	
Baker, Thomas	1	1	1		
Bicknall, Freeborn	1		1		
Allen, Samuel	3	1	2		3
Andrews, William	2		2		
Greene, Richard	1		1	1	
Townsend, Solomon	1	2	1		
Kinnecutt, Josiah	2		2		
Allen, Racheal		1	4		
Humphry, Josiah	1		1		

BARRINGTON TOWN—con.

NAME OF HEAD OF FAMILY.	Free white males of 16 years and upward, including heads of families.	Free white males under 16 years.	Free white females, including heads of families.	All other free persons.	Slaves.
Humphry, Josiah	1	1	5		
Humphry, Elknah	4	2	4		
Barnes, John	2	1	3		
Loyal, Edward	1		2		
Barnes, Samuel	2	3	5		
Tripp, Consider	1	2	2		
Ladue, Curtis	1	1	2		
Drowne, Caleb	1	2	2		
Heath, Annar	1	1	2		
Heath, Nathaniel	2	3	5		
Peck, Sollomon	3		4		
Peck, Kesiah	2		1		
Peck, Ebenezar	1	3	2		
Young, Charles	1		2		
Stanley, Comfort	1		2		
Remmington, Enoch	2	1	6		
Peck, Noah	3	1	1		
Peck, David	1		4		
Peck, John	1		4		
Armington, Joseph	5	3	4		

BRISTOL TOWN.

NAME OF HEAD OF FAMILY.	Free white males of 16 years and upward, including heads of families.	Free white males under 16 years.	Free white females, including heads of families.	All other free persons.	Slaves.
Hale, Amos	3	1	4		
Hale, Coomer	1	1	2		
Burr, Rufus	2	2	1		
Jolles, Sarah	1	1	2		
Vance, James	1		2		
Burr, Samuel	3	1	2		
Munroe, Nathan	1	3	2		
Hill, Jonathan	2	1	2		
Grant, Richard	1	2	2		
Throop, John	2	3	3		
Comas, John			2	1	1
Comas, John, Junr	1	1	4		
Comas, Thomas K	1	3	2		1
Gosham, Isaac	2	2	5		5
Finney, Loring	1	1	2		
Davis, Jessee	1		5		
Finney, Jeremiah	3		4		
Luther, Benjamin	1	2	4		
Coggeshall, Nubey	3	1	1		1
West, Lawrence	1	1	3		
Ball, Sarah			3		
Peck, Thomas	1	1	1		
Peck, Nathaniel	3		1		
Peck, Jonathan	3		6		7
Peirce, Nathaniel	1	2	2		
Peirce, Thomas	2	2	3		
Coy, Mary			2		
Peirce, Nathaniel, Jun	1		3		
Peck, Nicholas	1	2	2		
Cole, Ephraim	1	1	5		
Reynolds, Joseph	2	1	6		1
Carey, Anna			1		
Peck, Loring	2	3	4		3
Church, Peter	3		3		
Bradford, Daniel	2	3	2		
Peirce, Isaac (Negro)				2	
Throop, William	2		1		
De Woolf, Mark Anthony	2	3	2		
Reynolds, George	2	2	3		
Throop, Esther			2		
Reynolds, Lydia	2		7	1	2
Maxwell, David	1	1	5	1	
Reed, Joseph	2		2		
Bullock, Simeon	1		1		
Reed, Benjamin	1	3	1		
Brown, James	1	1	2		
Grimes, John	1		2		
West, Lydia	1	2	3		
Bosworth, William	2	2	5		
Harden, William	1	4	3	5	
Bourne, Ruth			2		
Manchester, Cebra	3	1	4		
Church, Samuel	4	2	3		
Peck, Samuel	2	3	4		
Greene, Joseph	3	3	3		1
Gardnier, William	2	5	4	1	1
Usher, Hezekiah	2	1	4		
Bosworth, Samuel	1	2	1		
Wardwell, Phebe			3		
Wardwell, Allen	1	1	2		
White, Allin			1		
McCartey, Clarissa			1		
McQuim, Molly			2		
Bourne, Aaron	2		4		
Burt, Ann			2	2	1
Usher, Allen	3		2		
Usher, Edward	1		2		
Munroe, Sarah			4		1
Munroe, Abigail			4		
Ingraham, Sarah			3		

BRISTOL TOWN—con.

NAME OF HEAD OF FAMILY.	Free white males of 16 years and upward, including heads of families.	Free white males under 16 years.	Free white females, including heads of families.	All other free persons.	Slaves.
Gladding, Joshua	1	3	4		
Gladding, Samuel	1	3	1	5	
Gladding, Daniel	1	3	5		
Bosworth, James	1		5		
Dimon, Jonathan	1	3	1		
Dimon, Jeremiah	2		5		
Lollis, William	1		1		
Dimon, Thomas	2	1	2		
Norris, John	3	2	4		
Bosworth, Benjamin	2	4	5		
Fales, Thomas	2	3	4		
Church, Thomas			2		
Usher, Allen, Junr	1	1	2		
Richardson, Molly			2		
Peirce, Thomas	2	4	2		
Holmes, Ruth	2		2		
West, Thomas	1	1	1		
Esleech, Isaac	1	1	3		
Dimon, James	1	2	4		1
Oxx, Prudence			2		
Usher, John	3		5		
Dimon, Timothy	1	3	3		
Coggeshall, Sarah			1		
Walker, Nabby			1		
Smith, Samuel	2		3		
Smith, Jemima			1		
May, Elisha	1		2	1	
May, Sarah			1		
Howland, John, Junr	1		3		
Coggeshall, William	2		5		
Munroe, Edward	2	2	1		
Eslech, Isaac, Junr	1	2	1		
West, William	1		4		
Cox, William	1	1	6		
DeWoolf, William	1	3	2		
Bailles, Gustavas	1		2		1
Bosworth, Elizabeth			2		
Woodberry, Lydia			1		
DeWoolf, James	1		1		
Pain, Samuel Royal	1	2	3		
Martindale, Sarah			2		
Russell, Jonathan	1		3		1
Wardwell, Stephen	1	2	3		
Wilson, Jeremiah	2		1		
Wilson, Thomas	1	2	3		
Phillips, Nathaniel	2	3	4		
Townsend, Samuel	1		1		
Wardwell, Samuel	1	3	6		2
Wardwell, Isaac	1		2		
Lindsey, William	1	4	5		
Swann, Thomas	1	6	2		
Swann, Margarett			2		
Wood, Joseph	1	1	2		
Finney, Josiah	2		4		
Waldron, Sarah		2	2		5
Martin, Hannah	1	1	3		
Wardwell, Benjamin	2		2		
Wardwell, Samuel, Jun	1		2		
Waldron, Newton	2		2		
Parker, Williams	1	5	2		
Lindsey, Joseph	1	3	7		
Gwin, Mary			1		
Murray, Anthony	1	2	4		
Sanford, William	1		3		
Hathgill, Sarah			1		2
Hathgill, Charles				3	
Smith, Josiah	3	3	6		
Munroe, Nathaniel	1	4	3		
Esterbrooks, Aaron	1	4	3		
Peck, Nicholas, Jun	1		3		
Lefavor, Daniel	1		1		
Vandorren, Joshua	1		5		
Vandorren, Ruth			3		
Vandorren, Mosses	1	3	2		
Norris, John	1	1	2		
Oxx, Samuel	1	2	4		
Ingraham, Jeremiah	1	1	1		
Brownwell, Thomas	1	1	2		
Smith, Nathaniel	2	2	3		1
Usher, Hezekiah	1		2		
Smith, Stephen	1	3	6		1
Fales, William	1	2	2		
Fales, Jonathan	1		6		
Munroe, Amerentia			2		
Drowne, Jonathan	1		2		
Drowne, Richard	1	1	2		
Drowne, Sollomon	1		2		
Edminster, James	1		4		
Hoar, Benjamin	1	1	4		
Sanford, Royal	1	1	2		
Waldron, Betsey			2		
Sanford, Wait	2		2		
Cook, Elizabeth			2		
Gladding, William	3		3		

[1]No attempt has been made in this publication to correct mistakes in spelling made by the deputy marshals, but the names have been reproduced as they appear upon the census schedules.

BRISTOL COUNTY—Continued.

BRISTOL TOWN—con.

NAME OF HEAD OF FAMILY.	Free white males of 16 years and upward, including heads of families.	Free white males under 16 years.	Free white females, including heads of families.	All other free persons.	Slaves.
Munroe, Archibald	2	1	6		
Waldron, Billings	2	1	1		
Waldron, Thomas	1	1	2		
Waldron, Isaac	2		2		
Gladding, William	1	5	1		
Gladding, John	1	2	2		
Few, William	1	4	2		
Clarke, Samuel	1		2	1	5
Dimon, Nathaniel	3		3		
Munroe, Charles	2		2		
Munroe, Nathaniel	2	2	3		
Waldron, Ambrose	2	2	2		
Lescum, John	1		3		
Munroe, Thomas	1	2	4		
Lescum, Samuel	3		1		
Liscum, Nathaniel	1		4	1	
Nooning, Rebeckah	1	2	4		
Callimore, Peleg	1	3	3		
Ingraham, Simeon	1	2	5		
West, Nathaniel	1	1	3		
Ingraham, Joshua	1		5		1
Richmond, Aletheas		1	3		
Gladding, Samuel	1		2		
DeWoolf, Charles	3	3	6		1
Talbey, Edward	1		1		
Talbey, Stephen	1	1	6		
Allin, James	2		3		
Munroe, William	3		2		
Dimon, Joseph	2	1	3		
Lawless, John	1	1	1		
Ingraham, Jeremiah	1	1	3		
Ingraham, John	3		3		
Gladding, John	1	1	6		
Smith, Nathaniel J	1	1	2		
Salsbery, Barnard	1		2		
Holdridge, Joseph	2		1		
Manchester, Nathaniel	2	2	5		
Munroe, William	1		2		
Oxx, George	1	2	2		
Young, John	1		1		
Wardwell, Pattey			2		
Wardwell, Joseph	2	2	4		
Smith, Richard	1		1		
Lindsey, Samuel	1		3		
Smith, Richard, Junr	2	1	3		
Waldron, Nathaniel	4	1	3		
Howland, Daniel	1	1	1	2	
Hathaway, Asa	2		3		
Bourne, Shearshairb	2	3	7	1	2
White, Revd Henry	1	2	2	1	
DeWoolf, John	1	2	2		
Reynolds, Mary			2		
Peirce, William	2	2	1		1
Peirce, Lydia	3	2	4		
Peck, Jonathan, Jun	1	2	4	1	
Ingraham, George	3	1	4		
Bradford, Honl William	4	2	9	2	2
Sanford, George	1	1	3		
Reynolds, Thomas (Negro)				9	
Bosworth, Timothy	1	3	2		
Bosworth, William	1		2		
Wing, Naomi				6	
Bosworth, Benjamin	1	3	1		
Wilson, William	1	1	3		
Waldron, John	2	1	1		2
Gray, Thomas	1		2		1
Gray, Pardon	1	1	2		
Munroe, Hezekiah	2	1	3	1	
Munroe, Elizabeth			1	1	
Blake, Ebenezar	4		5		
Coggeshal, William	1	2	1		1
Coggeshall, James	1	2	2		
Coggeshall, George	2	2	3		
Coggeshall, Hannah			2		
West, Nathaniel Hicks	2	2	2		
West, Asa	1	2	2		
Maxfield, Daniel	2		2		
Willard, Hezekiah	2	3	2		
Howland, John	2	5	4		
Reynolds, Jonathan	1		3	1	
West, Oliver	1		1	1	
Cranston, Stephen	1		1		
Fales, Nathaniel	2	1	4		
Fales, John	1	2	4		
Fales, Nathaniel, Jur	1	4	4		1
Munroe, Daniel				8	
Munroe, Nathan	4	1	3		
Munroe, Joseph	1	3	2		

WARREN TOWN.

NAME OF HEAD OF FAMILY.	Free white males of 16 years and upward, including heads of families.	Free white males under 16 years.	Free white females, including heads of families.	All other free persons.	Slaves.
Barton, William	3	2	5		
Burr, Nabby			1		
Consines, John	1	2	2		
Wheaton, Hannah		1	2		
Witmarsh, Joseph	3	1	2		1
Cole, Peter	1		1		
Eddey, Joseph	4	1	2		
Wheaton, Peres	1	1	6		
Bardine, Nathan	1	1	4		
Hale, Barnett	1		2		
Salsberry, Luther	1	2	2		
Bowen, Nathan	1		1		
Ormsbe, Ezra	2		1		
Childs, William	1	4	2		
Phillips, Nathaniel	1	4	2		
Cranston, Saml	1	1	4		
Sparks, Joseph	1	2	1		
Gott, James	1	3	3		
Estabroks, Thomas	2		1		
Ormsbee, Isaac	1		2		
Barton, Rufus	2	3	3		
Luther, Barnaby	1	2	5		
Cole, Thomas	1		2		
Maxwell, Level	1		2		
Carr, William	1	1	1		
Carr, Jonathan	1	1	6		
Cranston, Benjamin	1	2	2		
Hicks, Samuel	3	1	5		
Harris, John	1		1		
Bowen, Nathan	1		6		
Turner, Moses	1		5		
Vaune, James	1	1	2		
Bliss, Jonathan	1	1	5		
Hoar, Phebe	2	2	3		
Curtis, Mr	3	2	4		
Davis, Marey			1		
Saunders, David	1	1	1		
Childs, John	2		3	2	
Childs, John Throop	2	1	2		
Carr, Caleb	3	2	2		
Brown, Samuel	1	2	4		
Luther, John	1	2	2		
Esterbrooks, Benja	2		1		
Hale, John	2	2	3		
Ervenshire, Thomas	1		2		
Coles, Benajah	1	1	1		
Carr, Lydia	3	1	4	2	
Carr, Ruth			1		
Hill, Barnett	1	1	3		
Collins, Charles	2	1	2		
Bliss, William	1		1		
Snell, Seth	2	4	5		
Turner, Caleb	2	2	5		
Turner, Hannah			3		
Bowen, Josiah	4		3		
Baker, Jessee	4	2	5		
Hill, Elizabeth			1		
Chace, Edward	3		2		
Maxwell, James	2		5		
Bowen, Benjamin	1	1	2		
Brayton, James W	1	1	5		
Esterbrooks, Abiel	1	4	4		
Esterbrooks, Susannah			6		
Esterbrooks, Edward	1	5	2		
Hale, Mary			2		
Esterbrooks, John	1		1		
Witaker, Simeon	1	1	1		
Childs, Jeremiah	2	4	3		
Simmons, Sampson	1	2	2		
Miller, Samuel	1	1	1		
Childs, Hall	1	3	2		
Kelley, John	1	1	1	1	
Kelley, Joseph	1	2	2		
Kelley, Daniel	2	2	5	1	
Kelley, Joseph	2	2	3		
Bliss, William	2		7		
Champlin, Bettey	2	1	4		
Jones, John	2	1	3		
Salsberry, William	2		4		
Miller, William Ton	1	1	1	1	
Kelley, Duncan	2	1	1		
Miller, Rebeckah	2	1	2		2
Wheaton, Charles	3	1	1		
Cranston, Caleb	4	1	4		
Eddey, Edward	1		1		
Childs, William	1		2		
Fish, Samuel	1	1	3		
Childs, Crommel	2	1	2		

WARREN TOWN—con.

NAME OF HEAD OF FAMILY.	Free white males of 16 years and upward, including heads of families.	Free white males under 16 years.	Free white females, including heads of families.	All other free persons.	Slaves.
Childs, Caleb	1	4	3		
Burr, Simon	3		3		
Harding, John	3	1	3		
Saunders, Jacob	4	2	3		
Whiteing, Roba			1		
Tibbits, Susannah			2		
Miller, Bristol				6	
Childs, Crommel	1	3	3		
Childs, Simeon	1	1	2		
Childs, Sylvester	1	2	3		
Croad, John	2	1	4		
Adams, Joseph	1	1	3		
Thurber, Caleb	4	1	3		
Shoals, Cyrus	1	2	1		
Salsberry, Jonathan	2		2		
Cole, Allen	2	2	5		
Cole, Ebenezer, Jr	1	1	2		
Hoar, William	1		2		
Luther, Martin	1		5		5
Childs, Samuel	1	2	3		
Cole, Ebenezar	2		4		
Eddey, Sarah	1		1		
Smith, Joseph	3	5	5	1	
Bowen, Jonathan	1		3		
Lewis, William	1		4		1
Carpenter, Nathan	1	3	3		
Esterbrooks, Daniel	1	2	4		
Burr, Shubal	2		2		2
Bowen, Stephen	3	2	2		
Peck, Thomas	1	1	3		
Banas, James	2		3	1	
Miller, Barnett	2	2	4		
Ormsbee, Joshua	2	1	3		
Stephens, John	1		3		
Bowen, Samuel	1	1	1		
Wheaton Spencer	1	1	1		
Bowen, Smith	2	1	4		
Hale, Richard	4		3		
King, Elijah	2	3	4		
Luther, Ebenezar	1	1	1		
Miller, James	1	1	1		
Luther, Patience		2	1		
Hale, Mary			1		
Cole, Isaac	1	1	3		
Peirce, Jeremiah	1	2	4		
Peirce, Samuel	1	1	3		
Peirce, Saml, Junr	1	1	2		
Arnold, William	1		4		
Arnold, William, Jun	1	1	4		
Luther, Martin, 2d	2	1	2		
Rounds, John	1		2		
Kinnecutt, Shubal	2	2	2		
Kinnecutt, Hannah			2		
Richards, Peter	1	1	2		
Cole, Ichabod	2	1	2		
Finney, Elisha	3	2	4		
Cole, Benjamin	1	1	3		
Esterbrooks, Nathl	1		6		
Esterbrooks, Royal	1		2		
Cole, Landle	1	2	2		
Cole, Daniel	2	1	2		
Cole, Seth	1	3	3		
Short, James	1	4	3		
Barton, Richard	1	4	1		
Hicks, Jonathan	1		4		
Rounds, Oliver	1	2	2		
Burden, Thomas	1		1		1
Barton, David	1	2	7		1
Barton, Benjamin	2	1	3		
Barton, Lydia			3		
Barton, Benja, Jun	1		3		
Sissell, George	2		4	1	
Sisson, James	2	1	2	1	
Gardnier, Edward, 2d	2	2	4		
Gardnier, Edward	4	1	4	2	
Mason, John	2	1	5		4
Mason, Gardner	1	1	2	1	
Mason, Holden	1		2		
Mason, Samuel	1	1	5		
Read, Abigail			3		
Tripp, Susannah			2		
Sisson, Gidion	2	2	5		
Sisson, Molly			4		
Daggett, Job	1	2	3		
Barton, Joseph	1		4		
Butterworth, Hezekiah	2	1	3		
Butterworth, Patience			1		
Brown, John	1	1	3		

BRISTOL COUNTY—Continued.

Column key for all tables: **M16** = Free white males of 16 years and upward, including heads of families; **Mu16** = Free white males under 16 years; **F** = Free white females, including heads of families; **Other** = All other free persons; **Slaves**.

WARREN TOWN—con.

Name of head of family	M16	Mu16	F	Other	Slaves
Bosworth, Benjamin	4	4	5		
Luther, Jabez	1		3		
Luther, James	1	1	2		
Dorr, Peace		1	1		
Handy, Samuel		1	1		
Martin, Ebenezar	1	1	4		
Luther, Frederick	3		3		
Mason, James	1	6	2		
Mason, Edward	2	5	3		
Saunders, Benjamin	1	3	2		
Franklin, John	1	3	1		
Chase, Jacob	1	2	3		
Salsbury, John	1	3	1		
Hale, Nathan	4	3	3		
Mason, Marmaduke	1		2		
Sisson, George	1	1	4		
Peirce, John	2	3	1		
Peirce, Ephraim	1		2		
Winslow, Job	2	2	4		
Bowen, Peleg	2	2	3		
Alger, Preserved	1	1	4		
Bowen, James	1	4	4		
Bowen, Nathaniel	1		2		
Cole, Thomas	1	2	3		

KENT COUNTY.

COVENTRY TOWN.

Name of head of family	M16	Mu16	F	Other	Slaves
Ramsdel, Pheby			3		
Fenner, Anna	4	1	3		
Arnold, Philip	1	2	2		
Green, William	1	3	5		
Arnold, John	3		3		
Green, Job	2		3		
Green, John	2	1	1		
Green, Stephen	1	2	4		
Green, Job, Junr	2	5	4		
Levally, Joseph	1	3	2		
Burlingame, Stephen	2		7		
Burlingame, Reubin	1	1	1		
Burlingame, Ebenezar	1	1	1		
Burlingame, Joseph	2	1	7		
Burlingam, Russell	1	2	3		
Colvin, Mrs Meriba			4		
Colvin, Daniel	1		1		
Colvin, James	2	2	3		
Andrews, Griffin	3		3		
Colvin, Anna			1		
Abbitt, Pardon	5	5	4		
Colvin, Peter	2	3	4		
Fisk, Nathan	3	4	3		
Colvin, Colonel	2		3		
Stone, James	2	5	5		
Colvin, Thomas	1	1	5		1
Wall, John	3	2	2		
Potter, Pardon	1	1	4		
Weaver, Robert	1	1	1		
Burlingame, Benjamin	2		4		
Burlingame, Eseck	2	2	3		
Stone, William	2	1	3		
Westcoat, Benjamin	1		1		
Bucklin, David	2		2		
Bucklin, Benjamin	1	2	3		
Stone, Westcoat	1		2		
Stone, William, Junr	1	3	2		
Weaver, Langford	3	6	3		
Colvin, Joseph	1		3		
King, Ebinezar	1		1		
King, Jessee		2	3		
Fisk, Nathan, Junr	1	2	2		
Cooke, William	2	2	5		
Ralph, Hue	1	3	3		
Bowen, Asa	2	1	2		
Westcoat, Elisha	1	4	2		
Arnold, Benjamin	2	4	3		
Reed, Benjamin	2	3	1		
Reed, Mrs Elizabeth	2		4		
Briggs, William	1		1		
Bailey, Samuel	1	3	4		
Mathewson, Daniel	3	3	5		
Potter, Ichabod	3	1	3		
Johnson, Benedict	1	1	2		
Briggs, Benjamin	3	2	4		
Cumstock, Charles	1	3	2		
Briggs, John	1	1	3		
Corey, John	1	2	2		
Roberts, Eseck			3		
Brayton, William	2	3	3		
Brayton, Jonathan	3	1	4	1	
Johnson, Christopher	1		2		
Brayton, Rufus	2	2	3		
Brayton, Frances	2	2	4		
Mathewson, Nicholas	1	3	3		
Wait, Elvin	2		3		
Ward, Mary		1	5		
Colvin, Joshua	1	1	3		
Johnson, Antes	1	1	1		
Remmington, Thomas (of Prudence)	2	1	2		
Remmington, Thomas	2	2	3		
Potter, Josiah	1	4	2		
Kilton, John	1	3	5		
Utter, Thomas	3	3	4		
Manchester, Job	2	3	2		
Colvin, Edmund	1	1	2		
Capwell, Betty	1		3		
Philips, William	1		2		
Green, John	1		2		
Green, Sandwich	1	3	1		
Mathewson, Thomas	2	2	3		
Waterman, Thomas	5		3	2	
Westcoat, Frelove	2	1	5		
Westcoat, Ephraim	1	1	3		
Potter, Jessee	2		5		
Potter, Philip	1	1	1		
Tyler, William	2	2	3		
Mathewson, Benjamin	2	2	6		
Ellis, Nicholas	3		2		
Bowen, Benjamin	1		1		
Dunn, Dennis	1		1		
Bowen, Aaron	4	4	6		1
Bowen, Israel	4		5		
Bowen, Ichabod	3		3		
Bowen, Philip	3	6	3		
Waterman, Benjamin	3	3	3		
Waterman, William	3	2	5		
Knight, Ezra	1	1	3		
King, William	2	5	2		
Stone, Jabez	2		3		
Stone, Jabez, Junr	1	1	1		
Bapett, Samuel	2	3	4		
Ellis, Nicholas, Junr	1	3	2		
Litson, Jeremiah	1		2		
Scott, Simon	1	2	2		
Green, Jedadiah	4	2	5		
Scott, Joseph	1	1	1		
Scott, Ichabod	1		3		
Scott, Nathan	2	3	4		
Scott, Joseph, Junr	1	1	2		
Weeks, Abel	1	3	3		
Carnel, Latham	1	5	3		
Weeks, Benedict	2	2	3		
Green, Increase	2		3		
Carr, Edward	1	1	3		
Perry, Amos	2	3	3		
Green, John	2	3	3		
Green, Job	1	1	2		
Green, Charles	1	3	2		
Andrew, James	1	2	3		
Briggs, Ephraim	2	3	2		
Roberts, Jonathan	3	1	3		
Litson, Robert	2		2		
Ray, William	3	2	3		
Parker, Peter	1	2	4		
Johnston, Ezekiel	1	3	2		
Brock, Ezekiel	1	1	2		
Tillinghast, Pardon	1				
Nichols, Reubin	2	3	2		
Mathewson, Joseph	6		5		
Cooke, Charles	3	4	6		
Green, John	5	2	3	1	
Green, Manser	1	1	2		
Bennett, Joseph	2		3		
Bennett, William	1	1	2		
Bennett, Mary	1		3		
Bennett, Hezekiah	1	1	5		
Fox, John	3	4	6		
Jorden, Edmund, Junr	2	3	4		
Briggs, Jonathan	2	2	1		
Peirce, Ezrikam	2		3		
Rice, George	2	2	3		
Hammond, James	2		3		
Bates, James	3	4	3		
Bates, William	1		3		
Remmington, Benjamin	1	1	4		
Blanchard, Pheby			2	1	
Stafford, Martha	1		2		
Forster, Lemuel	2	1	2		
Hall, Ebinezar	1		2		
Brayton, Caleb	1		3		
Love, John	2	3	7		
Lewis, John	2	3	6		
Blanchard, Samuel	1	2	8		
Mathewson, David	1	1	3		
Mathewson, Solomon	2	2	3		
Davis	1		4		
Mathewson, Samuel	1		3		
Hill, William	1	1	7		
Mathewson, Jonathan	2	2	2		
Mathewson, Thomas	2	1	4		
Black, Jack				3	
Gorden, Johnson	2	3	3		
Green, Mrs Infield			4		
Jagness, James	1	1	2		
Moss, Lydia	1	1	3		
Rice, John	3		3		2
Rice, Rebeca	1		2		
Rice, Thomas	1		2		
Rice, Richard	1		2		
Burlison, John	3	3	6		
Waterman, Richard	4	3	3		
Vaughn, Caleb	1	1	4		
Vaughn, Caleb, Junr	3	3	4		
Roberts, Elizabeth			3		
Love, John, Junr	1	1	1		
Bennett, Ezekiel	1	3	6		
Kelly, Nancy		4	1		
Clarke, Benjamin	1	2	1		
Bennett, Abel	3	3	3		
Wilbore, Jonathan	3	3	3		
Potter, Reuben	1	2	3		
Love, Susanna	1	2	2		
Peck, Samuel	1	3	4		
Wilbore, Stephen	2	2	2		
Love, Adam	1		3		
Corey, Anthony	1		2		
Corey, Anthony, Junr	1	3	3		
Bates, John	1	1	3		
Love, Arthur	1	2	2		
Dixon, Thomas	1		2		
Eddy, Thomas	1	1	3		5
Peirce, Pardon	1		1		
Peirce, Benjamin	1	2	2		
Peirce, William	1	1	2		
Hammond, Ezekiel	1	1	3		
Franklin, David	1	3	4		
Perkins, Ebinezar	1	1	4		
Herrington, Francis	2	1	1		
Love, Mrs Martha	1		4		
Weaver, John	2		1		
Weaver, John, Junr	1		1		
Gibson, James	4		3		
Gibson, James, Junr	4	3	3		
Young, Andrew	4	3	4		
Shaw, John	2	2	4		
Greger, John W	1	3	3		
Gibbs, Samuel	3	3	3		
Gibbs, Josiah	2	2	4		
Colegrove, John	3	3	5		
Allen, Ebenezar	2	1	5		
Allen, Noel	2	4	5		
Allen, Joseph	1	2	2		
Johnson, Samuel	3	2	3		
Kasson, Archibald	3	2	2		
Congdell, John	3	2	3		
Rice, Joseph	2	3	3		
Ladd, John	2	3	5		
Rice, John, Junr	2	3	5		
Headly, William	1	2	2		
Rice, Ebinezar	2	3	6		
Jarden, Edmund	2	2	4		
Potter, John	1	3	2		
Codman, Nathan	1	2	1		
Rice, Samuel	1		8		
Aylesworth, James	1	3	8		
Vaughn, Job	1	1	6		
Aylesworth, Philip	1	1	5		
Arnold, Joseph	1	1	2		
Arnold, Charles	2		2		

KENT COUNTY—Continued.

COVENTRY TOWN—con.

NAME OF HEAD OF FAMILY.	Free white males of 16 years and upward, including heads of families.	Free white males under 16 years.	Free white females, including heads of families.	All other free persons.	Slaves.
Cook, Robert	2		3		
Young, James	1	1	2		
Bennett, William	1		2		
Arnold, Nathaniel	1		4		
Austin, Joseph	2	2	2		
Bennett, Abel	2	4	2		
Weeks, Joseph	2	3	3		
Johnson, Watty	2	3	3		
Whitford, Nicholas	1	3	7		
Capwell, James	2	3	4		
Whitman, Caleb	1	2	3		
Litson, Michael	1	2	2		
Price, Samuel	1	2	2		
Capwell, Stephen	1	1	2		
Capwell, Jeremiah	1	3	5		
Garton, George	2	3	4		
Carr, Benjamin, Junr	1		2		
Carr, Benjamin	1		2		
Green, Robert	1	2	5		
Green, Ebinezar	1		2		
Capwell, Henry	1	1	8		
Mathewson, Richard	2	1	3		
Carr, Peleg	2	4	2		
Burlingame, William	3	2	6		
Green, Samuel	2		3		
Wood, Robert	1	2	3		
Weaver, Jonathan, Junr	2	2	3		
Wood, John	2	3	2		
Wood, Thomas	1	2	4		
Andrews, Charles	5	1	6		
Weaver, Jonathan	2	1	6		
Collins, Benjamin	1	2	2		
Johnson, Obadiah	2	1	3		
Weeks, Ichabod	1	2	1		
Weaver, John	1		6		
Wilson, Joseph	2		1		
Weaver, Daniel	1		2		
Weaver, Nathan	1	1	3		
Allerton, Mrs. Rosann			3		
Garton, Slade	1	2	3		
Dorrance, Samuel	2	2	3		
Green, Thomas	2		3		
Brayton, Benjamin	2	2	5		
Green, Joseph	1	1	2		
Philips, James	3	3	3		
Philips, Thomas	1		2		
Brown, Nicholas	1		2		
Rice, Daniel	1		5		
Hopkins, Elisha	1		2		
Mathewson, Eleazer	2	2	3		
Green, Isaac	3		2		
Green, Nathaniel	2	1	4		
Green, John					
Whaley, Job	1	5	3		
Whaley, Thomas	1	1	3		
White, Joseph	1	2	3		
Commins, Daniel	1		2		
Sweet, Benjamin	2	3	3		
King, John	1	2	4		
Stone, Oliver	2	1	3		
Green, Stephen	1		1		
Colvin, William	1	1	1		
Stafford, John	1	2	4		
Nichols, Jonathan	1	2	2		
Havens, Robert		2	2		
Green, James	3	4	6		
Potter, George	1	2	5		
Green, Henry	1	1	2		
Andrews, Benjamin	1		5		
Green, Usnal	1		1		
Green, Henry, Junr	1		2		
Green, Timothy	2	3	4		
Cummins, Remmington	1	1	2		
Green, Robert	1		1		
Collins, Henry	1	1	3		
Johnston, Henry	1	2	4		
Johnson, Ebinezar	2	1	2		
Johnson, Hosea	1	2	2		
Johnson, Ezekiel	2	2	2		
Mathewson, Jonathan	3	1	3		
Mathewson, Stephen	1	2	3		
King, Amaziah	1	2	2		
Briggs, Henry	2	5	3		
Letson, William	1	2	1		
Hackstone, Benjamin	1	1	2		
Green, James	1	1	2		
Andrews, John	2	2	2		
Green, Hardwell	2	2	4		
Green, Othniel	1	2	4		
Green, Mary			1	1	1
Green, Russell	1		2		
Green, Elisha	1	2	3		
Mathewson, Thomas	3	2	5		
Wall, Samuel	3	1	3		

COVENTRY TOWN—con.

NAME OF HEAD OF FAMILY.	Free white males of 16 years and upward, including heads of families.	Free white males under 16 years.	Free white females, including heads of families.	All other free persons.	Slaves.
Whitford, Solomon	1	1	3		
Johnson, John	2	2	3		
Mathewson, Job	2	3	3		
Stafford, John	2		2		
Stafford, Joseph	3	3	4		
Mathewson, Moses	4	1	3		
Andrews, William	3		5		
Andrews, Nathan	3	1	2		
Mathewson, Joseph	3		6		
Whitford, Stweet	1	2	2		
Streight, John	1	1	5		
Andrews, Timothy	1	1	5		
Roberts, James	1		2		
Roberts, Calib	1	2	2		
Johnson, Jonathan	3		3		
Potter, Mrs Eunice	1		2		
Johnson, Samuel	2	2	5		
Whitman, Caleb	1	3	6		
Colvin, Joseph	2	2	4		
Colvin, Benedict	1	1	7		
Johnson, Isaac	1	1	4		
Wood, James	1	1	1		
Johnson, Joseph	3	2	2		
Johnson, Benjamin	3	5	5		
Johnson, Reubin	2	3	3		
Johnson, John	3	1	4		
Pendock, Sarah			1		
Batty, Nicholas	2		3		
Manchester, Joseph	3	3	4		
Streight, Samuel	1	3	2		
Potter, Ezekiel	2	2	2		
Potter, Fonas	1	3	3		
Tarbox, Sphink	2		3		
Merithew, Samuel	1	3	3		
Slocom, John	1	1	2		
Mathewson, Nancy		1	2		
Mathewson, Benjamin	1		2		
Lawton, Job	2	3	3	1	
Bartholick, Thomas	1	2	2		
Bartholick, Abner	1		2		
Nichols, Thomas	1	1	2		
Wood, John	1	1	4		
Wood, William	1	2	2		
Nichols, Richard	2		2		
Peirce, Daniel	2	1	2		
Capwell, Stephen	2	5	3		
Stafford, James	2	2	3		
Rice, Caleb	3	3	5		
Lindon, Nathaniel	1	3	2		
Shippy, Caleb	2	4	3		
Arnold, Mary	1	3	4		
Wood, Olney	1	2	2		
Shoemake, Abraham	1		2		
Manchester, Thomas	2	3	8	1	
Potter, Stephen	2	3	6		
Burgis, Joseph	1	4	1		
Arnold, Christopher	1	3	2		
Brayton, Caleb	1	1	3		
Warner, Elisha	1	2	2		
Leonard, Zepheniah	3	2	2		
Green, Gideon	3	4	4		
Green, Jeremiah	1		4		1
Green, Jacob	9	2	2	2	
Edmonds, William	2		2	1	
Potter, Nathan	2	1	3		
Edmonds, Anthony	1	2	3		
Burlingame, Moses	2	2	4		
Tubbo, Zephaniah	3	3	3		
Carpenter, Borton				5	
Green, Fortune				5	
Roberts, Francis				3	

EAST GREENWICH TOWN.

NAME OF HEAD OF FAMILY.	Free white males of 16 years and upward, including heads of families.	Free white males under 16 years.	Free white females, including heads of families.	All other free persons.	Slaves.
Nichols, Mary			2		
Reynolds, Samuel	1	3	4	1	
Briggs, William	1		5		
Mawney, Pardon	3	3	8	2	1
Briggs, John	1		3		
Briggs, Richard	2	2	6		
Hamilton, William	2	3	3		
Brown, Charles	2		2		
Briggs, Gardiner	2	7	2		
Briggs, Benjamin	2	2	2		
Briggs, Nicholas	1		1		
Carr, Isaac	1	2	4		
Briggs, Caleb	1	1	5		
Wells, George	1	2	4		
Austin, David	3	1	2		
Northup, David	3	1	2		
Vaughn, John	2	1	4		
Sweet, Paul	2		4		
Nichols, George	3		3		
Andrew, Samuel	1	1	3		

EAST GREENWICH TOWN—con.

NAME OF HEAD OF FAMILY.	Free white males of 16 years and upward, including heads of families.	Free white males under 16 years.	Free white females, including heads of families.	All other free persons.	Slaves.
Hill, Nathan	1	1	2		
Jones, Amos	2	1	6		
Jones, Seth	4		2		
Plice, Thomas	3	1	4		
Cole, Samuel	1	1	2		
Tillinghast, Thomas	2	1	3	3	
Clark, Cornelius	3		2		
Corey, Joseph	1	3	2		
Brigs, John	1		1		
Brigs, William	1	1	3		
Corey, Benjamin	1	3	2		
Cobb, John	1	1	4		
Vaughn, Thomas	1	4	5		
Vaughn, David	4	3	3		
Place, Philip	1	4	1		
Card, Job	3	2	2		
Sweet, Sylvester, Junr	1	3	2		
Place, Stafford	1		2		
Sweet, James	1		2		
Spencer, Gardiner	1	1	3		1
Pierce, William	1		4		
Place, John	1	2	3		
Tibbits, Elizabeth			1		
Tibbitts, Henry	1	1	2		
Green, Prince				3	
Whitman, James		1	2		
Whitman, Samuel	1	1	4		
Gardiner, John	3		3		
Gardiner, William	2	2	4		
Whitman, Benjamin	2	1	1		
Whitman, James, Junr	1	1	5		
Whitman, John	1	1	2		
Whitman, Joseph	1	1	1		
Johnson, Isaac	2		2		
Pitcher, John	3		2		
Whitford, Caleb	2	2	7		
Spencer, John	3	1	4		
Carr, Elizabeth			1		
Vaughn, Robert	3	2	3		
Capran, Green	1	4	4		
Bailey, William	3		3		
Godfrey, James	1		2		
Vaughn, David	1		1		
Vaughn, David, Junr	2	2	2		
Vaughn, Amos	1	1	6		
Briggs, Yelvesten	2	2	5		
Walker, Stephen	2	1	3		
Corven, Morgan	1		1		
Corven, Dennis	1	1	3		
Tarbox, David	3	2	3		
Nichols, Richard	4	2	5		
Vaughn, Nathan	3		4		
Whitford, George	1		6		
Healy, Benoni	1		4		
Whitman, Henry	2	3	3	1	
Carpenter, John	2	2	1		
Carpenter, Thomas	1	1	1		
Howland, Joseph	1	1	2		
Bailey, Robert	3	3	7		
Vaughn, Benjamin, Junr	1	2	2		
Wood, Benjamin	1	2	9		
Spencer, Silas	2	3	5	3	
Shippey, Thomas	1		5		
Shippey, Thomas, Junr	3	3	4		
Elsworth, Sarah			2		
Marks, William	1		6		
Briggs, Anderson	1	1	2		
Spencer, Anthony	1	3	3	3	
Sweet, Samuel	1	2	2		
Andrew, Benjamin	1	2	4		
Spencer, Wilson	2	1	3		
Spencer, Wilson, Junr	1	3	2		
Spencer, Amos	1	3	2		
Spencer, Michael	3	2	6		
Andrew, James	1		3		
Andrew, Mary			3		
Hall, Abiel	3		2		
Hall, Thomas	1	2	2		
Vaughn, Christopher	3	1	4		
Andrew, Caleb	1	1	3		
Weaver, Duty	1	2	2		
Spencer, George	2		6		
Northup, Ichabod				7	
Spencer, Mary			4		
Fry, Joseph	4	1	9	2	1
Spencer, William	2	2	5		
Green, Stephen	2	3	6		
Tillinghast, Benjamin	2	5	3		3
Green, Elisha	1	7			
Green, William	1	2	8		
Johnson, Allen			8		
Johnson, Mrs Bathsheba			2		
Johnson, Mrs Christian	3	2	4	1	1
Sweet, Sylvester	1	1	1		

KENT COUNTY—Continued.

EAST GREENWICH TOWN—con.

NAME OF HEAD OF FAMILY.	Free white males of 16 years and upward, including heads of families.	Free white males under 16 years.	Free white females, including heads of families.	All other free persons.	Slaves.
Tillinghast, George	2	4	2	1	
Carr, Daniel	2	4	5		
Davis, Mumford	1	1	8		
Davis, William	1	2	3		
Briggs, Thomas	1		3		
Cooper, Stephen	3	2	5		
Kinsyon, Remington	3	1	4		
Gardiner, Jack				5	
Hall, Robert	2	1	3		
Weeden, Edward	1	2	5		
Wall, Samuel	1		2		
Tafft, George	1		5		
Tanner, Nathan	1	4	4		
Spynk, Mrs Ollin		2	7		
Tafft, Hannah			2		
Johnson, William	1	1	1		
Spencer, Ebinez	1	3	2	2	
Spencer, Henry	1	5	4		
Nichols, James	1	1	4		
Nichols, Sarah	1		2		
Fry, Benjamin	6		3	2	
Nichols, John	1	5	4		
Howland, Daniel	3	1	3		
Arnold, Joseph	1	3	4		
Andrews, Jonathan	1		2		
Andrews, Whipple	1	1	1		
Card, Joseph	2	1	1		
Carnel, Joseph	1	6	4		
Langford, Joseph	1		2		
Weaver, William	2	1	1		
Spencer, Rufus	3		5	1	
Godfrey, Joshua	4	3	3		
Weaver, Christopher	1	4	5	1	
Weaver, Jonathan	1	2	4	1	
Sisson, Joshua	1		3		
Langford, Jonathan	1	1	2		
Bennett, Thomas	1		4		
Langford, John	1	2	3		
Weaver, Clement	1		2		
Spencer, Grace				5	
Essex, Richard	1	2	6		
Ballou, Joseph	3		2		
Spencer, Jeremiah	2	1	6		
Spencer, George	2		3		
Pierce, John	3	1	6		
Aldrich, Thomas	3	1	3	3	
Pierce, John (son of Benj)	1	3	3		
Reynolds, Shibney	2	1	2		
Lippitt, Benbo				8	
Hammond, Prince				2	
Hall, Isaac	1		1		
Garzia, John	1		6		
Corey, Joseph	1	1	2		
Langford, Benjamin	1		3		
Wilcox, Stephen	1		2		
Hatch, Samuel	1	5	3		
Mott, Stephen	1	1	1		
Green, Joseph	3	1	7		
Spencer, Stephen	1	5	3		
Proud, Samuel	2	2	5		
Weeden, Lydia			2		
Crary, Archibold	2	1	6		
Mumford, Pomp				3	
Howland, Benjamin	2	3	4		
Pierce, Moses	1	1	3	1	
Pierce, Stephen	1	6	4		
Stafford, Arnold	1		1		
Shaw, Mary		1	2		
Sweet, William	2	1	3		
Whitmarsh, Micah	2	1	3	3	
Corey, Oliver	1	2	6		
Comstock, Job	2		3		
Sprague, John	1	2	3		
Sprague, William	1	1	5		
Sprague, Caleb	1	1	3		
Holden Anthony	1		2		
Collins, William	1	3	3		
Weeden, Caleb	1	3	4		
Brown, Polly			3		
Simmons, Ezra	1	7	3		
Martain, Lemuel	1	1	2		
Burlingam, Chandler	1		1		
Miller, John	2	1	4		
Gorton, Mary			3		
Mumford, Ruth			3		
Cozzens, Anna		2	2		
Corey, Ebenezer	1	2	1		
Graves, Martha			2		
Flogg, Miss Betsey			1		
Green, James	1	3	2		
Proud, John	1	2	2		
Arnold, William	5	1	5	1	3
Peirce, Preserved	1		3		
Mathews, Caleb	1	1	4		
Peirce, Peggy	2		1	1	

EAST GREENWICH TOWN—con.

NAME OF HEAD OF FAMILY.	Free white males of 16 years and upward, including heads of families.	Free white males under 16 years.	Free white females, including heads of families.	All other free persons.	Slaves.
Peirce, Jeremiah	1	1	3		
Spencer, Thomas	2		2		
Fry, Samuel	1		6		
Cooke, Hopkins	2		2		
Reynolds, John	1	2	5		
Turner, Peter	2	4	5	1	
Brown, Clark	2	3	5		
Corey, John	3	1	2	1	
Stone, Joseph	2	2	2		
Joslin, Mrs Hope			3		
Gould, Samuel	1				
Arnold, Mary			4	1	2
Miller, Spice	2		4		
Bent, Nathan	1	3	3		
Coggeshall, Caleb	1	3	3		
Reynolds, Peirce	1		3		
Green, Mary	1		3		
Green, Russell	1		3		
Bailey, Jeremiah	1		3		
Green, Barbary			3		
Green, William	1	2	4		
Mumford, Gideon	2		2		
Mumford, John F	1	2	1	1	
Bentley, Mary	1	1	1		
Bentley, Christopher	1		3		
Peirce, Temperance		1	1		
Aylesworth, John	1	1	2		
Peirce, Philip	2	4	2		
Green, Caleb	1		2		
Nicholas, Martain	1		3		
Burlingam, Susanna	1		2		
Green, Nathan	3	2	4		
Weeks, Oliver	3		5		
Westcoat, Silas	1	2	2		
Spencer, Nathan	6	2	1		
Miller, James	1	3	2		
Smith, John	3	2	5		
Warner, Ezekiel	2	1	2		
Corey, Mrs Abigail	1		2		
Johnson, Elijah	1	1	3		
Capron, Nathan	1	3	1		
Peirce, Edward	1	2	1		
Rice, Samuel	1	1	3		
Peirce, Jonathan	2	2	3		
Wall, Hannah			3		
Frebourne, Gideon	2		2		
Andrews, Jonathan	1	1	4		
Boyd, Andrew	3	1	7		
Briggs, Charles	8	2	2		
Fry, Sarah	1	1	5		
Spencer, Hannah			3		
Spencer, John	4	1	4		
Winslow, Isabella	4		2		
Smart, Molly		1	2		
Glazier, John	1	1	5		
Hatch, Eleazer	1	1	2		
Spencer, Michael	1	1	2		
Sweet, James	1	1	3		
West, Samuel	1	2	2		
Tripp, Samuel	1	1	4		
Blair, William	2	2	3		
Corey, Mrs Frelove	1	1	5		
Mott, Elizabeth			4		
Peirce, Thomas	2	1	4		
Goddard, Nicholas	1		2		
Briggs, Jonathan	1	2	2		
Slocom, Sarah	1	1	2		
Potter, Jonathan	1	2	3		
Spencer, Richard	1		2		
Brion, Mrs Acena		1	1		
Mott, Joseph	1		4		
Spencer, Griffin	1	2	2		
Pierce, James	1	3	1		
Aylesworth, Richard	2	4	4		
Capron, Jonathan	2	2	5		
Niles, Jonathan	1	1	6		
Studson, Caleb	1	4	2		
Wilcox, Smyton	1	1	3		
Mumford, Stephen	2				1
Spencer, Ruth		2	2		
Arnold, Mrs Lois			3		
Weeden, Peleg	1	2	1		
Coggeshall, John	3		3	1	
Arnold, Thomas	1	2	5		
Spencer, Seneca	1	3	1		
Jones, Timothy	1	1	7		
Salisbury, Jonathan	2	4	2	1	

WARWICK TOWN.

NAME OF HEAD OF FAMILY.	Free white males of 16 years and upward, including heads of families.	Free white males under 16 years.	Free white females, including heads of families.	All other free persons.	Slaves.
Scranton, Daniel	1		4		
Essex, Hugh	2	1	8		
Green, Christopher	5	4	6	3	
Mathewson, Richard	4	2	5		
Green, Paul	5	1	5	1	

WARWICK TOWN—con.

NAME OF HEAD OF FAMILY.	Free white males of 16 years and upward, including heads of families.	Free white males under 16 years.	Free white females, including heads of families.	All other free persons.	Slaves.
Sweet, Daniel	1		2		
Spencer, John	4		1		
Spencer, Cuff				8	
Slocum, Mary			1	2	
Hall, Preserved	1	2	2		
Borton, Benjamin	2	2	3	1	1
Nicholas, Benjamin	3		4	3	
Morley, Henry	1	1	2		
Bennitt, David	1	4	6		
Church, William	1		4		
Gardiner, Nathan	1	1	3	1	2
Foster, Thomas	1	1	5		
Johnson, Mattey			2		
Green, William	4	1	4	5	
Pierce, Giles	1	1	5		
Green, David	1	1	4		
Holden, John	2		4		
Brown, Samuel	1	1	3		
Spencer, Nathan	6	2	1		
Green, Stephen	1	4	3		
Holmes, Samuel	1	4	1		
Wilcox, Gideon	1	1	2		
Olin, Peleg	3	3	4		
Gardiner, Oliver	1	6	7		
Lilley, John	1		1		
Whitford, George	3	4	5		
Rhodes, Holden	2	5	5		
Gorton, John	1		1		
Gorton, John, Junr	1	2	2		
Gorton, William	1	1	3		
Hammett, Thankful		1	3		
Andrew, Silas	1		2		
Stafford, John	1	2	6		
Spencer, Gardiner	2	1	2		1
Reynolds, Henry	1	1	3		
Rice, William	1	3	3		
Rice, Nathan	1	3	1		
Gerauld, Duty	3		3		
Miller, Nathan	1	1	3		
Miller, Nathan, Junr	1	3	3		
Carr, Caleb	2		4		
Gerauld, James	1	4	3		
Pierce, Thomas	1	2	3		
Rice, Henry, Junr	1		3		
Melowney, Michael	1		1		
Rice, Henry	3	1	4		
Arnold, Nicholas	2	1	2		
Miller, Squire	3	1	3		
Miller, Samuel	1	4	3		
Miller, John	1	2	1		
Straight, Joseph	1	2	7		
Briggs, Joseph	3	5	5		
Carpenter, Job	1	1	1		
Coggeshall, Thomas	1		1		
Carpenter, Wilbore	2	1	3		
Carpenter, Daniel	1	1	2		
Andrew, Frelove	2		3		
Spencer, Corey	1	2	2		
Briggs, Miss Susanna			2		
Dowd, Noah	1		2		
Arnold, Joseph			2		
Arnold, John	1	2	1		
Arnold, Joseph, Junr	2	2	1		
Shero, Abraham				4	
Whitman, David	1	1	3		
Price, Benoni	1		3		
Price, Mathew	1	1	4		
Remington, Henry	1		1		
Gorton, Benjamin	1	3	6		
Gorton, Joseph	2		3		
Gorton, William	1	1	2		
Gorton, Othniel	2	1	2		1
Weeks, Stently	1	2	9	1	
Weaver, Philip	1	2	2		
Bently, Caleb	2	2	3		
Remmington, Thomas	1		2		
Remmington, Benjamin	1	3	3		
Waterman, William	2	2	5	1	
Arnold, James	1	1	3		
Arnold, Frelove	1		3		
Carpenter, Elisha	2	2	3		
Sweet, Samuel	1		3		
Sweet, Whitman	1		1		
Green, Peter	1	3	4	2	
Salisbury, Peleg	1	3	2		
Hall, John	1	3	2	1	
Green, Ebenezar	1	4	3		
Allen, John	1	1	2	1	
Green, Giles	1	1	3		
Allen, George	1		3		
Whipple, Joseph	1	4	3		
Allen, Charles	2	3	5		
Tiffany, Thomas	2	2	7		
Tiffany, James	1	1	2		

KENT COUNTY—Continued.

NAME OF HEAD OF FAMILY.	Free white males of 16 years and upward, including heads of families.	Free white males under 16 years.	Free white females, including heads of families.	All other free persons.	Slaves.
WARWICK TOWN—con.					
Slocom, John	1		3		
Slocom, Thomas	2	2	6		
Bliss, Obadiah				7	
Sweet, Cesar				4	
Whitaker, Thomas	1	1	2		
Arnold, Stephen	3	2	5		
Clapp, John	1	5	4		
Clapp, Daniel	1	1	2		
Arnold, Thomas	5	2	4		
Arnold, Pheby	1		1		
Arnold, William	1	2	3		
Arnold, Gideon	1	3	3		
Rice, William	2	1	2	1	
Arnold, George	1	4	3		
Arnold, Nathaniel	1		2		
Arnold, Anthony	1	1	3		
Green, James	1		3		1
Green, James, Junr	1	1	3		
Green, Job	2	1	4		
Lippet, Sam				8	
Green, Ann	1		3		1
Lippitt, Cuff				4	
Eldrich, Thomas	1	1	2		
Hathaway, Caleb	1	1	3	1	
Levolly, John	1	2	3		
Levolly, Amey	1		4		
Dexter, Stephen	1		1		
Levolly, William	1	1	2		
Levolly, Peter	3		5		
Hathaway, Nathan	1	1	5		
Rice, Anthony, Junr	1	2	2		
Arnold, Nathan	1	2	3		
Arnold, Richard	1	1	1		
Arnold, John	2	2	5		
Ladd, Ann	2		1		
Whitman, Othniel	1	1	4		
Arnold, Harris	1	1	2		1
Church, Loring	1		2		
Bourk, William	1	4	2		
Gorton, Samuel	3	2	4	3	
Tibbets, Waterman	3	3	2	1	
Remmington, Mrs Wilkey			3		
Curtis, Elisha (Negro)				6	
Rhodes, Dick				4	
Spencer, Gideon	1	3	3		
Arnold, Andrew	2	2	3		
Arnold, Henry	1	2	3		
Rice, Thomas	3	1	3	2	
Rice, Thomas	1	1	1		
Weaver, Abiel	3		2		
Weaver, Caleb	1	2	1		
Tibbitts, John	2	5	3		
Tibbitts, William	1	1	1		
Tibbitts, Thomas	3		3		
Arnold, Philip	1	3	1	4	
Rice, Thomas, Junr	2		4		
Rice, Josephus	1	2	5		
Rice, Anthony	1		3		
Holden, William	1	1	2		
Atwood, Mary		3	2		
Bennett, Samuel	1	2	4		
Snell, Daniel	2	1	4		
Atwood, Caleb	2	4	1		
Abbett, Pardon	1		4		
Atwood, Nehemiah	1	1	2		
Shaw, Peleg	1	3	1		
Chace, Loring	1	2	3		
Chace, Abraham	1	1	3		
Andrew, George	1	4	3		
Burlingame, Samuel	1	2	2		
Brown, Elisha	2		2		
Levally, Benjamin	1		4		
Dowd, Ezekiel	1	2	4		
Baker, Daniel	3		3		
Baker, George	1	1	2		
Baker, William	2	1	1	1	
Ellis, Jonathan	1		5		
Kimball, Amos	3	1	4		
Potter, William	3	1	2		
Arnold, Benjamin	3	1	1	1	
Arnold, Duty	1	1	3		
Reynolds, Moses				6	
Stafford, Stently	2		2	3	
Holden, Charles	1	1	2	2	
Holden, Thomas	3	1	9		
Baker, Joseph	5	4	7	3	
Edmonds, Robert	3		5		
Gorton, Caleb	1	1	2		
Baker, Olney	1	1	3		
Allen, Lemuel	1	4	1		
Arnold, Henry	1	2	2		
Stone, Samuel, Junr	1		1		
Clemens, John	1		5		

NAME OF HEAD OF FAMILY.	Free white males of 16 years and upward, including heads of families.	Free white males under 16 years.	Free white females, including heads of families.	All other free persons.	Slaves.
WARWICK TOWN—con.					
Tibbitts, Jonathan	1	1	1		
Merrill, Spencer	2		4		
Hackstone, John	1	1	3		
Arnold, Caleb	1		4		
Arnold, Joseph	1	3	2		
Arnold, William	1	1	3		
Tibbitts, Job	1	1	1		
Westcoat, Caleb	1	1	5		
Green, Christopher	2	2	6		
Gerauld, Gorton	1	4	4		
Tripp, James	1	1	7		
Green, Caleb	4	2	5		
Gorton, Jonathan	1	1	4	1	
Corps, David	2		3		
Gorton, Samuel	1	1	2		
Whipple, James	1	1	1	1	
Havens, William	2	1	7		
Briggs, Stephen	1	3	3		
Arnold, Thomas	4	1	3		
Arnold, Gideon	5	2	3	1	
Freeman, Peter	1	1	4		
Arnold, Rebecca			2		
Green, Thomas	1	4	4		
Havens, Alexander	1		1		
Webb, William	4	2	5		
Gammitt, Isaac	2	3	3		
Wood, Pardon	1	2	3		
Harrison, George	1	2	4		
Remmington, Ruel	1		1		
Bathe, John	1	1	3		
Brown, Joseph	2	2	2		
Westcoat, Thomas	3	2	4		
Baker, Abraham	2	3	5		
Baker, Silas	1	1	3		
Baker, Moses	1	1	2		
Gorton, Nathan	1		1		
Gorton, Joseph	1	2	3		
Gorton, John	1		4		
Budlong, James	1	5	2	1	
Green, James	2		1		
Green, James, Junr	1	2	2	1	
Budlong, John	2	1	4		
Green, Thomas	2		1		
Budlong, Benjamin	1	5	5		
Budlong, Stephen	1	1	2		
Archer, Susanna			1		
Davis, Samuel	1	5	5		
Bennett, Joseph	1	4	5		
Brigg, Job	1	5	4		
Eldrich, Robin				6	
Watt, Thomas				8	
West, Benjamin				3	
West, Ishmael				2	
Holden, George				3	
Remmington, Gerauld	1	1	2		
Budlong, Rhodes	1	2	4		
Budlong, Nathan	1	2	3		
Wood, William, Junr	1	1	6		
Baker, Pardon	1	3	3		
Stone, Josiah	1	1	8		
Stone, Benjamin	1		2		
Rhodes, Primus				6	
Jacobs, Moses				6	
Carder, Jones	2	1	4		
Carder, Jones, Junr	1	4	6		
Budlong, Moses	2		2		
Howard, Benjamin	1		2		
Batty, Sampson	2	1	7	1	
Arnold, Simon	4		5		
Budlong, Samuel	4	4	5		
Arnold, Sion	2		2		
Westcoat, Jeremiah	3	2	3		
Philips, Caleb	1	1	4		
Roberts, Reubin				3	
Low, Tim				6	
Philips, Jeremiah	1	1	5		
Whipple, Job	2	2	4		
Rhodes, Esop				3	
Lippitt, Cesar				7	
Lippitt, Will				3	
Knapp, David	2	2	9		
Arnold, Stephen	1	1	1		
Straight, Henry	1				
Lippitt, Prime				5	
Lockwood, Cesar				4	
Bates, Benoni				2	
Briggs, Isaac	1	3	4		
Profit, James				8	
Littlefield, Samuel	1	2	3		
Howard, Solomon	3	1	2		
Remmington, Thomas, Junr	1	5	3		
Davis, Samuel, Senr	1	1	2		
Peck, Thomas	1		3		

NAME OF HEAD OF FAMILY.	Free white males of 16 years and upward, including heads of families.	Free white males under 16 years.	Free white females, including heads of families.	All other free persons.	Slaves.
WARWICK TOWN—con.					
Remmington, Thomas	1		2		
Barton, Rufus	1		1	1	
Edmonds, Joseph	1	4	2		
Johnson, Peleg	1		1		
Patt, David	1		5		
Hackstone, Nathaniel	1		2		
Hackstone, William	1	2	1		
Lockwood, Benajah	1	1	3		
Lockwood, Nathaniel	1		2		
Weeks, Barney				6	
Weeks, Harry				3	
Holden, Prince				2	
Low, John	4		5	1	
Low, Anthony	3		4		
Low, Benjamin	1		2		
Morris, Charles	1	3	3		
Hammitt, Malachiah	3	2	6		
Gorton, William	3		6		
Green, Caleb	2	1	3		
Hudson, Samuel	1		4		
Holden, Anthony	2	2	4	2	
Wells, John	2	1	3		
Green, John	1	5	6		
Stone, James	1	1	3		
Warner, Hannah			2		
Cole, John	1	2	3		
Green, Godfrey	5	1	4		
Green, Thomas	4	3	6	1	1
Arnold, David	3	4	6		
Brayton, Daniel	2		7		
Holden, Randal	3	1	7		
Arnold, Benedict	1	1	5		
Barton, Stently	4		3		
Westcoat, Nathan	3	1	8		
Weeks, Thomas	2	1	1		8
Lippitt, William	1		2		5
Lippitt, Thomas	1	1	4		1
Gorton, Benjamin	3	2	3	2	
Barton, Sarah			1	1	
Waterman, Prince				4	
Congdon, Charles	1		3		
Weeks, John	2	1	1		
Green, Benjamin	2	3	2		2
Gorton, Francis		1	2		
Lippitt, John	1		2		7
Lockwood, Amos	1		3	4	
Green, Caleb	1	3	4		
Warner, John	4	4	6		
Green, Mary	1		2		
Lockwood, Adam	1	2	4		
Lockwood, Abraham	1	2	4		
Cole, Nathaniel	1	1	2		
Cole, Sarah	1	1	3		
Waterman, John	3	1	4	3	
Waterman, Cuff				4	
Taylor, Ambrose	2		3		
Warner, John, Junr	2	1	5		
Warner, William	3	2	6		
Low, Stephen	1	2	5		
Low, Bennett	1		2		
Stafford, Thomas	2	1	8	2	
Green, Stephen	3		2		
Lippitt, Abraham	2	2	7		1
Lippitt, Moses	1	1	6	1	
Green, Benjamin	2		2		
Green, William	1	2	4		
Green, Philip	3	4	5	1	
Arnold, Benjamin	3	3	3		
Card, Stephen	1	4	3		
Utter, Zebulon	1		1		
Arnold, Josiah	3		1		
Arnold, Moses	2	3	4	2	
Corey, Daniel	1		3		
Arnold, George	2	2	2		
Lippitt, Murry				3	
Arnold, Simon	2		2		
Arnold, Israel	1	1	5		
Arnold, Susanna	2		2	1	
Sweet, Thomas	1	1	2		
Sweet, Benjamin	1	4	4		
Batty, Joseph	2	2	4		
Smith, Job	1	1	5		
Arnold, James	1	1	2		
Green, Stephen	1	1	3		
Remmington, Thomas	1	2	1		
Remmington, Mrs Wait	1		1		
Slocom, Abel	1	2	6		
Corps, Caleb	1	1	3		
Stone, Mrs Dorcas			2		
Holdrich, William	1		2		
Arnold, Remmington	1	2	3		
Randal, Mrs Bathiah	2		2	2	
Whitney, James	2	5	4		
Aborn, John Anthony	1		2		

KENT COUNTY—Continued.

WARWICK TOWN—con. / WEST GREENWICH TOWN.

NAME OF HEAD OF FAMILY.	Free white males of 16 years and upward, including heads of families.	Free white males under 16 years.	Free white females, including heads of families.	All other free persons.	Slaves.
WARWICK TOWN—con.					
Thornton, Solomon....	9		4		
Price, Mary...	1	2	3		
Remmington, Peleg...	1		1		
Rhodes, Mary...		1	3		
Rhodes, James...	1		1		
Rodes, Malachi...	2	2	4		
Barton, Andrew...	1		4		
Cardner, Esther...		1	3		
Aborne, Samuel...	3		2	1	
Donville, Peter...	1	3	3		
Rhodes, Robert...	1	3	1		
Rhodes, James...	1		1	1	
Howard, Thomas...	1	2	5		
Smith, Stephen...	2	1	6		
Rhodes, Peter...	2	2	2		
Rhodes, Benjamin...	1	1	2		
Smith, Simon...	1	5	2		
Ormsby, John...	1		1		
WEST GREENWICH TOWN.					
Corey, Sanford, Junr...	1	1	3		
Johnson, Elijah...	1	2	5		
Arnold, Pheby...	3		2		
Johnson, John...	2	3	4		
Mathewson, Josiah...	3		3		
King, Samuel...	5	4	6		
King, Paul...	1		2		
Hopkins, Alice...	2	2	2		
Herrington, Job...	1	5	2		
Mathewson, John...	3	1	5		
Mathewson, Jonathan...	1		2		
Mathewson, Job...	2	2	3		
Mathewson, Ezekiel...	2	2	6		
Potter, George...	1	2	4		
Mathewson, William...	2		2		
Mathewson, Obadiah...	1	4	3		
Whitford, Carmer...	2	2	4		
Manchester, Thomas...	2	3	5		
Green, Daniel...	1	2	1		
Mathewson, Thomas...	1	1	3		
Sweet, Henry...	1		2		
King, Susanna...		1	2		
Whitford, George...	1	1	1		
Tarbox, Joseph...	1	3	1		
Wethers, John...	1		2		
Briggs, Daniel...	1	2	1		
Kettle, Edward...	5		3		
Kettle, Edward, Junr...	5	3	3		
Hopkins, Henry...	1	4	2		
Sweet, William...	3	5	3		
Colegrove, Thomas...	2	1	4		
Whitford, Thomas...	2	1	2		
Hopkins, William...	2		1		
Whitford, Simon...	2	2	2		
Carr, Joshua...	2		2		
Arnold, Nathaniel...	2		2	1	
Herrington, Rebecca...	2		3		
Whitford, Job...	3	3	2		
Mathewson, Jeremiah...	3	2	3		
Briggs, John...	1	2	6		
Johnson, Edmond...	1	1	1		
Mathewson, Uriah...	2	2	5		
Mathewson, Silas...	3	5	5		
Burlingham, Eleazer...	2	2	4		
Whitford, Levi...	3		2		
Mathewson, Rufus...	2	3	6		
Mathewson, Abel...	2	2	2		
Sweet, Isaac...	1	2	3		
Mathewson, Jonathan...	3	1	5		
Mathewson, David...	3	3	8		
Mathewson, Edmund...	2	5	3		
Hall, Caleb...	2	5	6		
Hall, John...	2	2	2	1	
Comstock, Jonathan...	2		2		
Sweet, John...	2	8	2		
Sweet, Penticoast...	1	5	5		
Austin, Robert...	1	2	3		
Fry, Joseph...	3	3	4		
Olive, Henry...	1		4		
Olive, Henry, Junr...	2	5	6		
Arnold, Jeremiah...	2		3		
Sisson, Caleb...	1	3	2		
Oumstock, Ann... }	2		2		
Oumstock, Elizabeth... }					
Rowse, Sandy...	2	2	3		
Arnold, Elisha...	1	5	3		
Weaver, Joseph...	3	3	6		
Weaver, James...	2	3	5		
Mathewson, Nathan...	2	2	3		
Mathewson, Nathan, Junr...	1		1		
Mathewson, Bowen...	1		2		
Brown, Nicholas...	1		2		

WEST GREENWICH TOWN—con.

NAME OF HEAD OF FAMILY.	Free white males of 16 years and upward, including heads of families.	Free white males under 16 years.	Free white females, including heads of families.	All other free persons.	Slaves.
Austin, Brayton...	1	2	1		
Wait, Rufus...	2	3	6		
Richmond, William...	2	5	5		
Walker, Ezra...	1	2	1		
Hill, Robert...	1	5	2		
Hall, David...	1	2	8		
Hall, Thomas...	1	1	1		
Dyer, George...	1	1	2		
Kittle, Amos...	1		1		
Comstock, Patience...		1	1		
Mathewson, Henry...	2	1	3		
Brusley, Joseph...	2	3	5		
Richmond, Adam...	1	2	5		
Brown, Weaver...	1	2	1		
Austin, Jeremiah...	1	3	3		
Austin, Ellis...	3	3	3		
Straight, Nathan...	3	2	3		
Watson, Braddock...	1	2	3		
Streight, Job...	1	1	3		
Rowse, Benjamin...	2	2	2		
Rowse, Benjamin, Junr...	1	1	3		
Gorton, Benjamin...	1	2	4		
Gorton, Thomas...	4	1	3		
Austin, Brayton...	1	1	1		
Mathewson, Warner...	1	1	1		
Capwell, Benjamin...	1	3	3		
Brand, Robert...	2	2	2		
Wait, John...	1	3	2		
Youngs, Thomas...	1	2	1		
Mathewson, Oliver...	1	2	2		
Stafford, Thomas...	5	2	3		
Spink, William...	3	2	5		
Spink, John...	1	2	6		
Spink, Henry...	2	2	3		
Streight, John...	2	1	6		
Streight, David...	2	2	5		
Wood, Joab...	1	2	2		
Allen, Stephen...	2	1	3		
Nichols, Joseph...	1		3		
Nichols, Ishmael...	2	3	2		
Collins, Thomas...	2	4	1		
Hudson, Stently...	1	3	5		
Hudson, Benoni...	1		2		
Ellis, Rufus...	1	6	3		
Green, Eleazer...	1		2		
Rowse, Benjamin, Junr...	1	1	3		
Litson, Ephraim...	2	3	6		
Aylesworth, David...	1		2		
Aylesworth, David, Junr...	1	5	3		
Johnson, Elisha...	1	2	2		
Tanner, Samuel...	2	2	6		
Montgomery, John...	1	3	3		
Johnson, Elisha, Junr...	1	2	3		
Wait, Gideon...	3	6	3		
Baker, Solomon...	2	3	5		
Converse, David...	1	2	4		
Reynolds, Joseph...	2	3	2		
Hyems, Pardon...	1	1	3		
Bennett, Jonathan...	1	1	2		
Baker, William...	1	1	3		
Tyler, William...	1	1	2		
Wilcox, George...	2	5	1		
Converse, James...	2	2	2		
Whitboard, Isaac...	1		2		
Pulman, Nathaniel...	3	2	4		
Parker, John...	3	1	2		
Ross, Thomas...	1	2	2		
Burlisson, Joseph...	2	3	2		
Montgomery, Ebinezar...	1	1	3		
Austin, Jeremiah...	2	2	2		
Kenyon, Gardiner...	2	2	3		
Burlison, Edward...	3	4	3		
Iagnais, Amos...	2	2	3		
James, Allen...	3	3	4		
Hopkins, Jeremiah...	2	4	2		
Anderson, William...	1	2	3		
Tillinghast, Thomas...	2	2	3		
Rathbane, Clark...	2	2	2		
Codner, Samuel...	2	2	4		
Tillinghast, John...	2	3	5		
Croswell, Mingo (Negro)...				6	
Sweet, William...	1	1	3		
Young, Benjamin...	2	3	4		
Sweet, Elisha...	2	2	2		
Gates, Simon...	2	1	3		
Gates, Simon...	2	4	3		
Gates, Israel...	2	1	3		
Haszard, John...	1	2	6		1
Watson, Robert...	2	2	3		
Hoxney, Joseph...	1		3		
Casey, John...	3	1	3		
Young, Benjamin...	2		2		
Targee, Smith...	1	2	3		

WEST GREENWICH TOWN—con.

NAME OF HEAD OF FAMILY.	Free white males of 16 years and upward, including heads of families.	Free white males under 16 years.	Free white females, including heads of families.	All other free persons.	Slaves.
Tanner, Mrs Wait...	2	1	3		
Bailey, Jared...	1	2	1		
Watson, Samuel, Junr...	1	4	3		
Watson, Nicholas...	1	2	3		
Wilcox, John...	2	5	2		
Stone, Thomas...	5	2	2		
Wilcox, Stephen...	1		3		
Johnson, Benedict...	1		1		
Tillinghast, Benjamin...	2	2	2		
Bates, John...	1	2	2		
Watson, Samuel...	2		1		
James, Benjamin...	2	3	7		
Gardiner, Joseph...	3	1	2		
Tillinghast, Pardon...	1	1	2		
Gorton, Hezekiah...	2	3	6		
Gorton, Samuel...	3	1	5		
Tillinghast, Joseph...	1	2	2		
Tillinghast, Charles...	1	1	1		
James, Paul...	1	4	3		
Mathewson, David...	3	3	2		
Draper, Joseph...	1	1	6		
Reynolds, John...	2		2		
Tanner, Henry...	2	1	3		
Mathewson, Josiah Junr...	2	2	1		
Wood, Joseph...	2	3	5		
Sweet, Peleg...	2	3	8		
Green, Benjamin...	1	1	1		
Green, Clark...	1	3	4		
Green, Weltham...	2	2	5		
Carpenter, John...	2	3	5		
Manchester, William...	2	1	4		
Brown, Josiah...	2	2	2		
Green, Elisha...	2	2	3		
Green, Caleb...	2	4	3		
Lewis, Simeon...	2	2	2		
Austin, Beriah...	1	1	2		
Lewis, Daniel...	5	3	8		
Bailey, Silas...	1	3	3		
Streight, Solomon...	1	1	4		
Lewis, Jacob...	2	3	4		
Green, Lodowick...	1	4	3		
Austin, Rufus...	1		2		
Austin, Stephen...	1	3	3		
Northup, Joseph...	1		2		
Farlind, Mrs Experience...			2		
Eldrich, Samuel...	1		2		
Moon, James...	2	1	1		
Moon, Oliver...	2	2	3		
Spencer, Job...	1	1	2		
Culner, David...	2	2	5		
Lewis, William...	1	2	2		
Reynolds, Mrs Penelope...	1	3	5		
Ellis, Gidion...	4	3	3		
Crandal, John...	1	3	1		
Codnar, John...	1		4		
Peirce, Benjamin...	1		3		
Ellis, Jeremiah...	1	2	2		
Ellis, William...	1	1	5		
Gardiner, Samuel...	2	3	5		
Ellis, Augustus...	2	3	6		
Crandal, Peter...	2	2	5		
Bailey, Caleb...	2		3		
Austin, Benjamin...	2	4	5		
Benjamin, Silas...	2	2	2		
Nichols, William...	5	4	5		2
Boss, Haszard...	1	2	3		6
Barker, William...	1	2	2		
Dawley, James...	1	2	2		
Green, John...	2	3	3		
Philips, Philo...				4	
Essex, John...	2	3	5		
Niles, John...	1	2	4		
Niles, Joseph...	1	2	2		
Nichols, Henry...	1	5	1		
Bokes, John...	1	1	1		
Congden, James...	1	2	2		
Niles, Joseph, Junr...	3	3	5		
Barton, Simon...				6	
Dean, Jonathan...	2	3	3		
Aylesworth, Arthur...	2		1		
Spencer, William...	2	1	2		
Niles, Nathaniel...	1	2	2		
Hopkins, Beriah...	1	2	4		
Briggs, John...	3	2	3		
Vaughn, George...	2	3	4		
Austin, Silas...	2	3	3		
Reynolds, James...	1	3	2		
Boss, William...	1	2	2		
Case, John, Junr...	1	2	2		
Case, John...	1	2	3		
Cobb, John...	1	2	2		
Hopkins, Robert...	1		5		
Hopkins, Alexander...	1		1		
Albro, John...	3	2	4		

KENT COUNTY—Continued.

NAME OF HEAD OF FAMILY.	Free white males of 16 years and upward, including heads of families.	Free white males under 16 years.	Free white females, including heads of families.	All other free persons.	Slaves.
WEST GREENWICH TOWN—con.					
Case, John, Junr	1		4		
Reynolds, Amos	3	3	4		
Hill, Thomas	1		3		
Reynolds, Robert	2	1	5		
Rogers, Thomas	3		3		
Case, Sanford	3	2	3		
Johnson, Benjamin	3	3	5		
Davis, William	2	3	3		
Tillinghast, Pardon	3		2	2	
Andrews, Thomas	2	3	4		
Carr, Caleb	3	5	6		1
Carr, Robert	1	2	1		
Carr, Eseck	5	3	6		
Sweet, Thomas	1	1	1		

NAME OF HEAD OF FAMILY.	Free white males of 16 years and upward, including heads of families.	Free white males under 16 years.	Free white females, including heads of families.	All other free persons.	Slaves.
WEST GREENWICH TOWN—con.					
Hopkins, John	2	1	2		
Whitman, Rhodes	2	2	2		
Fairbanks, William	3	1	3		
Mott, Robert	1	2	3		
Jenkins, Benjamin	1	5	6		
Hopkins, Joseph	3	1	5		
Hopkins, Thomas	1	1	2		
Philips, Deborah			3		
Spynk, Nicholas	1	2	2		
Hopkins, Ebinezer	1	4	2		
Green, Abel	5	3	3		
Hopkins, Joseph, Junr	1	1	1		
Hall, Robert	1	1	1		
Mathewson, Thomas	3		3		

NAME OF HEAD OF FAMILY.	Free white males of 16 years and upward, including heads of families.	Free white males under 16 years.	Free white females, including heads of families.	All other free persons.	Slaves.
WEST GREENWICH TOWN—con.					
Brown, Gideon	3	2	8		
Hopkins, Samuel	3	3	3		
Briggs, John	1	2	7		
Howard, Elizabeth	1	1	3		
Hopkins, William, Junr	1	1	3		
Bentley, Caleb	2	3	3		
Cobb, Daniel	1	2	2		
Jorden, Miles	1	1	1		
Stafford, Michael	1	1	2		
Dolliver, Joseph	1	1	1		
Dolliver, Joseph, Jun	2	3	2		
Manchester, Job	2	3	2		
Mins, Nicholas	2	3	5		

NEWPORT COUNTY.

NAME OF HEAD OF FAMILY.	Free white males of 16 years and upward, including heads of families.	Free white males under 16 years.	Free white females, including heads of families.	All other free persons.	Slaves.
JAMESTOWN TOWN.					
Howland, John	2	2	3	1	3
Haszard, Thomas	2	2	2		
Martin, William	1		3		
Stanton, Renewed	3	1	6		
Cotterell, Nathaniel	2		1	2	
Knowles, Haszard	1	2	4	1	
Armstrong, George	1	2	3	1	
Fowler, Josiah	1	1	3		
Austin, Joseph	1	2	7		
Weeden, York				4	
Manchester, Joseph	1	3	1		
Franklin, John	1	2	5		
Franklin, George	1	1	2		
Franklin, Abel	1	1	3		
Martin, Bersheba			1	1	3
Reynolds, Benjamin	2		4		
Remmington, Stephen	1	2	3		
Remmington, Clark	1		1		
Remmington, Benjamin	2	1	2	1	
Fowler, Jonathan	1		1		
Battey, John	1	2	4		
Carr, Bristol				5	
Greene, Joseph	2		4		
Greene, Jonathan	1	2	2		
Potter, Peleg	1	2	3		
Lewis, Mr	1		1		
Brown, Jeremiah	1	3	6		
Weeden, Arnold	1	2	3	1	1
Weeden, Daniel	1	1	4		
Weeden, John	1	2	3	1	
Douglass, Joseph	1	1	8		
Fowler, Thomas	1	1	3		
Fowler, Christopher	2		3		
Tew, John	1	3	6		
Tew, Elisha	1	2	5		
Eldrich, Cuff				6	
Weeden, Tobey				8	
Carr, Benjamin	1		1		
Carr, Benjamin, Junr	1		3		
Fowler, Henry	1	1	1		
Carr, Isaac	1	1	4		
Hopkins, Samuel	1	1	4		
Haszard, Thomas	1		2		
Eldrich, John	2	3	7	5	
Howland, Isaac	1		2		3
Grinnell, Mathew	1		1		
Grinnell, Robert	1	2	3		
Armstrong, Oliver	1	2	2		
Carr, Robert	1	1	2		
Carr, William	1	1	2		
Brightman, Isaac	2		2		
Remmington, Jershom	3	1	5		
Tiers, Benjamin	1	1	1	1	
Eldrich, Plimouth				6	
Remmington, John	2	2	4	1	
Carr, Peleg, Junr	1	3	6		
Carr, Peleg	2	3	6		
Carr, James	4		3	2	
Hull, Tiddeman	1	3	6		
Remmington, Tiddeman	1		3		
Slocom, Peleg	2	2	4		
Battey, William	1	3	7	1	
Carr, Nicholas	3		4		3
Mathewson, John	2	3	4		
Weeden, Daniel	1		6	2	
Weeden, Peggy		1			
Weeden, Peleg	1	1	3		
Fowler, Henry	1		3	1	
Hopkins, Jonathan	5		4		
Watson, Job	5	1	2	3	
Underwood, Joseph	1	2	2		
Underwood, Mary	1		2		
Fowler, Oliver	1	2	1		
Howland, Quam				6	

NAME OF HEAD OF FAMILY.	Free white males of 16 years and upward, including heads of families.	Free white males under 16 years.	Free white females, including heads of families.	All other free persons.	Slaves.
JAMESTOWN TOWN—continued.					
Townsend, Harwick					5
Carr, Samuel	2	2	5		
Carr, Ebinezar	1	4	1	1	
Hammond, Nathaniel	1	2	2		
Remmington, Orman					5
LITTLE COMPTON TOWN.					
Almey, Sanford	1	5	3		
Bailey, Samuel	1	6	4		
Woodman, Edward	2		4	1	
Woodman, John	3	4	2		
Woodman, Ruth			3		
White, Peregrine	1	2	2		
Little, Fobes	1		2		
Little, Fobes, Junr	2	2	4		
Allen, William	1	1	5		
Woodman, Robert	1		2		
Brown, Thomas	2	4	6		
Grinnell, Billings	1	1	8	1	2
Grinnell, Aaron	1	1	4	1	
Rouse, Hannah			3		
Irish, Ann			2		
Irish, David	1				
Dring, Nathaniel	1	1	2		
Shaw, Seth	1	2	2		
Hunt, William	1	4	4		
Irish, Samuel	2	2	2		
Irish, David	1	1	3		
Irish, Charles	1		3		
Brown, Robert	1		2		
Brown, Moses	2	3	3		
Salsberry, John	1		3		
Ballantine, John	1		2	1	
Brown, John	1	1	2		
Brown, Sylvanous	1	1	7		
Brown, William	1	1	2		
Brown, George	1	4	2		
Wood, Ichabod	2	1	3		
Head, Fobes	2	1	3		
Davis, John	2		3	4	
Clapp, Deborah			2		
White, Christopher	2	1	2		
Brown, William	1	4	4		
Gray, Samuel	2	4	5		3
Gray, John	1	2	3		
Bailey, Molly			2		
Richmond, William	3	1	2	2	2
Wood, George	2	1	4		
Coe, Samuel	1	4	2		
Bliven, John	1		1		
Brownell, Pierce	1		3		
Coe, William	1	2	4		
Richmond, Peres	3		5		
Richardson, Thomas	1	1	4		
Church, Ebinezar	3		2		
Simmonds, Adam	1	1	2		
Simmonds, Isaac	1		3		
Church, Nathaniel	2		3	1	
Church, William	4	1	2		
Sheppard, Mace	1	2	1	1	
Wood, Isaac	1	1	6		
Taylor, Philip	3		3		
Taylor, Andrew	2		5		
Lynn, Sarah			2		
Church, Caleb	1	1	1		
Pain, Richard	1	1	3		
Brownell, George	1	1	5		
Brownell, Stephen	1		1		
Head, Job	1				
Sampson, Dolly (Negro)				2	
Hilyer, David	1	1	3		4
Hilyer, David, Junr	2	1	3		
Peckham, John	3		1	1	
Peckham, Isaac	1	2	1		

NAME OF HEAD OF FAMILY.	Free white males of 16 years and upward, including heads of families.	Free white males under 16 years.	Free white females, including heads of families.	All other free persons.	Slaves.
LITTLE COMPTON TOWN—continued.					
Head, David	2	1	3		
Brownell, Gideon	2	5	5		
Shaw, Benjamin	1	1	2		
Shaw, Noah	1	1	2		
Wood, Reuben	2	3	2		
Shaw, Isreal	1		3		
Wood, Peleg	1		1		
Shaw, William	1	5	1		
Head, Gamaliel	1	1	3		
Brownell, John	2	1	3		
Woodman, Sylvester	1	2	1		
Wilbore, Aaron	3		2		1
Brownwell, James	1	1	5		
Manchester, Charles	1	1	3		
Durfee, Wing	2	2	6		
Brightman, Thomas	1	3	3		
Manley, William	1	1	2		
Palmer, Rescome	3	4.	4		
Wood, Abner	2	2	4		
Head, Benjamin	3		1		
Head, Henry	2	2	5		
Brownell, Charles	1	6	2		
Manchester, Brazil	1		3		
Brownell, James	1	6	2		
Richards, Mary			3		
Manchester, Gilbert	1		2		
Manchester, Joseph	1		3		
Brownell, William	1	1	1		
Parmer, Job	1	1	4		
Pierce, Isaac	1	1	2		
Stoddard, Nathaniel	1		5		
Stoddard, Benjamin	1	1	5		
Stoddard, Brownell	1		2		
Stoddard, Zebediah	2		2		
Davenport, Jonathan	1		1		
Snell, Job	2	2	3		
Wilbore, Champlin	1	1	4		
Parmer, Thomas	3	2	4		
Palmer, Elkanah	3	1	3		
Palmer, Benedict	1	1	4		
Wilbore, John	2		4		
Wilbore, Brownell	1	2	4		
Manchester, Edward	1	2	2		
Sanford, Rescomb	1		2		
Woodman, William	1	2	4		
Richmond, Benjamin	2	6	6		
Head, Benjamin	1	5	3		
Searle, Nathaniel	3	1	4	1	
Richmond, William	1		4		
Bennett, John	1	1	5		
Clapp, Barnabus	1	2	1		
Simmonds, Zara	1	1	4		
Simmons, John	3	1	4		
Simmons, Ichabod	1	3	2		
Simmons, Mary			2		
Simmons, Aaron	2	1	6		
Phillis (Negro)				5	
Wilbore, William	3	1	2		
Simmonds, Caleb	1		7		
Dring, Philip	1	1	3		
Browning, Gardner	1	2	3		
Grinnell, Zebede	2		3	1	
Layer, Josiah	1	1	4		
Pierce, Wright	3	2	3		
Pierce, Nathaniel	2	1	2	1	
Pierce, Ezekiel	2				
Pierce, Priscilla			1	1	
Pierce, John	1	2	2		
Briggs, Arnold	1	1	1		
Tomkins, Sarah			2		
Seaburry, William	3	3	5		
Tomkins, Nathaniel	1	4	3		
Sawyer, Lemuel	1	2	2		
Sawyer, Josiah	1	2	1		
Tomkins, John	1	1	2		

NEWPORT COUNTY—Continued.

LITTLE COMPTON TOWN—cont'd.

NAME OF HEAD OF FAMILY.	Free white males of 16 years and upward, including heads of families.	Free white males under 16 years.	Free white females, including heads of families.	All other free persons.	Slaves.
Pierce, Giles	1		4		
Seaberry, Gideon	1	4	2		
Snell, Pardon	2	1	5		
Stoddard, Arnold	1	1	2		
Briggs, Lovett	1	2	3		
Simmons, Gerge	2	1	3		
Fowler, Cynthia			2		
Pierce, Stephen	1	1	3		
Davenport, Thomas	1	1	2		
Wilbore, William	1	2	3		
Carr, William	2	1	1		
Woodman, Sarah	1	1	3		
Hyliard, Jonathan	1	2	3		
Hilyard, Samuel	1	1	3		
Taylor, William	2	2	5		
Wilbore, Sylvanous	1	4	7		
Simmons, Nathaniel	1	1	4		
Taylor, Jonathan	1	2	2		
Chace, Timothy	1	3	3		
Wilbore, Joseph	1	2	3		
Wilbore, Samuel	1		2		
Wilbore, Clarke	1	2	2		
Wilbore, Anthony	1	2	4		
Gray, Job	1	4	4	1	
Wilbore, William	4		7		
Coe, Benjamin	1	3	4		
Wilbore, Daniel	4	1	4		
Southworth, William	1	1	6		
Burgis, Thomas	1				2
Wood, Constant	3		1		
Wood, Mordecai	1	1	1		
Chace, James	1	1	1		
Chace, Ezra	2		5		
Hunt, Samuel	2	2	4		
Simmons, Benoni	1	1	2		
Bailey, Ephraim	4	4	3	1	
Grinnall, Aaron	1	1	2		
Bailey, John	2	2	5	1	
Bailey, Isaac	2	2	5	2	
Bailey, Thomas	1		2	3	
Grinnall, Owen	1		2		
Chace, Philip	1	1	1		
Bailey, William	2	3	4		
Davenport, Jeremiah	1	1	5		
Austin, Jeremiah	2	1	4		
Austin, James	1	1	3		
Shaw, Isreal	1		2		
Southworth, Constant	3	1	1		
Wilbore, William	1		1		
Woodworth, Elisha	1		1		
Head, Lovell	1	1	5		
Wood, Molly			1		
Wilbore, Charles	1		6		
Wilbore, Isaac	1	1	2		
Davenport, William	1	3	4		
Wilbore, Burden	1	2	1		
Gibbs, John	1		1		
Hunt, Adam	1	2	8		
Davis, Aaron	1		2		
Wilbore, Joseph			4	1	
Pierce, James	3		3		
Hicks, Eunice			2		
Simmons, Joseph	1	2	4		
Simmons, Benjamin	1	2	3		
Taylor, James	1	1	6		
Simmons, Gideon	1	2	3		
Shaw, Peter	2	3	5		
Brownell, Thomas	3	1	4		
Briggs, William	2		1		
Briggs, Job	1	1	4		
Briggs, Thomas	2	2	2		
Palmer, Joseph	2		7		
Brownell, Joseph	2	3	6		
Briggs, Cornelius	1		1		
Briggs, Anna		1	2		
Wilbore, Samuel	1	2	1		
Taylor, Robert	1	1	3		
Grinnell, Lydia			3		
Simmons, William	2	1	4		
Tompkins, James	1	2	2		
Tompkins, Gamaliel	1	1	7		
Simmons, Jonathan	2	3	3		
Simmons, Ephraim	2	1	6	1	
Snell, Sarah		1	2		
Salsberry, Anthony	1	2	2		
Manchester, Jabez	1		2		
Brownell, William	2	3	3		
Snell, Susannah			2		
Miller, Robert	1		2		
Wilbore, Thomas	2	3	5		
Wilbore, Walter	4		2		
Wilbore, Hannah		1	2		
Simmons, Ivory	1	4	3		
Childs, Jeremiah	1		2		

LITTLE COMPTON TOWN—cont'd.

NAME OF HEAD OF FAMILY.	Free white males of 16 years and upward, including heads of families.	Free white males under 16 years.	Free white females, including heads of families.	All other free persons.	Slaves.
Stoddard, David	1	1	4		
Springer, John	1		3		
Wilbore, Isaac	1	1	3		
Manchester, Job	1	1	5		
Gifford, Noah	2	1	2		
Gifford, Enos	3	3	6		
Gifford, Joseph	2	1	5		
Gifford, Jonathan	1	1	2		
Gifford, John	1		2		
Gifford, William	1	2	3		
Manchester, Zebediah	2	4	3		
Ladd, William			3	1	
Tabor, David	2	4	3		
Tabor, William	1				
Brownell, Stephen	2	3	4		
Hart, Richard	1	1	3		
Manchester, John	3	4	3		
Tabor, Philip	2	5	3		
Hart, Joseph	2	3	5		
Hart, Sarah			2		
Hart, Noah	1	2	3		
Seaberry, Benjamin	1		3		
Seaberry, Constant	1	4	4		
Woodman, Susannah	1		1		

MIDDLETOWN TOWN.

NAME OF HEAD OF FAMILY.	Free white males of 16 years and upward, including heads of families.	Free white males under 16 years.	Free white females, including heads of families.	All other free persons.	Slaves.
Chace, James	2	2	3		
Slocomb, Fortune				3	
Hathaway, Elizabeth	1	1	2		
Bowler, Charles	2	3	3		
Irish, George	9		9	2	2
Peckham, Isaac	1	2	3		
Bailey, Hannah	1	1	2		
Anthony, Gould	1		2		
Peckham, Daniel	2		1		
Anthony, Elizabeth	1	1	2		
Gould, Thomas	2	1	7		
Gould, Daniel	1	2	6		
Weaver, Thomas	3	1	1		
Gould, John	4		7		
Rodgers, John	3		4		
Babcock, Nathan	1	1	1		
Coggeshall, Clark	1	1	2		
Weaver, Job	1	3	2		
Brown, William	3	5	6		
Brown, Peleg	1	4	4		
Brown, Gideon	2	3	6		
Brown, Pardon	2		3		
Weaver, Thomas, Junr	2	1	2		
Coggeshall, Josiah	2	1	2		
Weaver, Mathew	1	2	5		
Stoddard, Isaac	2		7		
Shearman, Thomas, Junr	1	1	2		
Cornell, Samuel	2		2		
Coggeshall, Sarah			5		
Cornell, Robert	1	1	5	2	
Slocomb, Peleg	1	2	2		
Wilcox, Sarah	3		2		
Olivet, James	1		2		
Weaver, Rosanna	1	1	2		
Durfee, Oliver	2	4	5		
Albro, John	2	1	5	1	
Worden, Anna			4		
Coggeshall, Thomas	3	1	2		
Potter, James	2	1	5		2
Coggeshall, Jonathan	2	4	6		
Coggeshall, Jonas	1	1	1	1	
Coggeshall, Joseph	2	3	5		
Sheffield, Aaron	5	1	5	6	1
Anthony, Jonathan	3	1	2		
Weaver, Ruth	1		1		
Anthony, Daniel	2		4		
Slocom, John	3		3	2	
Dyer, James	2	1	3		
Durfee, James	2	1	3		
Clarke, Weston	2		1		
Gould, Thomas	1	1	3		
Lake, David	1		1		
Stoddard, Salesberry	3	1	3		
Peckham, Silas	2		4		
Peckham, Isaac	1	1	2		
Peckham, Samuel	1	3	3		
Peckham, Levi	1	3	4		
Wyatt, Samuel	1	2	4		
Bailey, Easton	1	1	3	2	
Hathaway, Aaron	1		3		
Wood, John	2	1	2		
Manchester, John	1		4		
Allen, Samuel	2	2	3		
Slocom, Giles	1		3		
Lawton, Isaac	1		4		
Mitchel, James	1		3		

MIDDLETOWN TOWN—cont'd.

NAME OF HEAD OF FAMILY.	Free white males of 16 years and upward, including heads of families.	Free white males under 16 years.	Free white females, including heads of families.	All other free persons.	Slaves.
Mitchel, Richard	2	4	5		
Manchester, Hannah	5	3	3		
Coggeshall, Thomas	2	3	3		
Allen, Peleg	1	2	8		
Allen, Elisha	3		2		
Allen, Sarah			4		
Taggart, Clarke	1	2	2		
Macomber, Lois			3		
Ward, Philip	3	1	1		
Holmes, John			8		
Weaver, John	3	1	2		
Barker, Samuel	1	1	2		
Smith, Edward	1	1	3		
Reider Joseph	1	4	2		
Ward, Richard	1	1	4		
Pabodie, Benjamin	2	1	4		
Albro, David	2		3		
Lake, Jonathan	2		3		
Hopkins, Thomas	2	4	2		
Pabodie, Caleb	1	2	1		
Pabodie, Joseph	1		1		
Pabodie, John	1	1	2		
Smith, Benjamin	2	1	3		
Barker, David	1	6	5		
Smith, Philip	4		5		
Clarke, Samuel	3				
Gardiner, Benjamin	1	4	3	4	1
Peckham, Peleg	2	3	5		
Shearman, Solomon	1	1	2	1	
Eston, Nicholas	2		8	2	2
Peckham, Stephen	2	4	4		
Tew, Mary			2		
Barker, Elisha	1	2	4		
Hall, Parker	1	2	3		
Peckham, William, Junr	1		4		
Barker, Benejah	1	1	3		
Barker, Mary	1		3		
Barker, Peleg	1		5		
Barker, Mathew	1	3	5		
Slocom, William	1	4	4		
Barker, Edward, Junr	1		3		
Barker, Edward	3		1		
Reider, William	1	3	5		
Barker, Gideon	1	1	3		
Barker, Joshua	1	1	6		
McWater, John	1		1	1	4
Turner, Peleg	1		2		
Vars, John	3	4	5		
Peckham, Richard	1	3	3		
Peckham, Daniel, Junr	1	3	3		
Peckham, Joseph	3	2	7		
Weeden, Jonathan	2		1		
Card, Richard	3		4		
Bliss, William	3		5		
Peckham, Joshua	1	3	4		
Peckham, William	2	1	1		
Peckham, Felix	2		4		
Easton, Edward	2	1	7		
Barker, Jeremiah	1		2		
Weeden, William	2	1	4		
Peckham, Mary			2		
Easton, Walter	2		2	1	

NEW SHOREHAM TOWN.

NAME OF HEAD OF FAMILY.	Free white males of 16 years and upward, including heads of families.	Free white males under 16 years.	Free white females, including heads of families.	All other free persons.	Slaves.
Sands, John	2	2	5	1	6
Clark, Ichabod	3	2	2		1
Dodge, James	1		2	6	
Dodge, Hezekiah	1		2	6	
Wyllis, Hnry	1	1	2	6	1
Connelly, Edward	3	1	4	8	
Card, Job	3	2	2	3	
Mitchel, Sarah			2	5	
Rathbone, Walter	3		4	5	1
Mott, Lodowick	1	3	2	1	
Rose, Thomas	1	1	2		
Angel, William	5	2	8		
Milligan, Archibold	1	2	2		
Dodge, Mark	1		3	6	1
Pain, William	1	1	7	1	1
Cartwright, Edward	1	1	2		
Rose, James	3	1	4		1
Dodge, Samuel	1		7	4	
Sands, Ray	1	3	3		
Littlefield, Nathaniel	5	2	5		2
Mitchel, Alexander	1	1	2		
Mitchel, Solomon	1	1	2		
Mitchel, Joseph	1		7		
Ball, Isaac	1	1	2		
Ball, Fanny			2		
Frankling, Abel	3		4		
Franklin, John	2		2		
Rose, Daniel	1		3		1
Rose, Enock	1	1	2		1

NEWPORT COUNTY—Continued.

NEW SHOREHAM TOWN—continued.

NAME OF HEAD OF FAMILY.	Free white males of 16 years and upward, including heads of families.	Free white males under 16 years.	Free white females, including heads of families.	All other free persons.	Slaves.
Littlefield, Anthony	3		1		1
Littlefield, Benjamin	1	5	3		
Russell, Robert	1	2	2		
Rose, John	1	2	4		
Rose, Sarah	2	2	3		
Crandal, Azariah	1	3	5		
Sheffield, Edward	1	1	3		1
Dodge, Nathaniel	3	4	3		
Sprague, John	4	2	3		
Dodge, Nathaniel, Junr	1	1	1		
Wright, John	1	4	4		
Ball, Edward	2	3	7		
Ball, John	1	2	3		
Ball, Peter	3	4	3		
Dodge, Edmund	1		2		
Dodge, Samuel	1	1	2		
Sprague, William	1		1		
Dodge, Thomas	2		4		
Littlefield, Thomas	1	3	4		
Rose, Ezekiel	3		4		
Dickins, Daniel	2		1		
Dickins, Amos	2		2		
Dunn, Lucy	1	1	2		
Beckwith, Anderson	1	2	3		
Rose, William	1	1	4		
Rose, Dorry, Junr	1		2		
King, John	1		3		
Rose, Dorry	1	1	4		
Rose, John	1	2	3		
Rose, Gurden	1		2		
Dodge, Edmond	1		2		
Mott, Daniel	2	4	1		
Mott, Mm Waitstill	2	2	1		
Pocock, Mary	1	2	3		
Dickins, Thomas	3	1	1		2
Dodge, Tristram	2	1	5		
Mitchel, John	3	4	5		
Mitchel, Joseph	3	2	3		
Mitchel, Johnathan	1	3	2		
Mitchel, Thomas	3	1	8		
Ayres, Hannah			3		
Honeywell, Abijah	1	2	3		
Pain, John	2		6	3	
Sands, Edward	2	1	3	6	
Franklin, Stephen	2		1	9	
Gorton, John	4	2	2	6	
Dodge, Joshua	3	4	7	1	
Rose, Hancock	1	1	3		
Dodge, Joshua, Junr	1	2			
Littlefield, Caleb	3		3		5
Sheffield, Edmund	1	1	1		
Littlefield, Solomon	2		6		
Miner, George	1	2	5		
Briggs, Mm Margery	4		2		
Dodge, Jane	3	1	2		
Paine, Peggy			2		
Rose, William	1	1	2		
Briggs, Joseph	1	1	1		
Littlefield, John	2	1	5	6	2
Eldrich, Daniel	2	1	3		
Littlefield, Henry	2	1	4		4

NEWPORT TOWN.

NAME OF HEAD OF FAMILY.	Free white males of 16 years and upward, including heads of families.	Free white males under 16 years.	Free white females, including heads of families.	All other free persons.	Slaves.
Dyre, Samuel	3	2	2		
Freebourne, Robert	4	1	4		
Miller, Mary			3		
Finch, Joseph	1		4		
Hoxsie Lodewick	1	1	2		
Greene, Patience	2	2	5		
Butts, Bershaba	1		1		
Hoxsie, Benjamin	2	4	3		
Crandal, Ezekiel	1		2		
Weaver, James	2		2		
Stoddard, Jonathan	4		2		
Stoddard, Salsebery	1		2		
Marvil, Jonathan	1	1	4		
Taylor, Anthony				2	
Currie, Mary		1	4		
Pollock, Abigail		1	3		
Sheffield, Mary	3		1		
Amory, Molly			3		
Wallace, James	1	1	7		
Taylor, Robert	2	2	4		
Challoner, Charles				6	
Dunham, Benjamin	2		2		
Lawton, Mathew	2		1		
Rodman, Samuel			6		
Hull, Samuel	1		3		
Dennis, William	1	5	5		
Wescott, John	1	2	2		
Hoase, Benjamin	2	4	3		
Roggers, John	1	1	2		
Warren, Joseph	3	3	4		

NEWPORT TOWN—con.

NAME OF HEAD OF FAMILY.	Free white males of 16 years and upward, including heads of families.	Free white males under 16 years.	Free white females, including heads of families.	All other free persons.	Slaves.
Thurston, Cato				3	
Dennis, Thomas	2	3	6		1
Finch, Margarate	2	1	5		
Southwick, Joseph	1	3	5		
Goddard, Stephen	2	1	3		
Goddard, Hannah			3		
Goddard, Thomas	1		2		
Austin, Daniel	3	3	3		
Coffin, Sally	1		2		
Hervey, Ruth			2		
Weaver, Eliphalet		1	1		
Gabbord, John	1		2		
Parmer, William	1	2	2		
Brown, Phillip	1	1	2		
Jacobs, Belah	1	2	2		
Gardnir, Joseph	1	1	3		
Weaver, Thomas, Junr	1		5		
Champlin, Joseph	1	3	5		
Case, Abigail			2		
Jack, Alexander	1	2	2		
Hill, Jeremiah	1		2		
Perrey, John	1	1	2		
East, William	1	2	1		
Sisson, Robert	2		4		
Bliss, Clark	1		1		
Thurston, Mary	2		2		
Stanhope, William	1		5		
Carson, William	2	1	2		
West, William	1		2		
West, John	3		2		
Butts, Coggeshall	2	3	5		
Spencer, Phebe		1	7		
Weaver, Gideon	1	4	4		
Witherly, Joshua	2		1		
Brown, Joseph	2	3	3		
Brown, William	1		3		
Buliod, Lewis	3		1		
Axtol, John	1		1		
Spear, Elias	1	1	3		
Davis, Mary			1		
Crandal, Phillip	1		1		
Chapple, Scranton	1	4	4		
Gibbs, Elisha	1	3	7		
Lamphier, Elizabeth	1	1	3		
Clark, Sally			2		
Crandall, Joseph	1	1	3		
Stephens, Zirgo				3	
Thurston, John	1		1		
Peckham, Deborah		2	2		
Douglas, William	1		2		
Viol, Samuel	1		1		
Dockray, Margaret				3	
Fry, Thomas	1		3	1	
Chadwick, Jonathan	2	2	7		
Engs, William	1	1	4	1	
Dayton, Henry	1	2	5		
Howland, Ann		2	6		
Fish, Caleb	1	1	2		
Nickols, Joseph	1		1		
Robinson, Thomas	2		7	3	
Mumford, Paul	1	2	1	1	
Warren, John	2		4		
Howland, Sarah	2	4	3		
Tillinghast, Joseph	1	2	3		
Dillingham, Edward	1	2	4		
Boss, Joseph	2		4		
Huntington, David	3	3	2		
Simpson, Richard	1		2		
Thurston, William	1	2	4		
Simpson, John	1		1		
Grafton, Nathaniel	1		1		
Anthony, Elizabeth			1		
Wilson, William			2		
Smith, Marcy		1	5		
Luther, Nathan	5	1	2		
Lawton, Benjamin	1	3	7		
Borden, Thomas	1	2	3		
Borden, Molly			1		
Townsdend, Cato				2	
Boss, William				6	
Crandall, Joshua	1		3		
Topham (Widow)	1		5		
Townsdend, Job	2	1	2		
Anthony, Daniel	1	1	4	1	
Boss, Martin	1	2	4		
Anderson, Francis	1	2	4		
Vaughn, Elizabeth			1		
Morse, Agnes	2		3	2	
Dedrich, John	1		2		
Gardner, Pomp				2	
Gardner, Cudge				4	
Baker, Benjamin	3		4		
Low, Sarah			2		
Slocum, George				6	

NEWPORT TOWN—con.

NAME OF HEAD OF FAMILY.	Free white males of 16 years and upward, including heads of families.	Free white males under 16 years.	Free white females, including heads of families.	All other free persons.	Slaves.
Potter, William	3	2	7		
Sawyer, Betsey			2	1	
Cornell, Thomas	1	2	1		
Freeborn, Henry	1	3	3		
Johnson, Clark	1	2	3		
Luther, Benjamin	1		1		
Sears, George	2	1	3	1	
Goddard, Ruth			2		
Lewis, Richard	1	1	2		
Manchester, Anna	1		2		
Levi, Pomp				6	
Bush, Richard			1		
Talman, Samuel	1	1	1		
Lawton, Jonathan	1	1	6		
Rodman, Catherine			2		
Burras, Elizabeth			3		
Almey, Prince				6	
Murray, Anthony	2	2	2		
Peabody, Benjamin	3		4		
Roggers, Mary			5		
Heath, Jonathan	2	2	3		
Hammilton, Alexander	1		1		
Powrs, Micheal	1		2		
Roggers, Jonathan	1		2		
Pettiface, Rebeckah			1		
Newton, Simeon	1		4		2
Ward, Benoni	1		2		
Roggers, John	1		1		
Crafts, William	1	2	4		
Lyndon, Caleb	3	2	4		
Bilot, John	1	2	1		
Roggers, Josias	1		1		
White, Isaac	1		1		
Johnson, Meriam	1		2		
Dunham, Daniel	1	1	2		
Newton, John	1	1	4		
Larley, Mr	1		2		
Ingraham, Benjamin	2		2	1	1
Fowler, Clarke	1	1	2		
Gardner, William	3	1	4		
Williams, John	1	3	2		
Loyd, William	2		2		
Handley, Molly	1		2		
Cooper, William	2	2	1		
Parker, William	2		2		
Greenwood, Holmes	1		2		
Cranston, Peleg	2	2	3	1	
Simpson, Samuel	1	1	1		
Grinman, William	1		2		
Townsdend, Edmund	1	4	3		
Coit, John	1	4	4		
Clarke, George	3	1	4		
Phillips, Sarah	1		1		
Crosby, Mrs			1	5	
Crandall, Thomas	1	1	5		
Shermon, Peleg	1	1	2		
Lillibridge, John	1	2	4		
Hammett, Dolly			1		
Townsdend, John	1	4	3		1
Townsdend, Christopher	1	1	2		
Thurston, Abigail	1	3	3		
Milward, James	1	1	3		
Wilson, John	1	1	4		
Fish, Alice	1		2		
Friend, John	2	2	1		
Potter, Thomas	1	2	3	1	
Nerbourne, John	2	2	3		
Atwood, Sheffield	2	4	5		
Boss, John	1	4	3		1
Bois, Joseph	2		2		
Nickols, Benjamin	2		3	1	
Williams, John	5	2	6		
Dayton, Isaac	1	1	1		1
Pettice, Amey			1		
Clarke, Nathaniel	3	3	7		
Oldfield, John	1	1	6		
Munroe, George	1		4		
Remmington, Auther				4	
Mowatt, Quash				5	
Challoner, Cudge				3	
James, Flora				5	
Littlifield, Henry				5	
Shermon, Cash				5	
Rivera, Abram	1	1	5	1	4
Clarke, Jeremiah	4	3	5		
Slocum, Samuel	1	3	5		
Cooke, William	1		3		
Franklin, Robert	1		2		
Chapman, Britain	1	2	2		
Stoddard, Mary	1		3		
Tillinghast, Thomas	1		1		
Carter, James	1		1		
Carter, Robert	2	3	2		
Topham, John	2	5	2		

NEWPORT COUNTY—Continued.

NEWPORT TOWN—con.

Name of head of family	Free white males of 16 years and upward, including heads of families	Free white males under 16 years	Free white females, including heads of families	All other free persons	Slaves
Godfrey, Amtice		2	7		
Robinson, William	2	1	3		
Geers, Richard	1	1	1		
Ashton, Thomas	1	1	2		
Hull, Jonathan	1		2		
Hill, Mary			2		
Billington, Elisha	1	1	2		
Carle, Sarah			1		
Card, William	1	2	4		
Matts, Barney	1		4		
Orsborne, Thomas	1	4	2		
Bond, Miles	1	1	2		
Helme, William	1	1	2		
Helme, James	1		1		
Wilbore, George	1		1		
Austin, Job	1	1	6		
Helme, Samuel	1		1		
Watts, Daniel	1		2		
Southwick, Jonathan	1	2	1		
Shaw, John	3	1	5		
Knapp, Elijah	1	2	3		
Swan, Richard	2	2	2		
Lillibridge, Jonathan	2		2		
Dunham, Robert	1	6	4		2
Anthony, James	1	3	3		
Brier, Elias	2		1		
Brown, Mary			3		
Burnett, Andrew	3	1	3		
Bush, Richard	1	3	5		
Jenkins, Nathaniel	1	7	2		
Barber, Henry	2	4	4		
Dewett, Oliver	1	4	3		
Dedio, Mehitible		2	3		
Cotton, Patience				2	
Dyer, Joseph	2	4	5		
Beebe, Nathan	2	3	7		2
Jeffers, Jonathan	1	3	2		
Omer, Henry	1		2		
Goddard, Mary			3		
Holloway, Daniel	3	1	9		
Monks, Daniel	1		1		
Langley, George	1	1	1		
Cozzens, Joseph	2	5	3	1	
Cozzens, William	1		1	1	
Haswell, Martha	2	3	2		
Pike, Joseph	1	2	6		
Devenport, Charles	2		8		
Ferguson, Thomas				6	
Moulton, Micheal	1	4	3		
Young, Samuel	1	1	3		
Edy, Micheal	1		2		
Gion, Thomas	1	2	2		
Flagg, Auther				9	
Hicks, Cudgo				4	
Wickam, Mark				4	
Brawon, David	1	3	7		
Hall, Benjamin	3		3		
Hall, George	3	3	3		
Batang, Margaratt			4		
McClish, Margaratt		1	4		
Bowers, Quam				2	
Stevens, John	1	3	4		
Keith, Robert				2	
Keith, Limus				3	
Thurston, Gardner	1		2	1	
Macomber, Ephriam	1		1		
Cole, Sarah		2	3		
Wiatt, Standfast	1	3	3		
Fry, George	3		3	1	1
Perrey, George	1		5		
Marshall, Nancy			1		
Phillips, Elizabeth		1	3		
Oakler, Mrs			1		
Freebourne, Joseph	1	4	2		
Trevitt, Eleazar	4	2	4		
Bourroughs, Pompey				2	
Lawton, Samuel	1	1	5		
Lawton, Jonathan	1	1	4		
Cutler, Thomas	2	1	3		
Mumford, Thomas	3	3	2		
Forrester, Thomas	1		5		
Sanford, Samuel	1	1	3		
Barker, Benjamin	1	2	2		
Merchant, Henry	1	3	5	1	1
Bentley, Ann		3	6		
Slocum, William	1	1	2		
Hookey, Daniel	1		1		
Billings, Benjamin	1		1		
Wise, Adam	2		3		
Hookey, William	1		2		
Vose, Thomas	1				
Soal, Abigail		3	2	1	
Gofrong, Elizabeth		1	3	1	
Kenyon, Remmington	3		3		
Wallen, Alice		2	2		
Weaver, Perrey	2	5	4		
Walden, Rebeckah	2		3		
Wanton, Gideon	4				2
Nickols, Samuel	1	2	2		
Wate, Ann			1		
Beebe, Joseph	1	3	4		
Williams, Mrs			2		
Jennings, Temperance			2		
Murphy, Edward	1	4	4		
Nightingale, George	1	1	3		
Drew, Cuffee				2	
Vickery, Dick				3	
Lawton, Jeremiah	1		1		
Esten, James	1	2	5		
Hardin, James	1	1	2		
Engs, William	1	2	5		
Pierce, John	1	2	3		
Isaacks, Jacob	1	2	6		
Dunham, Barbary			2		
Coddington, Catherine			4		
Coddington, Edward	2	1	3		
Waldron, George	1	3	2		
Woodard, Robert	1	1	2		
Vose, Edward	1	3	5		
Richardson, Hannah	1		4		
Horn, Mrs Mary	1	4	3		
Wilson, Caleb	1	1	1		
Robinson, William	2		1	1	
Card, Sarah	2		1		
Richardson, Josias				2	
Heath, Record	1	2	4		
Warner, Oliver R	3		4	1	2
Young, Samuel	1	1	5		
Center, James	2	1	5	1	
Tripp, Abiel	1	2	1		
Cornell, Peace			3		
Anthony, William	1	2	3		
Downer, Phobe			1		
Fowler, Samuel G	1	1	3		1
Jacobs, Joseph	1	3	4	1	
Fryers, Elizabeth			3	1	
Nickols, Walter	2	3	7		1
Garrison, Nicholas	1	2	1		
King, Deborah			1	1	
Pinnegas, Mary			1	4	
Tew, Thomas	6	2	4		
Almey, Jonathan	2	1	3		
Clarke, Polly	1	1	3		
Goulding, Isaac	1		2	1	
Ayres, Elizabeth			2		
Harwood, John, Jr	1	1	2		
Clarke, Sarah			2		
Heath, Jonathan	1		2		
Perrey, Joseph	1	1	2		
Fell, Deborah			0		
Williams, John	1	2	3		
Maxson, Caleb	1	3	2		
Fry, James	1		3		
Stephens, Thomas, Junr	1	4	5		
Stephens, Thomas	2		1	1	
Channing, Anna			1	1	1
Larcy, Jeremiah				2	
Wheeden, Jeremiah	1				
Borden, William	1	3	2		
Beebe, Bush					5
Brown, Clarke			2	1	
Harwood, John, Jr	1		3		
Stearns, Samuel	1	2	2		
Challoner, Joseph			2		
Perkins, Phebe		1	2		
Champlin, Phebe			4	1	
Coddington, Nathaniel	1		2		
Church, Benjamin	2		4		
Ambrose, Israel	2		3		
Greenman, Joseph	2	1	3		
Kennedy, Nancy			2		
Tripp, Thomas	1		1		
Storer, Zebediah	3		5	1	1
Allen, Joseph	1	2	8		
Coffin, Paul	2		2		
Fish, Preserved	1		1		
Northup, Margery			1	1	
Wey, James	1	2	2		
Carter, William	1		1		
Gardner, Isaac	1	2	1		
Juba, Lewis W	1	2	4		
Sevier, Mrs					2
Bailey, Constant	1		1		
Bailey, Benjamin	1	1	1		
Irish, Charles	1		4		
Barker, Benjamin	4		5		
Barker, Joseph	1		3		
Roggers, Martin	2	2	2		
Cornell, George	1		4		
Lillibridge, Alice	2	1	3		
Martino, Martha	1	2	3		
Scoett, Elizabeth			2		
Miller, Elizabeth	2		5	1	2
Hammond, Pain	1	3	4		
Hardin, Abram	1	1	1		
Gardner, Mary			4		
Bryer, Jonathan	1		2		
Cowell, John Anthony	1		5		
Davis, Edward	1	2	3		
Allen, Joseph	1	3	5		
Brown, Sarah			3		
Omer, William	1		3		
Waterhouse, Timothy	1	1	2		
Stall, William	1	2			
Peckam, Henry	1	3	4		
Potter, Robert	1		3		
London, Priscilla			1		
Davis, William	2	2	4		
Bliss, Thomas	1	1	5		
Scudder, Mary		1	2		
Turner, Sarah		1	5		
Taylor, James	3	3	2		
Wilson, Jonathan	1	2	4		
Proud, Phebe		1	5		
Hazzard, Foner	1				
Clarke, Audley	2	1	2		
James, Annis			4		
Portolo, Richard	3				
Hawkins, Stephen	2	1	4		
White, Noah	1	4	3		
Phillips, Hannah			2		
Sherman, John	1		3		
Bennit, James				2	
Phillips, Phebe	1		1		
James, Benjamin	2	4	2		
Pierce, Sally		1	2		
West, Nathan	1	3	5		
Read, Oliver	2	1	2		
Arnold, Alfred	1		3		
Davenport, Gideon	4		3		
Jeffard, Jonathan	3		3		
Haswell, Pierce	1		1		
Marshall, Elizabeth	2		2		
Crossing, Sarah			1		
Thurston, Primus				3	
McKinzey, Mr	1		1		
Coggeshall, Bacchus				3	
Peterson, Swain	1		2		
Spear, Pierce	1	1	2		
Munroe, John	1	2	3		
Clarke, Richard	1		3		
Jenson, John	1		1		
Shermon, Benjamin	1		3		
Reed, William	1	4	3		
Lovey, William	1	1	1		
Helme, Thomas	1		2		
Heath, Mary	1	1	3		
Netcher, Thomas	3	3	2		
Haswell, Thomas	1		4		
Barney, Daniel	1	2	4		
Perrey, Edward	3	1	4		
Sims, William	2		2		
Taylor, Newport				2	
Bailey, Richard	3	1	3		
Wilbore, Sarah	1	1	4		
Taylor, James	1		2		
Bradley, James	1		1		
Peabody, Benjamin				2	
Anthony, Samuel	1	3	6		
Stanhope, Edward	4	1	6		
Manchester, Isaac	2	3	2		
Pike, Joseph	1		1		
Simmonds, Jonathan	2	4	5	1	
Kirber, John	1		6		
Simmonds, Edward	1	1	3		1
Cranston, Samuel	1	4	3		
Gorton, Edward	1	2	3		
Tew, James	1		1		
Coggeshall, Thomas	1	3	3		
Remmington, John	1		2		
Robinson, Thomas R	3		3		
Atkins, James	1		2		
Champlin, William, Junr	1	4	2		
George, Thomas	1		2		
Tripp, William	4	1	6		2
Peckam, Thomas	1	3	4		
Cornell, Benjamin	1		3		
Peckam, Benoni	1	1	7		
Hull, Samuel	1		3		
Holt, Sarah			4		
Harding, Prudence			2		
Roggers, James	2		3		

NEWPORT COUNTY—Continued.

NEWPORT TOWN—con.

NAME OF HEAD OF FAMILY.	Free white males of 16 years and upward, including heads of families.	Free white males under 16 years.	Free white females, including heads of families.	All other free persons.	Slaves.
Bennit, Christopher	1	1	4		
Briggs, William	1	2	2		
Webb, Hannah	1		3		
Carpenter, Cato				2	
Cornell, Gideon	3		1		
Stoddard, Fortune			•	4	
Swasey, Gregory	1	1	2		
Kidd, Richard				2	
Tabor, George	3	1	5		
Easton, Samuel				5	
Jeffard, Joseph	1		5		
Reed, Eleazar	2	3	3		
Webb, James	2	1	1		
Seabury, Thomas	1		1		
Gavit, James	1	1	2		
Cadman, Robin				2	
Hazzard, Bristol				6	
Hampshire, George				3	
Marshall, Samuel	2	3	5		
Brittain, William	1	1	3		
Shaw, Asa	1	4	1		
Yeamons, Peggy	1		1		
Nickols, Elizabeth	1		1		
Bell, Charles	1	2	1	1	
Pitman, Samuel	1	1	3		
Sambo, Marsa				2	
Earle, Caleb	2		1		
Pendleton, William	1	1	6		1
Kilborne, Caty		2	4		
Pitman, Moses	2	1	3		
Lawton, Elisha	1		2		
Pinnegas, Rebeckah	1	1	1		
Sisson, Lavis	1		2		
Taggart, William	3	3	3		
Burdick, James	3	1	3		
Bissell, Job	1	1	4		
Stone, William	2	3	3		
Pitman, Thomas	2	1	2		
Pitman, Benjamin	1		1		
Easton, Jonathan	1	2	2	2	
Stratton, John	2	1	3		
Smith, Elisha	1	4	2		
Bull, John	1	2	3		
Pitman, John	1		2		
Hargill, Joseph	2		2		
Woodard, Martha			1		
Grealea, John	1	1	3		1
Wilcocks, Robert	1		3		
Adencourt, William	2		4		
Dunham, Daniel, Jun	2	1	2		
Carey, Hannah	1		2		
Allen, William	1	4	1		
Dunham, Joseph	1		2		
Reed, Mary			2		
Clarke, William	1		1		
Brown, Auther	1	1	2		
Woodard, Robert	1		1		
Luther, Nathan	1		1		
Silvester, Mary	2		3		
More, William	2	3	7		
Wanton, John G	1		1		
Lyman, Daniel	1	1	7		1
Hosier, Giles	2	2	3		
Murphy, John	1	1	2		
Easton, Mary		1	3		
Easton, John	1	3	1		
Lawton, Rebeckah		1	5		
Brayton, Robert	2	1	4		
Lawton, John	2	4	7		
Barker, Peleg			2	1	
Barker, Richard	1		2	1	
Howard, William	1	1	2		
Tripp, Samuel	3	1	1		
Harden, Anna	1		1		
Brayton, Elizabeth			2		
Potter, Naomi			2		
Bliss, William	1	3	2		
Brown, Samuel	1		1		
Sisson, Job	1	1	5		
Cowen, William	2		1		
Bardin, Anna			1	1	
Mandsley, Mary		1	2		
Dennis, Sarah			3		
Feaks, Charles	3		5	2	
Cozzens, Peter	2	2	4		
Tares, William	1	1	4		
Buffom, Samuel	1		4		
Clarke, Joseph	3		5		
Jewel, Benjamin	1	1	3		
Gibbs, Cudgo				2	
Wilbore, Benjamin	2	1	4		
Dunbar, Robert	2	3	3		
Clarke, Mary			2		
Arnold, Thomas	1		3		1

NEWPORT TOWN—con.

NAME OF HEAD OF FAMILY.	Free white males of 16 years and upward, including heads of families.	Free white males under 16 years.	Free white females, including heads of families.	All other free persons.	Slaves.
Sanford, Samuel	1				1
Gibbs, Job	1	2	3		
Ellory, William	4	1	6		1
Gibbs, Lydia	1		2		
Vernon, Samuel	1	1	1		1
Thurston, Mary	3		4	1	
Earle, John	2	1	6		
Stanton, Elizabeth			1		
Billings, Samuel	1	1	5		
Peckham, Peter	1	1	3		
Carey, Elizabeth			3		
Paul, Mary			2		1
Lawton, Robert	3	1	3	1	
Elisier, Isaac	1		7		
Burrill, James	1		2		
Cornell, Clarke	1	1	1		
Cornell, Gideon	1	2	4		
Harris, John	1		1		
Redwood, Sally			2		
Stevens, Elizabeth			2		2
Miller, John	1	2	4		
Seaburg, Betsey			1		
Northup, Amey			2		
Davis, Amey			2		
Vernom, William	2	1	4		1
Potter, Henry	1		2		1
Roggers, Robert	3	6	5	2	
Champlin, Jabez	1	1	3		
Edes, Peter	1	3	5		
Simmons, Remembrance	1		3		
Bennit, Patience			1		1
Patten, William	2			4	
Barker, Mathew	1	2	3		
Brown, Esther			2		
Barney, Gideon	1		2		
Barker, Peleg	4	1	3		
Allen, Timothy	1		1		
Ash, Hannah		1	2		
Sanford, Nabby			2		
Pierce, John	1	1	2		
Anthony, John	3	2	6		
Levi, Moses	2	1	4		
West, William	1	1	4		
Still, George			3	4	
Richmond, Gamaliel	1		1		
West, John	1		2		
Wilson, Jonathan	1		2		
Center, Isaac	2	4	4	1	1
Gould, James	2	6	3		
Whitman, Valentine	1	2	2		
Tillinghast, Nicholas P.	1		6	1	
Wanton, Newport				2	
Brown, Sharp				2	
Easton, Walter	2		2	1	
Larcy, John				3	
Cornell, George J	1	2	2		
McCloud, Daniel	1		1		
Marvell, Charles	1		2		
Cornell, Gideon	1	1	1		
Algel, Nicholas	1	1	3		
Wanton, Sarah	2	1	2		
Lawton, John	1	1	1		
Williams, Obadiah	2		2		
Carpenter, Anna			4		
Williams, David	1		1		
Cowen, Isaac	1		3		
Robinson, Phillip	1	5	2		
Marsh, Jonathan	1	1	3	1	
Chadwick, Thomas	1		1		
Helmes, Coggeshal	1		2		
Marsh, Gould	1	3	7	1	
Marsh, Patty			1		
Wilcocks, Samuel	1	1	4		
Burns, Walter	1	2	3		
Richardson, Jacob	4	1	5		
Norman, John	1	1	2		
Norman, Moses	1	2	3		
Hull, Hanson	1	3	3		
Wanton, John	2	3	4		
Scoctt, Betsey	1		1	1	
Hadwen, John	4		9	1	
Wilson, Jane			2		
Hazzard, Lucretia			2		
Hazzard, Edward	2		2		2
Gibbs, George	5	3	8	4	
Mumford, Susannah	1		5	2	
Taber, Abner	1	2	1		
Sheffield, Ezekiel	1	1	1		1
Coggeshal, William	3		6		
Roggers, Daniel	1	3	3	1	1
Fenner, Freelove			3	1	
Greene, Caleb	1	1	2		
Langley, William	2		4		
Richmond, Gideon	1		3		

NEWPORT TOWN—con.

NAME OF HEAD OF FAMILY.	Free white males of 16 years and upward, including heads of families.	Free white males under 16 years.	Free white females, including heads of families.	All other free persons.	Slaves.
Baptist, Michael	1	2	3		
Cranston, John	1	1	3		
Coggeshall, John	1	3	2		
Mumford, Francis			3		
Bull, Phebe			1		
Allen, Mrs			1	1	
Greene, John				5	
Channing, Walter	1		4		2
Handy, Charles	1	3	4		
Weeden, Sarah			1	1	
Bates, Ann			2		
Bonos, John	1	3	4	2	
Champlin, Christopher	3		3	2	1
Horsfield, Israel	1		2		
Coggeshall, Peter	1		1		
Cotterell, Thomas	2	2	4		1
Fowler, Samuel	1		2	1	1
Coggeshall, Caleb	3		3		
Almey, Benjamin	3	1	4	3	
Clarke, Lawrence	1	1	3		
Hazzard, George	3	2	2	1	1
Lopez, Sarah	4	3	6		6
Lopez, Moses	3		1		
Cook, Margarett	1		4	1	
Champlin, George	1		3	1	
Clarke, Ethan	1	2	4		
Durffee, Elisha	2	1	3		
Freebody, Thomas	3		2		4
Freebody, Samuel	3		2		3
Mason, Benjamin	1	2	1		
Scoctt, Mrs				3	
Coggeshall, Mrs			1		
Rummeril, Thomas	1		5		
Nasson, David	1	2	3		
Session, Gideon	1	1	2		1
Tucker, Patience			1		
Briggs, Jethro	1	1	2		
Cowley, Mary		1	6	1	
Wescott, James	1		2		
Pierce, Rebeckah			1	2	
White, Elizabeth			3		
Shermon, Elizabeth			1		3
Ferguson, Adam	2		3		
Burroughs, William	1	2	5	1	
Briggs, Willard	2	1	4	1	
Babcock, William	1		2		
Freebody, Samuel	3		2		3
Fry, Benjamin	1	2	4	2	
Northup, John	1	2	3		
Davis, Mary			1	3	
Thurston, Joseph	1	1	4	1	
Pitman, Peleg	1	4	2		
Bastow, Levi	1	3	2		
Kelly, Robinson	1	1	1		
Sweet, Samuel	3		2		
Rodman, Clark	1	4	4		
Hazzard, Elizabeth	1		7		1
Cahoon, Abigail		1	4		
Sawyer, Jack				2	
Sawyer, Rebeckah		3	2		
Scoctt, Pomp				2	3
Mason, Benjamin	1	2	2	3	
Tew, Henry	1	2	6		
Buckmaster, George	1		1		
Hopkins, Samuel	2		4		
Vernom, Daniel	1	3	4		
Channing, William	3	5	6		2
Sanford, Giles	1	1	7		
Gray, Rhody			1	4	
Harkness, George	2	2	3		
Smith, William	1	4	2		
Arnold, William	1	2	3		
Roggers, Jeremiah	1	2	5		
Judah, Hillil	1	2	5		
Soxias, Moses	1	1	9	1	6
Hayner, Barnett	1	1	4		
Whitfield, Elizabeth	3	1	3		
Baker, John	1		1		6
Stockman, Ann	2		2		
Johnson, Mary			1	2	
Roggers, Patience			3		
Spooner, Peleg	1	1	2		
Tilley, William	3	4	5		
Hacker, Samuel	1				
Elwood, Samuel	1	1	6		
Brindley, Francis	2	2	3		4
Clarke, James	1	2	6		
Briggs, William	1		3		
Hunt, George	2	3	4		
Clarke, Peleg	3	2	4		6
Spooner, Samuel	3		2		
Melvill, David	1	3	4		3
Melvill, Thomas	1		1		
Melvill, Seth	1	1	3		

NEWPORT COUNTY—Continued.

NEWPORT TOWN—con.

NAME OF HEAD OF FAMILY.	Free white males of 16 years and upward, including heads of families.	Free white males under 16 years.	Free white females, including heads of families.	All other free persons.	Slaves.
Melvill, Samuel	1	2	2		
Melvill, Thomas	1				
Remmington, John	3	4	5		
Smith, Mary	1	1	3		
Jeffard, Joseph	1	1	2		
Clarke, Latham	1		1		
Anthony, Susanah			2		
Orsborn, Sarah		1	5		
Vernom, Lammet	2	3	5		
Melvill, Elizabeth			3		
Bissell, Lydia			3		
Wheeden, Lettice	1		2		
Rider, Phebe	2	1	1		
Merchant, Isabel			2		
Tanner, Scipio				2	1
King, Samuel	3		3		1
Vernom, Samuel	1		3	1	2
Oliphant, David	1	1	3		3
Smith, Ann			2		
Willis, William	1	1	1		
Smith, Mr	1		1		
Martin, Simeon	1	3	5	2	
Ayrault, Stephen	2		3		7
Clarke, John	3		3		
Wood, Peleg	6	1	3	1	
Brown, Daniel	2		4		
Dunbar, Charles	1	1	4		
Hammond, William	1	2	4	1	
Easton, Edward	1	1	2		
Thurston, Mary	1		2	1	
Briggs, John	1		1		
Hart, Nicholas	1	5	3		
Clarke, Katherine	1		2		
Macartey, Hugh		1			
Springer, John	2	1	3		
Bird, Nathaniel	1	2	5	1	
Goddard, William W	1	2	5		
Shermon, Mary			1		
Richards, John	1	2	6		
Eliot, Abigail	1	1	6	1	2
Chapple, James	3	4	2		
Downing, Rachel	2		4		
Clarke, Joseph	2	1	4	1	
Mumford, Henry	1		2		
Card, Joseph	1		3		
Peckam, Benjamin	1		2		
Sawyer, Benjamin	3	2	7	1	
Tanner, Hannah	1		2		
Norris, John	1	2	6		
Bannister, John	2	1	4		3
Card, William		2	2		
Fowler, Slocum	1		2		
Burden, Benjamin	1		2		
Mumford, Benjamin	2	5	3		
Pitman, John	1	3	1		
Averil, Ebenezar	1	3	5		
Woodman, Richard	3	4	5		
Henshaw, John	1		4		
Viol, Nathaniel	1	2	6		
Prior, Robert	1		3		
Thurston, John	1	2	1		
Smith, Nathaniel			3		
Burdick, James	1	2	1		
Varnum, Barney				2	
Varnum, Cudgo				3	
Thurston, Latham				2	
Babcock, Robert	1	3	4		
Tarbey, Peter	1		2		
Smith, William	1		4		
Pope, Israel	1		2		
Clarke, Catherine		2	4		
Lawton, Arnold	1		2		
Thurston, Samuel	1	2	3		
Wheatley, Molly			2		
Allen, Henry	1		1		
Peterson, Sally			3		
Easton, Nicholas W	1		3		
Newman, John			2		
Gardner, Caleb	1	1	5		9
Sanford, Esther	1		2	1	1
Allen, Mary			3		
Billings, Woodman			6		
Hull, John	2	3	4		
Wickam, Hannah		4	7	1	
Battey, Joseph	3		2		
Grealey, Samuel	1		2		
Shermon, Giles	1		2		
Tayer, Benjamin	2	1	3		
Mumford, John	1	1	3		
Lawton, Lydia		1	1		
Tayer, John			3		
Phillips, James	1	4	3		
Peterson, Edward		3	1		
Carr, Ebenezar	3	1	3		

NEWPORT TOWN—con.

NAME OF HEAD OF FAMILY.	Free white males of 16 years and upward, including heads of families.	Free white males under 16 years.	Free white females, including heads of families.	All other free persons.	Slaves.
Dupee, Mary			5		
Gardner, John		1	3		
Dean, Silas	1	2	4	2	
Yeamons, John	1	3	7		
Muenscher, John	1	3	3		
Jackson, Bartholemew	4		2		
Watson, Samuel	2	1	3		
Thomas, Mrs			1		
Carr, Samuel	2	1	3		
Mumford, Joseph	1		5	1	
Carr, Elizabeth	1		1		
Church, Benjamin	1	4	2		
Place, Samuel	1		2		
Greenwood, Isaac	1	2	2		
Greene, Thomas	3		5	1	
Burroughs, Green		3	4		
Perkins, Mehetible	1		4	1	
Hudson, Mary	2	2	4		
Phillips, Sarah	4	2	3		
Oxx, Catherine			1		2
Prior, William	7	2	7		
Mumford, Samuel	1		2	1	
White, Sarah		1	1	2	
Allen, William		3	2		
Carr, Samuel	1	3	2	1	
Davis, Benjamin	1	1	4		
Briggs, Joseph	1	2	7		
Freebody, William	1		3	1	
Tew, William	2	5	4		
Mumford, Peter	2	1	2	4	
Webber, Ann	1		5		
Bentley, Abigail			3		
Hoxie, William	2	1	3	1	
Littlefield, Sollomon	4	2	2		
Pierce, Israel	2	2	4		
Smith, Nathaniel	1		2		
Stockford, Elizabeth	1		1		
Duncan, James	2		4	2	2
Vaughn, John	1	1	2		
Grimes, John	2		6		
Wainwood, Godfrey	3	3	6	1	
Pierce, Stephen	1				
Thurston, Valentine	1	1	1		
Newman, Agustus	1	2	3		
Harkness, Elanor			1		
Read, Eleazar	2		1		
Griffiths, Charity		1	1		
Hervey, Peter	2	2	5		
Potter, Ichabod	1		2		
Nickolas, John	1		3		
Harkness, Isabel			2		
Church, Hannah			5		
Bannister, Pero				7	
Evans, Thomas	1	4	2		
Melvill, David	3		7		
Allen, Elizabeth			1		
Townsend, Thomas	4		4	3	1
Stevens, Robert	1	3	4	1	
Earle, Oliver	1	3	3		
Handy, Charles	4		3		3
Holt, Christopher	1	1	2		
Langley, Bethiah			1		
Vaughn, Daniel	1		2		
Hall, Mary			2		
Langley, John	2	1	1		
Howland, Henry	1	1	1		
Slocum, Samuel	1	2	1		
Jones, Jonathan	1		1		
Faxson, John	1	2	4	1	
Hazzard, George	1		3	1	
Webster, Nicholas	1	2	8		
Brown, Nathaniel	5	2	9		
Richardson, Thomas	3		9		
Cahoon, James	3	4	9		
Andrews, John	1	2	3		
Coats, Martin	1	2	2		
Coggeshall, Abigail	1		3		
Decoster, Mary			3		
Cornell, William	1	1	2		
Shaw, William	2	4	6		
Jones, Henrietta	1		1		
Handy, John	1	2	7	2	
Doubledee, Mary			3		
Brattle, Robert	2	1	2	1	
Orsborn, William	1	2	4		
Robinson, James	1	4	5	2	
Lyon, Joseph	1	3	5	2	
Geofroy, Andrew	1	1	1		
Gardner, Widow			3		
Evans, Isaac	1		2		
Tilley, Thomas	1		2		
Sly, John	1	2	2		
Stoddard, Jack					6
Donnahough, John	1	2	2		

NEWPORT TOWN—con.

NAME OF HEAD OF FAMILY.	Free white males of 16 years and upward, including heads of families.	Free white males under 16 years.	Free white females, including heads of families.	All other free persons.	Slaves.
Giles, William	1	3	5	1	
Anthony, Elisha	3	2	6	1	
Jepson, John	1		3	1	
Hart, Sally			3		
Goddard, Thomas	1		4		
Vickeroy, Joseph	1	2	4		
Thurston, Northum	2	2	3		
Burroughs, Samuel	2		4		
Cahoon, Charles	1		4		
Minthurn, Hannah			2		
Freebody, John	3	1	2	1	
Cleavland, John	1		2		
Tripp, Joshua	1	2	3		
Coudry, Mehetable			2		
Barker, Noah	1	2	2		
Gibbs, Samuel			2		
Morris, Esther			3		
James, Christiana			3		
Hart, Abigail			2		
Cabelee, Martin	1	2	2		
Easton, Susanna			3		
Weeden, John	1	4	3		
West, Elizabeth			3	1	
Brock, Thomas	3	1	4		
Swinman, Lydia			2		
Cahoon, Stephen	2		2		
Tillinghast, Nabby			2		
Burke, Richard	1		3		
Stillman, Ruth	3	1	4		
Hicks, Benjamin	1	2	4	1	2
Gardner, Joseph	2		6		
Stanton, John	1		6		
Vaughn, Mary			4		
Sherbourne, Henry	1		4	1	
Pierce, Benjamin	1	3	5	1	
Tweedy, Joseph W	1	1	2		1
Amboy, Peter	1	1	3		
Channing, Henry	1	1	3		
Weeden, Jonathan	1		3		
Ingraham, Timothy	1		3		
Malbone, Catherine			3		2
Malbone, John	1	2	3		3
Fairchilds, Major	1		3		
Hammilton, Sarah	1		5		
Lassells, Charles	1		5	1	
Lyon, William	3	2	6	1	
Shermon, John	1		3		
Coggeshall, Billings	4		5		
Price, Thomas	2	2	4		
Pettiface, Jonathan	1		4		
Arnold, Sanford	1		3		
Coddington, Mary			3		
Yeats, Samuel	1	2	3		
Russell, Thomas	1	1	3		
Yeats, Seth	1		5		
Vickery, Joseph	2		5		
Carr, Rhody			2		
Launders, John	3	2	6		
Spooner, Benjamin	2	3	6		
Norton, Elisha	1	2	4		
Hudson, Thomas	2		3		
Oxx, Samuel	1	1	3		
Hazzard, Richard	1		3		
Martin, Elizabeth			3		
Tabor, Constant	1		2		
Vaughn, Samuel	1	2	3		
Swineboune, Joseph	1		4		
Hammit, Benjamin	2	5	4		
Clanning, Edward	1		2		
Bliven, James	1	1	4		
Smith, Sovine	1		3		
Sanford, Mary			2		
Clarke, Anna			2		
Henderson, James	1	1	2		
Fairbanks, Molly			2		
Colt, Peter	1	1	2		
Christian, John			2		
Myers, Jacob			2		
Guireau, Mr	1	1	2		
Cozzens, Gregory	1		3		
Haywood, Joseph	1		3		
Hall, James	1		3		
Martin, John	2	3	2	2	
Roggers, Joseph	1		3		
Rathburn, Joshua	1	2	4		
Bennit, Mary			3		
Hicks, Betsey			4		
Wright, Rachel			3		2
Gibbs, James	1	1	3		
Greene, Thomas			3		
Austin, Daniel	1	1	2	1	
Bailey, Prince				3	
Fairbanks, Elizabeth			2	7	
Wilbore, John	1	2	5		

NEWPORT COUNTY—Continued.

NAME OF HEAD OF FAMILY.	Free white males of 16 years and upward, including heads of families.	Free white males under 16 years.	Free white females, including heads of families.	All other free persons.	Slaves.
NEWPORT TOWN—con.					
Peckam, Enos	1	1	1		
Greene, John	2		4		
Castoff, John	3	1	2		
Gurney, Thomas	1		2		
Shermon, Avis			2		
Wallace, Sarah			1		
Swinman, Daniel	1	1	2		
Swinman, Nathaniel	1	1	3		
Fairbanks, Benjamin	1		1		
Allen, Sally	2		1		
Young, Patty	1		2		
Stanton, Phebe	1		4		
Anderson, Paul	1	1	1		
Brown, Samuel				3	
Malbone, Toney				6	
Gould, Isabel				3	
Gibson, Prince				3	1
Crook, Robert	4	2	5		1
Wickam, Thomas	1	3	6		1
Corey, Abram				5	
Wanton, Patty			2	2	
Barned, Avis		1	4		
Hammit, Nathan	2	2	6		
Spooner, Wing	3	2	6		
Burges, Phillip	3	1	3		
Bliven, Henry	1		3		
Southwick, John	2	3	2		
Marvill, Robert	1		3		
Burges, Abigail	1		3		
Breeze, John	1	3	5		2
Deblois, Stephen	1	2	6		2
Witchorn, Samuel	2		5		1
Kennedy, John	1	1			
Slocum, John	6	2	4	1	
Reed, John	1	1	5		
Malbone, Francis	4	4	4	1	3
Auchmerty, Robert	1	1	3	2	1
Rodman, Kirby				6	
Weeden, Ephraim	4	1	6		
Shelden, John	1	1	4		1
Bliven, James	2	2	4		
Greene, Samuel	1	2	1		
Greene, Fones	1	2	3		
Greene, Fleet	1	1	5		
Smith, Sarah	1	2	3		1
Hitchcock, Joshua	1	3	3		
Burdick, Clark	1	1	2		
Ellery, Benjamin	2		4	2	2
Carpenter, Avis	1		4		1
Howland, Thomas	2		3		
Hathaway, Desire	2		4		
Sawyer, Lewis	1	2	2		
King, Mehetable			1		
Wilbore, Joshua	1		5		
Boon, James	1	2	4		
Lee, William	1	1	2		
Hunter, Henry	2	4	4		2
Smith, Patience	1	1	4		
Pratt, Joseph	1	2	3		
Childs, Oliver	1	1	4		
Liney, James	1	1	5		
Seney, Jeremiah	1		2		
Chesley, Mary			3		
Shearman, Pompey				3	
Pierce, Martha	1		2		
Peterson, Polly	1		2		
Stacey, Joshua	1		2		
Franklin, George	1		3		
Wilson, William	2		3		
Forster, Nancy		1	3		
Burgis, John	1		4		
Gladding, Henry	1	3	2		
Scoett, William	1	2	2		
Brayton, John	1		2		
Clarke, Simeon	1		5		
Jersey, Martha			2		
Devans, John	1	2	3		
Huddy, Thomas	2	1	3		
Harrison, Ann	1	1	1		
Tompkins, Samuel	1		2		
Morgan, William	1		3		
More, Hannah		1	3		
Harris, Samuel	1	2	1		
Luther, Mary	1		4		
Fitzgerrald, Edward	1		2		
Malbone, Cezar				2	
Fortune, Joseph				6	
Davis, Joshua	1	4	2		
Hudson, Peleg	1	4	6		
Beers, Elizabeth	1		2		
Howard, John	1		2		
Brown, Edmond	2	1	2		
Lee, William	2		3		
Benson, Martin	1	2	1	1	2
Larkin, James	1	1	3		
NEWPORT TOWN—con.					
Jewell, Cuffee				10	
Overing, Toby				2	
Bourne, Sharper				4	
Overing, Bacchus				1	
Collins, Barrey				2	
Coggeshall, London				1	
Newbe, Sollomon				1	
Walker, Jonathan	1		1		
Slocum, William	2		4		
Wilson, William	1		2		
Cahoon, John	1	1	2		
Cahoon, John	2	2	7		
Price, John	2	1	2		
Burdick, Henry	1		1		
Grinnall, Jedediah	1		1		
Peabody, William	1	1	3		
Albro, Clark	2	1	5		
Albro, Benjamin	1	2	4		
Lillibridge, Prince				2	
Boies, Joseph				3	
Sweet, Moses	1	1	2		
Maxson, John	1		4		
Lillibridge, Jessee	1		2		
Bull, James	1	1	1		
Tomkins, Elijah	1	3	2		
Rogers, Greene	4		2		
Johnson, Richard	1	1	4		
Mason, London				2	5
Overing, Polly	1	1	2		
Millard, James	1	1	4		
Rex, George	3	1	5		
Miller, John	1	2	3		
Holt, Benjamin	1	4	1		
Earle, Thomas	1	2	3		
Reed, John	1	2	3		
Marshal, John	2	1	2		
Whitwell, William	1		3		
Giladore, Daniel	2	3	4		
Barney, Jabez	2	1	5		
Gould, Martha			3		
Rummeril, Ebenezar	1	1	2		
Champlin, Henry G	1		3		2
Babcock, Nathan	2		4	2	1
Sisson, Edward	3	1	3	1	
Dunwell, Tennant	1		2		
Phillips, Mr	1		1		
Hubbard, John	1		4		
Peckam, Joseph	4	3	3		
Almey, Job	1	4	4		
Irish, Benjamin	1	3	5		
Weaver, Thomas	2		3		
Bliss, Henry	2		4		
Haswell, John	1	1	2		
Haswell, Nathaniel	1	3	2		
Stanton, Avis			2		
Gould, Benjamin	1		2		
Vaughn, Samuel	2	1	2		
Easton, Elizabeth	1	1	2		7
Irish, Edward	2	1	4		
Easton, John	1		5		4
Hazzard, Thomas G	7	1	4		
Tew, Joshua	1	1	2		
Clarke, Spooner	1	4	2		
Easton, Jonathan	1	1	3		1
Maxson, Jonathan	1	1	1		
Taylor, Joseph	2	1	4	1	
Taylor, Nicholas	1	1	2		
Hazzard, George	2	2	7		
Dixson, Anthony	2		2	1	
Anthony, Mary	2	1	5		
Coggeshal, Benjamin	5	1	4	1	
Collins, John, Jr	1	1	3		2
Hazzard, Mumford	2	1	1	1	1
Collins, Samuel	3	1	2	1	
Hazzard, Godfrey	1		2		3
Brenton, Benjamin	3	2	10		
Gardner, Amos	2	3	4		
Collins, John	1		2		13
Champlin, William	1	2	8		
Almey, John	1	3	2		
Coggeshall, Elisha	2		8		2
Clarke, Thomas	1	6	8	1	
Carr, John	3	1	4		
PORTSMOUTH TOWN.					
Elam, Samuel	3	1	2		
Barker, Izbon	1		4		
Spooner, John	2	1	1		
Parker, Peleg	1		2		
Tabor, Pardon	1		3		
Barker, Robert	1	2	3		
Allen, Rowland	1	3	6		
Sanford, Resguim	3		3	2	
Slocom, John	1	3	4		
PORTSMOUTH TOWN—continued.					
Chace, Aaron	2		5	1	
Ward, Nicholas	1	1	4		
Ward, Elizabeth		2	3		
Tabor, Philip	1	1	2		
Anthony, Giles	1	1	2	1	
Burrington, Daniel	2		2		
Gibbs, Jonathan	1	2	1		
Sisson, James	1	5	4		
Potter, Thomas	4	4	4		1
Cornel, Clarke	2		1		
Lawton, John	3		3		
Taylor, Reubin	2		4		
Lawton, George	4	2	3		
Anthony, Abram, Junr	2	2	4		
Clarke, Walter	1	2	4		
Lawton, Cuff				7	
Lawton, Robert	2	4	3		
Lawton, John	3		3		
Lawton, William	1	3	5		
Brightman, John	1	3	2		
Albro, Elizabeth	2	3	3		
Manchester, Peleg	3	1	9		
Albro, James	4		4		
Cornell, Nicholas	3	1	6		
Coggeshall, William	1		3		
Coggeshall, George	1	1	1		
Cornell, Jonathan	3		3		
Sisson, Richmond	1	1	5		
Shrieve, Thomas	2		4		
Peckham, Joshua	2		4		
Lawton, Joseph	1		2		
Brightman, William	1		2		
Lawton, Mary	2	1	3		1
Shearman, Thomas	3		4		
Chace, Zacheus	4		3	1	
Cobb, Elijah	1		4		
Lake, David	1	1	6		
Durfee, Christopher	1	1	2		
Albro, Robert	1	2	3		
Thurston, John	1	2	1		1
Carr, Robert	1	2	6	1	
Coggeshall, Robert	1	1	1		
Lawton, Isaac	3		4		
Lawton, Isaac, Junr	1	5	2		
Lawton, James	1	1	2		
Slocom, Stephen	1		1		
Freebourne, George				3	
Anthony, Abraham	3		3	1	
Shearman, Isaac	3	1	3		
Shearman, Christopher	2	2	3	1	
Davis, George	1	2	2		
Pearce, Jeremiah	1	2	4		
Sisson, Mary	1		2		
Almey, Job	2	1	4	2	
Almey, Isaac	1	1	3		
Lawton, David	3	4	5		
Thurston, Samuel	2	1	1	1	
Cornell, Elizabeth	1	1	2		
Mott, Jacob	3	1	5	1	
Hoadley, Hannah	2		2		
Anthony, Isaac	2	2	5		
Slocum, Mathew	1		1	1	
Shearman, Isaac	1	1	1		
Lake, Benjamin	1	2	2		
Thomas, Richard	1		1		
Freebourne, William	1	3	5		
Freebourne, Jonathan	1	4	2		
Chace, Nathan	2	2	3	1	
Freebourne, Mary			2		
Borden, Joseph	1		1		
Shearman, John	1	2	6		
Freebourne, Benjamin	1	2	2		
Pierce, Samuel	1	3	3		
Barrington, John	1	2	4		
Hicks, Samuel	2		6		
Burrington, Robert	1	3	2		
Burden, William	3		5		
Corey, Thomas	3	2	5		
Burden, William	1	2	2		
Burrington, Stephen	2	1	2		
Browning, Joshua	2		4		
Chace, Isaac	2	1	2		
Willcox, Daniel	1	3	2		
Wilcox, Cooke	1	3	2		
Durfee, Job	2		9	1	1
Durfee, Gideon	1	3	2		
Brownell, Joseph	2	1	3		
Brownell, Nathan	2	2	7		
Anthony, Burrington	1	3	3		
Anthony, Joseph	2		3		
Anthony, William	1	2	3		
Shearman, Giddeon	2	1	3		
Corey, John	2		3		
Hall, George	4	3	3	1	
Tolman, Benjamin	2		4		
Anthony, Giddeon	1		2		

NEWPORT COUNTY—Continued.

PORTSMOUTH TOWN—continued.

NAME OF HEAD OF FAMILY.	Free white males of 16 years and upward, including heads of families.	Free white males under 16 years.	Free white females, including heads of families.	All other free persons.	Slaves.
Chace, Holder	4	2	5		
Hicks, Thomas	1		2		
Almey, Tillinghast	1	3	6		
Anthony, Abigail	1	1	2	1	
Cooke, Job	1	1	2		
Irish, Isaac	1	5	6		
Burden, Henry	2	1	2		
Earle, John	3	2	3		
Gifford, Abigail	2	2	4		
Cooke, Mathew	2	2	2		1
Chace, Benjamin	1	4	5	1	
Cooke, Giles	2		3		
Corey, Samuel	1	2	4		
Corey, Patience	1	2	3		
Devol, Benjamin	1	2	5		
Brownell, Benjamin	1	3	1		
Brownell, Joseph	1	5	5		
Cooke, Thomas	3		2		
Brownell, Thomas	1		1		
Wilcox, John	4	6	5		
Brownell, George	1		5		
Faulkner, Thomas	2	1	5		
Hall, Benjamin	2	2	2		
Newman, Ann			3		
Slocom, Hannah		1	3		
Brownell, Stephen	1	5	4		
Cornell, Elizabeth			3		
Hall, William	2		2		
Fish, David	1	1	2		
Lake, Gideon	1	1	3		
Shaw, Thomas	1		2		
Talman, John	2		4		
Hall, George	1	3	5		
Talman, William	1	1	4		
Thomas, David	1	3	1		
Thomas, Sarah			5		
Thomas, Darcus		1	2		
Sanford, John	2	1	4		
Lawton, Henry	1	2	4		
Dennis, Gideon	1	2	2		
Huddlestone, William	1		2		
Strange, Ann	1		2		
Burden, John	2	4	5		
Shearman, Martha			2		
Lake, Daniel, Junr	3	1	5		
Thomas, Daniel	2	5	4		
Thomas, Richard	2	5	4		
Thomas, Alexander	1	1	4		
Burden, Stephen	1	1	2		
Dennis, Robert	3	2	4		
Fish, Preserved	1	5	8		
Dennis, Joseph	1	1	2		
Talman, Joseph	1	3	4		
Borden, William	1	1	2		
Hunt, John	1	1	3		
Yung, John	1	2	3		
Gray, Noah	1	1	2		
Fish, Lydia	1		5		
Fish, Robert	2	3	6		
Dennis, Robert	2	1	4		
Shearman, Parker	2		2		
Lawton, Giles, Junr	1	2	5		
Shearman, Preserved	1	1	5		
Sisson, George	1	1	5		
Almey, Holder	1	2	4		
Dulerisk, William	1	3	3		
Shearman, Christopher	3	3	1		
Shearman, Sampson	3	3	7		
Shearman, Walter	1	2	3		
Shearman, John	2	1	5		
Almey, Peleg	2	1	5		
Shearman, Richard	4	2	6		
Turner, Benjamin	1	2	4		
Curney, Mathew M	3		3	1	3
Sisson, George	4		4		
Sisson, Peleg	2	3	5		
Fish, Benjamin	1	1	2		
Shearman, Joseph	4	3	4		
Sisson, Richard	1	3	6		
Sisson, Job	2		2		
Shearman, Ruth			6		
Sisson, Abigail	2		4		
Wales, Peter T	2	3	4		1
Fish, John	1	2	3		
Sisson, Pardon	2		2		
Cooke, John	3		2		
Cundell, Abner	1	4	1		
Cundell, Joseph	4		4		
Sisson, Elizabeth	2	1	3		
Cooke, Job	3	2	5	1	
Sisson, Job	1	2	2		
Bachelor, Rupee	1	4	4		
Slocom, Mathew	2	2	5		
Slocom, Stephen	1	1	1		

PORTSMOUTH TOWN—continued.

NAME OF HEAD OF FAMILY.	Free white males of 16 years and upward, including heads of families.	Free white males under 16 years.	Free white females, including heads of families.	All other free persons.	Slaves.
Slocom, Susan		1	4		
Almey, Sarah	3	1	3		2
Tennant, James	1	4	2		
Coggeshall, Elisha	1	1	4		
Almey, William	1	4	3		
Anthony, Gideon	1	1	1		
Lawton, George	2		4	1	
Slocom, Giles	1	3	6		
Taylor, Peter	2	1	3		
Green, William	1		2		
Lawton, David	1	1	4		
Brown, Benjamin	1		2	2	
Sisson, Joseph	4	2	6		
Anthony, Beriah	1	1	3		
Kirbey, James	1	1	3		
Grinman, James	2	2	2		
Davenport, Jonathan	1		1		
Kirbey, Joseph	1		2		
Barker, John	1	2	2		
Lawton, Giles	4		4		
Lawton, Peleg	1	1	2		
Lawton, Peleg, Junr	1	1	3		
Haszard, Jeremiah	1		1		6
Easton, Benjamin	7	2	4	1	
Pierce, Samuel	1		1		
McNear, John	2	1	6		
McNear, Robert	1	4	4		
Allen, William	4		7	1	
Woodhull, John	1		2		
Taylor, Peter	2	1	3		
Wall, John R	1	1	2		
Pabodie, John	1	1	2		
Pierce, Samuel, Junr	6	5	4	1	
Pierce, Thomas	1	2	1		
Allen, Jonathan	1		2		
Allen, Barnet	1	3	2		
Bailey, Samuel	1	1	1		
Allen, James	9	4	5		2
Allen, Thomas	3		5		
Allen, Thomas, Junr	1	1	2		
Sheldon, Palmer	3	5	5		
Chace, Daniel	4	2	4	1	
Brown, Caleb	1	2	3		
Cooke, Daniel	1	2	1		
Allen, John	1	1	3		

TIVERTON TOWN.

NAME OF HEAD OF FAMILY.	Free white males of 16 years and upward, including heads of families.	Free white males under 16 years.	Free white females, including heads of families.	All other free persons.	Slaves.
Stilwell, Joseph	1	5	2		
Burden, William	2	1	5		
Shermon, Stephen	1	1	2		
Simmons, George	1		2		
Butts, Israel	1	3	2		
Durfee, Richard	2	3	3		
Durfee, James	2	4	7		
Pierce, James	1	1	5	1	
Perrey, Joseph	1	1	3		
Negus, John	2	1	6		
Earle, Thomas	1	1	2		
Bowen, John	3		3	5	
Bowen, John, Junr	1	1	6		
Corey, Roger	1	2	1		
Haswell, Luke	1	1	1		
Davis, Pardon	1	1	5		
Durffee, Joseph	2	3	7		
Burden, John	2	3	2	1	
Durffee, Benjamin	1		3	4	
Roggers, Jeremiah	1		3		
Borden, Louis		1	3		1
Davis, Torey	1	1	3		
Roggers, Patience			2		
Bailey, Edward	2		4		
Durffee, Abram	1		3		
Edey, Mrs Cynthia	1		3		
Corey, William	2	3	5		
Freeman, John	1	1	2		
Negus, Benjamin	1	1	4		
Durffee, Benjamin	2		2		2
Haswell, Benjamin	1		2		
Tallman, Stephen	2	2	5		
Smith, Toby (Negro)				5	
Borden, Richard	3	1	5	1	
Borden, Benjamin	1	2	4		
Manchester, John	1	2	3		
Church, Israel	1	1	1		
Borden, Aron	2	1	6		
Hicks, Weston	4		4		
Durffee, Prince	1	1	5		
Durffee, Thomas	1		3		
Bunington, Abram	1		2		
De Marville, John	1	2	1		
Hicks, Elisha	1				
Hicks, Abram	1	1	3		
Hicks, Stephen	1	1	2		

TIVERTON TOWN—con.

NAME OF HEAD OF FAMILY.	Free white males of 16 years and upward, including heads of families.	Free white males under 16 years.	Free white females, including heads of families.	All other free persons.	Slaves.
Robbins, Pardon (Negro)				8	
Shermon, Lot	4	1	3		
Crossin, Enoch	2		2		
Manchester, John	1	2	5		
Durffee, Lydia		3	5		
Durffee, Thomas	1	2	4		
Hamlin, Benjamin	1	2	7		
Osborne, William	4		3		
Wesgate, John	2	3	5		
Wesgate, Mary	1		2		
Maccomber, Michel	2	2	6		
Wanton, William (Negro)				5	
Domini, Esther (Negro)				6	
Experience, Hector (Negro)				8	
Domini, David (Negro)				5	
Wanton, William (Negro)				5	
Wanton, Jeremiah (Negro)				2	
Wanton, Jeremiah, Jur (Negro)				2	
Slocom, Cato (Negro)				3	
Martin, Mark (Negro)				4	
Lake, Giles	3		4		
Lake, Richard	1	1	1		
Barker, Susannah	3	2	7		1
Durffee, James	2	2	6		
Bennit, Godfrey	2	2	4		
Bennit, Molly		1	2		
Negus, John	1	1	3		
Negus, Isaac	1	2	5		
Slocom, Ebenezar	1	2	4		1
Manchester, William	3		4		
Devol, Stephen	4	4	3		
Hull, Charles	1		1		
Briggs, Nathaniel	1	1	2		4
Rounds, John	3	2	5		
Manchester, Peleg	4	2	2		
Manchester, William	1	2	3		
Butts, William	3		1		
King, Alpley	1	6	3		
Manchester, Edward	2		1		
Manchester, Giles	1	3	3		
Grinnell, Aaron	1	1	3		
Manchester, Phillip	1	2	5	2	
Devol, Daniel	2	4	4		
Corey, Caleb	2	1	4		
Howland, John	1	2	5	1	
Howland, Benjamin	1	1	2	1	
Slocum, Comfort			2		
Durffee, Abner	1	1	4		
Tabor, Phillip	1	4	3		
Gray, Gideon	1	4	3		
Gray, John	2	2	6		
Fisher, Patience		2	2		
Tabor, Ephraim	1	1	3		
Thurston, Thomas	1	3	2		
Durffee, Prince (Negro)				4	
Cornell, Thurston	1	1	3		
Wesgate, George	1		5		
Durffee, David	2	3	6		
Dyre, Benjamin	1		1		
Corey, Thomas	3		4		1
Humphry, William	1	3	2		
Brown, Abram	5		5	3	
Brown, David	1		1		
Brown, Elisha	2		1		
Hathaway, Betsey			3		
Gray, Pardon	5		4		2
Gray, Phillip	1		4		
Tabor, Admiral	2		4		
Manchester, John	2	1	4	1	
Gray, Phillip	4	3	9		3
Gray, William	1	2	4		
Manchester, Gilbert	1	1	3		
Manchester, Godfrey	1	3	3		
Manchester, Rebeckah			2		
Manchester, Rhoda		1	4		
Wilcocks, Gideon	2	4	5		
Soal, Abner	2	4	5		
Crandall, Nathaniel	1	2	5		
Murray, Mary	1	1			1
Perrey, Phineas	2		3		
Palmer, Sarah	1		2		
Palmer, Noah	1	2	2		
Davenport, Ephraim	4	1	3		
Davenport, Pardon	1	4	3		
Corey, William	1	2	1	1	
Corey, Phillip	4	3	3		
Brownell, Israel	2	4	4		
Cooke, Isaac	4	3	5		

NEWPORT COUNTY—Continued.

TIVERTON TOWN—con.

NAME OF HEAD OF FAMILY.	Free white males of 16 years and upward, including heads of families.	Free white males under 16 years.	Free white females, including heads of families.	All other free persons.	Slaves.
Wilcox, Thomas	1	4	2	1	
Davenport, John	3		2		
Tabor, Stephen	3	1	3		
Tabor, Job	1	3	2		
Amey, Holder	1	3	1	1	
Wilcox, William	5	2	4		
Beal, Joseph	1		6		
Lawton, Thomas	1	2	3		
Almey, Gidion	4	1	4		1
Almey, Sarah	2	2	2		
Gray, Phillip	3	1	5		3
Cooke, Jeremiah	3		2		
Almey, John	3	1	2		
Sisson, Joseph	2	1	4		
Cook, John	2	2	4	1	3
Cook, Abiel	4	2	3		
Seberrey, Lion	6	2	7		
Tabor, Lemuel	1	3	5		
Taber, Israel	1		1		
Tabor, Joseph	1		2		
Tabor, Jeremiah	2	4	4		
Bailey, Lemuel	4		3		
Sanford, William	1	2	3		
Borden, John	2	2	3		
Manchester, Stephen	1	1	3		
Williston, Ichabod	1	3	4		
Tabor, Thomas	1		1		
Hart, William	1	1	2		
Hart, Gilbert	1		3		
Devol, William	1	2	3		
Devol, Elijah	1	3	3		
Lameryon, Samuel	1	1	3		
Burroughs, Peleg	2	1	7		
Bailey, Robert	1		4		
Tabor, Samuel	1	1	6		
Manchester, Isaac, Junr	1	2	2		
Crandell, Joseph	1		2		
Whitrage, William	1	3	5		
Tripp, Abiel	3		3		
Manchester, Phillip	1	4	2		
Simmon, Samuel	2	1	3		
Sanford, Samuel	2	1	1		
Tabor, Edward	1	1	1		
Manchester, Christopher	3	1	2		
Dennis, Bedford	1	2	5		
Manchester, Isaac	2	1	4	1	
Cook, Abram (Negro)					8
Sanford, George	1	2	6		
Simmons, Peleg, Junr	1		1		
Simmons, Peleg	1	4	3		
Simmons, Moses	1	1	3		
Simmons, Thomas	3	2	7		
Sanford, Ephraim	2	4	6		
Tabor, Thomas	1	1	2		
Bennit, Susannah		2	5		
Crandall, Benjamin	2		2		
Cook, George	1	2	3		
Cranston, Walter	1		5		
Cook, Walter	2	1	1		
Tabor, Jacob	3	1	2		
Tabor, Joseph	1	1	2		
Bennit, Daniel	1		3		
Butts, William					
Corey, Peter (Negro)					5
Manchester, Mary		1	3		
Chace, Benjamin	2	1	2		2
Wilcox, William	2	1	3		
Wilcox, Abner	1	4	3		
Cook, William	1	2	2		
Gray, Peter (Negro)					3
Woodman, Emanuel					2
David, Sollomon (Negro)					5
Cook, Megg (Negro)					2
Gray, Fortune					5
Jack, Amey					1
Demas, Joseph					4
Gray, Jacob					7
Gray, Jacob, Junr					5
Brooks, John					5
Blossom, Bloomy					3
Manchester, Cyprian					8
Simmons, Deb					1
Barker, Peter					2
Warcomb, John					2
Month, Hannah					2
Almey, Sharper					1
Earle, Walter	2	1	5		
Lake, Joel	1		1		
Albert, John	1	1	3		
Lake, Richard	2	2	3		
Lake, Giles	1	2	1		

TIVERTON TOWN—con.

NAME OF HEAD OF FAMILY.	Free white males of 16 years and upward, including heads of families.	Free white males under 16 years.	Free white females, including heads of families.	All other free persons.	Slaves.
Lake, Edward	1	2	1		
Grinnelly, Daniel	2	1	4		
Grinnell, Gidion	2		2		
Cornell, Walter	2	1	2	3	
Clamon, Thomas	1	1	6		
Brayton, David	2	3	5		
Rounds, David	2	3	6		
Chamberlane, Ephraim	1	1	4		
Fish, Brownel	1	1	1		
Springer, Dursey	1	2	2		
Springer, Thomas	1		3		
Albert, John	2	2	3		
Brownell, Charles	1	2	3		
Brownell, Giles	1		1		
Remmington, Joseph	2		1		
Sawdey, Benjamin	2	2	7		
Dennis, Obadiah	1	2	5		
Dennis, Robert	1		1		
Manchester, Jeremiah	1	2	3		
King, Godfrey	2	4	3		
Eder, Samuel	1	1	1		
King, Benjamin	1		1		
King, Stephen	1	1	6		
Hart, Smitten	1		3		
Wilkey, Mary	2		1		
Bennit, Phillip	1	2	4		
Springer, Knight	1	1	3		
Tabor, Noel	1	2	4		
Slocum, Sarah	1	1	2		
Hart, Sanford	1	2	6		
Roggers, Mary			2		
Lake, Jonathan	4	2	4		
Lake, Noah	2	1	7		
Lake, David	1	1	2		
Grinnell, Lewis	1	1	2		
Lake, Job	2				
Lake, Daniel	1	3	1		
Argler, John	1	1	1		
Tabor, John	1	2	3		
Talman, Holder	1	1	1		
Wilcox, John	1	5	2		
Tabor, Thomas	1		2		
Hart, William	2	2	2		
Tabor, Moses	2		6		
Crandall, Ebor	2		1		
Crandall, Stephen	1		2		
Wait, John	1		2		
Wait, John, Junr	1	1	3		
Hart, Constant	1	5	2		
Sanford, Joseph	1	4	1		
Tripp, Thomas	1		2		
Mosier, Paul	1	1			
Mosier, Obadiah	2	1	3		
Davenport, Ephraim	1	2	5		
Sisson, Thomas	1	2	2		
Shaw, Nathaniel	1	5	2		
Hart, John	1	1	5		
Hart, Isaac	1		3		
Hart, Martha			4		
Manchester, Gardnier			3		
Maccomber, Ephraim	1	6	6		
Simmons, Ichabod	1	1	3		
Peckam, George	3		3		
Simmons, Abner	1	2	3		
Crandall, Abner	2	4	3		
Crandall, Joseph	1	1	2		
Fish, Sarah			1		
Tripp, John	1	2	7		
Fish, Robert	2		3		
Pitman, Joseph	1	1	3		
Sawdey, Benjamin	1	1	2		
Sawdey, Samuell	1	3	6		
Peckam, Samuel	1	2	1		
Hart, William	1	2	1		
Perrey, Walter	1	3	3		
Bennit, John	2	1	3		
Cook, Abner	1	2	6		
Lake, Pardon	1	1	2		
Cooke, Stephen	2	1	5		
Fish, William	2		2		
Fish, William, Ju.	1		2		
Fish, Ruth		2	2		
Fish, Zarimal	2	2	6		
Cook, Silas	1	1	5		
Corey, William	1	1	3		
Corey, Thomas	1	1	3		
Shrieve, John	1	1	1		
Cook, Abner	1		1		
Manchester, Lydia			3		
Sherman, Daniel	2	1	4		
Bailey, George	1	1	1		

TIVERTON TOWN—con.

NAME OF HEAD OF FAMILY.	Free white males of 16 years and upward, including heads of families.	Free white males under 16 years.	Free white females, including heads of families.	All other free persons.	Slaves.
Phillips, William	1	2	2		
Sherman, William	1	2	2		
Hamlin, Peleg	2		2		
Hunt, George	1	3	1		
Stafford, Joshua	2	6	3		
Jennings, Joseph	1	1	1		
Jennings, Deborah			3		
Stafford, Stephen	1	1	2		
Perrey, Pierce	2	1	4		
Eley, Joseph	3	4	6		
Borden, Josiah	1	1	3		
Jennings, Isaac	3	5	4		
Estes, Elisha	3	2	4		
Estes, Robert	2	2	5		
Durffee, William	1	1	3		
Stafford, Abram	5		5		
Cooke, Thomas	1	2	3	1	
Davis, Dinah		1	1		
Negus, Benjamin	3		3		
Negus, Henry	1		3		
Cook, Pardon	2		3		
Cook, Paul	2	2	4		
Negus, Silas	1		1		
Negus, Stephen	1	1	3		
Perrey, John	2	2	3		
Cook, Joseph	1		3		
Cook, Joseph	1		1		
Corey, Daniel	1		1		
Thomas, Gardiner	1		3		
Shermon, Silas	1		2		
Currey, David	1		3		
Negus, Thomas	2		3		
Durffee, Jack (Negro)				7	
Pierce, London				5	
Cook, Caleb	3	1	4		
Springer, Robert	1	4	4		
Wood, Abner	2	1	5		
Durffee, Mary	4	2	3		
Burden, Theophilous	1		3		
Durffee, John	2	1	3		
Durffee, Gidion	4	1	4		
Sanford, William	3	1	5		
Dwilley, Pierce	1		2		
Allen, Beriah	1	2	3		
Mosier, Amos	1		2		
Case, Ephraim			4		
La Morion, Phillip	1		4		
Tripp, Bettey	2	3	4		
Hart, Joseph	2	2	2		
Case, Isaac	1	1	2		
La Morion, John	1		2		
Dwilley, Richard	1	2	3		
Dwilley, Jeremiah	1	2	2		
Dwilley, Olivo			2		
Dwilley, Daniel	2	1	2		
Pettice, George	1	2	2		
Borden, Anne			3		
Stafford, John	1	1	6		
Stafford, Samuel	2		3		
Towle, Jacob	2	2	9		
Thasher, Peter	2	4	3		
Gifford, Richard	1	1	2		
Gifford, Elihu	1	1	2		
Sisson, Phillip	1	2	3		
Pettice, John	1	1	1		
Crossman, Paul	1	1	5		
Randall, Michael	1	5	2		
Lowdry, William	4	4	2		
Borden, Mary	1		4		
Durfee, Benjamin	1		2		
Perrey, Godfrey	1	2	5		
Borden, Christopher	1	1	2		
Woodle, Gershom, 2d	2	3	2		
Borden, Jonathan	1		2		
Woodle, William	5		2		
Shermon, Sampson	2	2	8		
Woodle, Gershom, 1st	2		8		
Richmond, John				2	
Mingo, Isaiah				5	
Croker, George			1	1	
Croker, George, Jur	1	2	3		
Towle, Joseph	2	5	3		
Towle, Peleg	1	1	2		
Warren, Gamalice	3	5	2		
Gifford, Anorariah	1		1	5	
Gifford, William	4	5	5		
Jenkes, Benjamin	2		2		
Borden, John	1		2		
Towle, Job	1	1	5		
Borden, Joseph	8	2	3		
Harrison, John	1	1	5		

PROVIDENCE COUNTY.

CRANSTON TOWN.

NAME OF HEAD OF FAMILY.	Free white males of 16 years and upward, including heads of families.	Free white males under 16 years.	Free white females, including heads of families.	All other free persons.	Slaves.
Arnold, Peleg	2	1	3		
Arnold, John	2	4	2		
Dubosey, Peter	1		1		
Smith, Israel	1		3		
Atwood, Thomas	1	2	4		
Aborne, Anthony	3		2	1	1
Randal, Jeremiah	1	1	3	1	
Aborne, Mary	1	1	4		
Remmington, Mrs Marcy			1		
Sheldon, Remmington	1	3	2		
Green, Rhodes	3		3		
Haynes, Barbary		1	2		
Carpenter, Thomas	1	3	2		
Fuller, Nathaniel	2	2	1		
Sheppard, Sally		1	4		
Dean, Ezra	1				
Smith, Elizabeth		3	4		
Hill, Allen	1		1		
Rhodes, Anthony	1	1	1		
Knap, Nehemiah	1		1		
Rhodes, Daniel	1	2	1		
Tucker, Zachariah	2		3		
Smith, Benjamin	3	4	2		
Rhodes, Joseph	2		2		
Andrews, Seth	1	2	2		
Brown, Stephen	1				
Rhoes, Zachariah			2		
Waterman, William	1	2	2		
Smith, Reuben	1	1	3		
Hunt, Zebediah	3	2	5		
Corps, Thomas	1		2		
Lorkwood, Pheby		1	5	3	
Potter, Stephen	2		2		
Rhodes, Nehemiah	4	1	5	1	
Smith, Stutley	1	3	3		
Arncld, Elisha	2	2	4		
Low, John	1	1	3		
Hawkins, Barned	2	3	2		
Corps, Mrs & Mrs Pyke			2		
Westcoat, James	2	3	5		
Field, William	3	1	7		
Nicholas, John	1	2	1		
Stently, William	1		3		
Field, James	2	1	3		
Burgis, Joseph	1	3	3		
Wamsley, Joseph				5	
Green, Cuff				2	
Waterman, Ann		1	3		
Burgis, James	3	2	4		
Clifford, Mrs Pheby			4		
Field, John	2	6	4		
Williams, Joseph	2	3	2		
Payne, John	3	1	3		
Waterman, Zuriel	2		6		
Williams, Nathaniel	2		3		
Williams, Ann			4		
Williams, James	1	1	5		
Sheldon, Philip	1		3		
Sheldon, James	1		5		
Carpenter, Elisha	2	4	5		
Harris, John	2	2	4		
Potter, Thomas	2		4		
Fenner, Stephen	1	2	2		
Fenner, William	2	2	4		
Salisberry, Pierce	1	1	3		
Williams, Frederick	2	5	4		
Carpenter, Nathaniel	2	4	5		
Corps, David	1		3		
Potter, Job	2		1		
Waterman, Stephen	1	6	3		
Pratt, Samuel	1	4	3		
Green, James	1	2	2		
Waterman, Christopher	1	1	1		
Williams, Caleb	1	5	4		
Dyer, Samuel	1		1		
Potter, Samuel	1		7		
Pierce, Mial	1	1	4		
Vaughn, Benjamin	1	3	5		
Bennett, William	1		1		
Harris, James	1	3	1		
Arnold, James	2	3	7		
Stone, Peter	1		1		
Stone, Andrew	1	2	3		
Waterman, George	2	1	4		
Potter, Mesheck	1	4	4		
Manning, Joseph	1		1		
Butman, Zebulon	1	2	2		
Potter, Abednego	1		2		
Potter, Zuriel	1	3	5		
Harris, Joseph	2		2	1	
Batty, Josiah	2	3	6		
Lockwood, Joseph	3	3	8		
Whitman, Peleg	1	1	2		
Bennett, Mrs Patience			1		

CRANSTON TOWN—con.

NAME OF HEAD OF FAMILY.	Free white males of 16 years and upward, including heads of families.	Free white males under 16 years.	Free white females, including heads of families.	All other free persons.	Slaves.
Tompkins, Frebourne				2	
Westcoat, Josiah	1		2		
Westcoat, Samuel	2	2	3		
Westcoat, Ryan	1	3	4		
Profit, Watt				3	
Profit, Watt, Junr				6	
Congdell, Benjamin	2		3		
Arnold, Philip	2	2	2		
Congdell, James	1	3	4		
Thornton, Charles	1	1	2		
Eddy, Mirah	1	1	2		
King, Asa	4		6		
Hinds, Nathan	1	2	2		
Profit, Caleb				4	
Profit, Thomas				7	
Stone, Joseph	1		2		
Salisberry, Nathan	2	3	6		
Eddy, Elephalet	2	1	2		
Burlingam, William	2	2	3		
Burlingam, Roger	1	2	2		
Stafford, Edward	2	2	5	1	
Stafford, John	3		4		
Potter, Andrew	1	1	3		
Cooke, Mingo				2	
Stone, Mrs Patience		1	3		
Stone, Amos		2	2		
Stone, Samuel	2		4		
Arnold, John Rice	2	1	2	1	1
Andrews, Anna		1	4		
Potter, Pardon	1	3	1		
King, Asa	4		6		
King, John	1	4	4	1	
Andrews, John	1	1	3	1	
King, Jeremiah	1		2		
Warner, John	1	1	2		
Turner, Joshua	1		2		
Turner, Reubin	1	2	2		
Congdell, Thomas	3	2	6		
Sarle, John	1		3		
Searle, Ezekiel	2	3	4	1	
Holden, Anthony	1	3	4	1	1
Potter, Anthony	2	5	6		
Brayton, Joseph	2	2	3		
Keech, Seth	1	3	5		
Mason, Thomas	1		2		
Tompkins, Somerset				2	
Potter, Thomas	3	1	2	1	
Potter, Joseph	1	4	3		
Potter, Sylvester	1	4	4		
Baker, Thomas	2	3	6		
Holden, Thomas	1	1	2		
Potter, Caleb	2		1		
Burlingam, Samuel	1	2	2		
Potter, William	1	3	2		
Whitman, Henry	2	1	4		
Tompkins, Samuel	2		2		
Williams, Elisha	1	1	2		
Allen, James	1	1	2		
Congdon, James	1		2		
Burton, John	2	2	4	1	
Burlingam, Philip	2	1	2		
Burlingam, Pardon	1	4	3		
Abbitt, Daniel	2		2		
Lippett, Moses	1	1	2		
Potter, Thomas	2		2		
Burlingam, James	3	3	2		
Potter, Betsey		1	4		
Parkerson, James	2		3		
Bennett, William	1		1		
Lippett, Christopher	2	3	3	2	
Potter, Andrew	1	2	1		
Knight, Robert	3	3	8		
Remmington, Sally			2		
Arnold, Edmund	1		3		
Congdon, Ephraim	3		3		
Sayles, Joseph	1	2	3		
Briggs, Pardon	1		2		
Brayton, Frebourne	2	2	6		
Knight, Benjamin	3	1	2		
Fisk, John	1	3	2		
Sayles, Edward	3		3		
Sayles, Silas	1		2		
Knight, Mrs Woltha			3		
Roberts, Ephraim	2		5		
Roberts, Hannah			3		
Knight, Joseph	2	1	4		
Blanchard, Benjamin	2		4		
Knight, Jonathan	1	1	4		
Whitman, Elisha	3	1	5		
Whitman, John	1	2	3		
Manchester, Israel	1	3			
Blanchard, Benjamin	1		4		
Roberts, Oliver	2		4		

CRANSTON TOWN—con.

NAME OF HEAD OF FAMILY.	Free white males of 16 years and upward, including heads of families.	Free white males under 16 years.	Free white females, including heads of families.	All other free persons.	Slaves.
Manchester, George	1	1	3		
Manchester, Gideon	1	3	4		
Collins, William	5	1	3		
Field, Stephen	1		3		
Roberts, Caleb	1	2	3		
Burlingam, Caleb	3	1	2		
Nicholas, John	3	3	5		
Weeks, Sylvester	1		2	1	
Shearman, Eleazer	3	4	5		
Tyler, William	1	1	3		
Baker, Caleb	1		3		
Sheldon, Stephen	3	2	10		
Sylvester, Amos	1	4	9		
Hammett, Caleb	1	1	1		
Potter, Caleb	1	2	3		
Waterman, Thomas	1	2	3		
Young, Amaziah	2	4	2		
Knowles, Robert	2	1	3		
Knight, Nathan	1	2	3		
Field, Thomas	2	4	2		
Henny, Samuel	1		2		
Knight, Stephen	3	1	3		
Knight, Reubin	1	3	3		
Knight, Richard	2	2	6		
Knight, Barzilla	2		3		
Hawkins, Jeriah	2	4	4		
Knight, Job	1	4	2		
Fenner, Rhodes	1	2	5		
Taylor, David	1	4	3		
King, Jonathan	2	4	4		
Fenner, Turner	1	1	2		
Ralph, Edward	3	1	3		
Waterman, John	3		3		
Westcoat, Stently	1		3		
Cruff, Thomas	2	2	3		
Stone, John	1	1	1		
Fenner, Samuel	3		2		
Fenner, Stephen	1		2		
Fenner, Jeremiah	1	1	1		
Dyer, Charles	3	1	6		
Chapman, Nathaniel	1	4	4		
Dyer, John	4		2		
Dyer, Eseck	1	1	2		
Knight, Olney	1	1	3		
Knight, Henry	2	1	4		
Salisbury, Martin	2	1	4		
Salisbury, Martin, Junr	1	1	2		
Salisbury, Mary			2		
Henry, Caleb	2	4	5		
Burton, John	2	1	5		
Henry, William	2		3		
Thornton, Eseck	1	1	3		
Sheldon, Nicholas	3		2	1	
Sheldon, Nicholas, Junr	2	3	4		
Sayle, Thomas	1	3	4		
Johnson, David	1		1		
Westcoat, John	2		3		
Edwards, Edward	2		4		
Pratt, Phineas	1	1	2		
Westcoat, Samuel	1	1	3		
Pitts, Rufus	1	1	3		
Jay, Job	3		3		
Ralph, Thomas	1		1		
Jay, Samuel	1		2		
Westcoat, Nathan	1		2		
Hudson, Hopkins	1	1	4		
Ralph, Sylvanus	1		2		
Lyppett, John	2		4		
Burton, William	3		4	2	
Burton, Edmund	1		1		
Hudson, Samuel	1	3	1		
Burlingame, Mrs Zerviah			2		
Gorton, Israel	2	1	4		
Gorton, Pardon	2		4		
Burton, John Anthony	3	4	7		
Randal, Benjamin	1		2		
Randal, John	2		2		
Jack, Cloe				6	
Fenner, George	1	3	2		
Potter, Dimmis		1	1		
Sheldon, John	1		1		
Sheldon, Pardon	1	3	4		
Colvin, George	2	2	5		
Randal, Rufus	1		4		
Potter, Arnold	1	1	2		
Warner, Ezekiel	3		2		
Warner, William	1	3	4		
Carpenter, William	4		4		
Merithew, Mary	1		2		
Westcoat, Mrs Pheby			6		
Westcoat, Reubin	1	4	5		
Randal, Nanny		1	1		
Congdel, Molly			5		
Randal, Uriel	1		3		

PROVIDENCE COUNTY—Continued.

CRANSTON TOWN—continued.

NAME OF HEAD OF FAMILY.	Free white males of 16 years and upward, including heads of families.	Free white males under 16 years.	Free white females, including heads of families.	All other free persons.	Slaves.
Randal, Waterman	1	2	2		
Smith, Randal	2	1	4		
Waterman, Stephen	1		2		
Knight, Nehemiah	1	4	3	1	2
Knight, Andrew	2	1	2		
Knight, Jeremiah	1		1		
Briggs, Mrs Barbary	1	3	3		
Randal, William	2	1	1		
Green, John C	1	3	5		2
Tower (Negro)				2	
Mowrey, Pero				3	
Sprague, Jonathan, Junr	1	2	4		
Sprague, Stephen	1	3	1		
Harris, Elisha	2		1		
Pinkney, Peleg	1	1	2		
Randal, Henry	2	2	3		1
Sprague, William	4	1	5		
Sprague, Nathaniel	1		5		
Sprague, Asa	1	1	5		
Williams, Christopher	2	1	4		
Williams, Benjamin	1		5		
Sprague, Jonathan	1		1		
Williams, John	2		4		
Williams, John, Junr	1		5		
Comstock, Andrew	1	3	3		
Davis, Mrs Alice			3		
Green, Cato				8	
Williams, Nathaniel	1	1	4		
Pitcher, John	2		2		
Williams, Nathan	2		1		
Thomas, William	1		4		
Harris, William	1	2	2		
Bennett, Weaver	1	1	4		

CUMBERLAND TOWN.

NAME OF HEAD OF FAMILY.	Free white males of 16 years and upward, including heads of families.	Free white males under 16 years.	Free white females, including heads of families.	All other free persons.	Slaves.
Whipple, Simon	2	2	6		
Whipple, Jeremiah	6		7	2	
Angel, Abram	3		4		
Potter, Hollaman	2	3	3		
Freeman, Job	1	1	4		
Ray, Daniel	1		2		
Jenkes, Daniel	2	4	4		
Jenkes, Gideon	1	1	1		
Whipple, Moses	3		6		
Jenkes, Jeremiah	1		2		
Jenkes, Jodediah	1	3	2		
Bly, John	1	1	1		
Chace, Samuel	2	1	2		
Wilkinson, Jeptha	3	1	5		
Scott, Jeremiah	3	1	6	1	
Scott, Nathaniel	2	2	2		
Follet, Amos	1	2	2		
Jenkes, John	3	1	8		
Brown, John	1	1	2		
Razy, Freelove			2		
Wetherhead, Amaziah	1		3		
Angel, Thomas	1		1		
Gardiner	2	4	6		
Coller, Jonathan	1	1	1		
Walcott, George	1		3		
Wilkinson, Jeremiah, Junr	6	1	6		
Bowen, Thomas	1	3	4		
Balou, Absolom	1	2	3		
Allen, Benjamin	1	1	2		
Alexander, Mary			4		
Bly, Oliver	1	1	6		
Ray, Henry	2		1		
Ray, Jonathan	1	2	4		
Ray, David	1	1	2		
Jenckes, David	2	3	4		
Jenckes, Peter	1	1	1		
Clein, John	1		3		
Brown, George	1		1		
Mason, Timothy	2	2	3		
Mowrey (wife of Philip)	2		2		
Sprague, Abraham	4	1	5		
Sprague, Gideon	1	2	2		
Alexander, Roger	2	1	2		
Jilson, Enos	2	2	4		
Brown, Stephen	3		2		
Brown, Elijah	3	3	4		
Lovett, Ruth	1		3	1	
Lovett, Whipple	1	2	3		
Rowland, William	1		3		
Whipple, Stephen	2	3	6		
Joslin, Thomas	3		5		
Joslin, Isreal	1	1	2		
Brown, Elihu	2	6	5		
Carpenter, Jotham	3	2	6		
Bartlet, Daniel	2	4	7		
Follet, Joseph	2	2	6		
Whipple, Ephraim	3		4		

CUMBERLAND TOWN—continued.

NAME OF HEAD OF FAMILY.	Free white males of 16 years and upward, including heads of families.	Free white males under 16 years.	Free white females, including heads of families.	All other free persons.	Slaves.
Newell, Thomas	1	2	2		
Lapham, George	1	1	1		
Sheldon, Roger	3	3	6		
Lovet, Eliphalet	1	3	5		
Peck, Benjamin	2		4		
Clarke, Barney	1	2	1		
Clarke, Wheaton	1	3	1		
Bartlet, Job	1	2	2		
Alexander, John	1		3		
Jeffers, Thomas	1	2	1		
Bartlet, Jeremiah	2	3	2		
Ramsdel, Moses	1	2	2		
Capron, Joseph	2	5	6		
Lapham, Abner	3		2	1	
Lapham, John	5	3	4		
Bartlet, Asa	2		4		
Bradford, Joel	1	3	4		
Fisk, Squire	1	4	2		
Bartlet, Rufus	6	2	2		
Lapham, James	1	3	3		
Fisk, John	2	2	2		
Fisk, Darius	2	1	2		
Capron, Charles	1	3	3		
Capron, Philip	3	4	5		
Inman, Amey	1	1	3		
Cooke, Eseck	1		2		
Bartlet, Zebiah	2		3		
Inman, Jeremiah	2		6		
Jilson, Uriah	1	2	5		
Jilson, Luke	2	2	2		
Baker, John	1	1	2		
Jilson, Nathaniel	1	6	2		
Gaskill, William	2	1	3		
Saunders, Jessee	1	1	3		
Bartlet, Jacob	1	2	6		
Darling, Peter	4	4	3		
Darling, Peter, Junr	1	1	5		
Bartlet, Abner	1	3	2		
Bartlet, Joseph	1		1		
Bartlet, Joseph, Junr	1	3	2		
Bartlet, Liven	1	1	3		
Estas, Zacheus	2		7		
Wilcox, John	1	1	4		
Wilcox, Stephen	1	3	4		
Arnold, Joseph	3	3	7		
Scott, David	1	1	3		
Aldrish, Amos	2	2	3		
Arnold, Luke	1	1	1		
Paine, James	1		4		
Aldrish, Robert	3		3		
Chace, Isaac	1		1		
Arnold, Levi	2	4	3		
Harris, Christopher	1	1	2		
Cooke, Ariel	2	4	4		
Cooke, Annanias	1	1	5		
Arnold, Samuel	2	1	3		
Arnold, Nathan	2	1	3		
Jilson, Nathan	2	3	4		
Cooke, Benjamin	1	1	4		
Bolou, William	2	3	3		
Sprague, Mrs (Widow of Amos)			3		
Bennett, Charles	1	5	3		
Aldrish, Moses	3	2	5		
Cooke, Abraham, Junr	1		2		
Estes, Samuel	2	3	3		
Cooke, Hezekiah	4		3		
Gaskill, Samuel	1	1	2		
Cooke, Abram	2	2	4		
Cooke, Eeazar	1	2	1		
Arnold, John	1	2	2		
Chace, William	1		2		
Arnold, James	1		2		
Hoxsey, Stephen	1	1	3		
Darling, John	1	1	5		
Prince (Negro)				2	
Mason, Jonathan	2	2	2		
Balou, Noah	3	1	2		
Ballou, Noah, Junr	1	1	1		
Tower, Levi	2	3	4		
Tower, Enoch	3		5		
Inman, Stephen	2	3	6		
Balou, Abner	4		5		
Jenckes, Joseph	1	1	3		
Jenckes, James	1	2	3		
Ballou, Edward	1	3	4		
Ballou, Joanna			1		
Ballou, Ezekiel	2		2		
Ballou, Reubin	1	3	3		
Ballou, Levi	2	3	7		
Ballou, Ariel	1		2		
Ballou, Ariel, Junr	2	2	3		
Darling, Ebinizar	1	2	3		
Newell, David	1	2	2		

CUMBERLAND TOWN—continued.

NAME OF HEAD OF FAMILY.	Free white males of 16 years and upward, including heads of families.	Free white males under 16 years.	Free white females, including heads of families.	All other free persons.	Slaves.
Trask, James	1	1	1		
Ballou, Ziba	2	2	1		
Scott, Charles	1	3	1		
Emerson, William	1	1	3		
Brown, Joseph	3	1	4		
Grant, Samuel	3	3	6		
Fisher, Jonathan	4		4		
Fisher, Darius	1	2	1		
Haskell, Abner	1	1	1		
Haskell, Comfort	1	4	2		
Aldrish, Asa	3	4	3		
Hawkins, Darius	1	1	2		
Crowninghill, Richard	2	2	4		
Haskell, John	1	2	4		
Fuller, Job	2	1	7		
Haskill, Samuel	1	3	3		
Wetherhead, Daniel	2		2		
Wetherhead, Levi	1	3	2		
Wetherhead, John	1	3	6		
Jilson, Nathaniel	1	1	3		
Ray, Joseph	3		3		
Ray, Joseph, Junr	1	2	3		
Whipple, Joseph	1		1		
Whipple, Asa	2	4	3		
Aldrish, Abel	1	1	3		
Whipple, Amos	2	1	4		
Chamberlain, Samuel	2	3	4		
Whipple, Joel	1	5	2		
Herrendon, James	1	1	3		
Whipple, Israel	1	3	3		
Cummins, Joseph	1	2	2		
Whipple, Simon	2	4	4		
Harris, Oliver	1	3	3		
Newell, Thomas	1		2		
Rhodes, John	1		2		
Fisher, Jeremiah	1	2	2		
Darling, John	2	2	2		
Darling, John, Junr	2	4	3		
Whipple, Job	1		2		
Hathway, Sylvanus	2		4		
Bosworth, Stacey	1	1	1		
Ballou, Richard	1	4	3		
Gould, Nathaniel	3	4	4		
Follet, William	1		4		
Bishop, Simon	3	1	1		
Whipple, Priserved	2	3	3		
Hyde, Timothy	2		3		
Chace, Charles	2		2		
Albertson, David	1		2		
Gould, John	2	1	5		
Gould, Sybell		1	1		
Sheldon, William	2	2	5		
Razy, David	1	2	5		
Ellis, Jessee	2		2		
Razy, Joseph	1	3	3		
Tingley, Benjamin	1	4	5		
Newell, Jason	2	4	4		
Butterworth, John	1	2	3		
Cole, Betty			2		
Cole, Patience		1	4		
Follet, Levi	1	1	2		
Sheperdson, Nathaniel	1	1	4		
Jones, Stephen	1		2		
Butterworth, Sarah		1	1		
Arnold, Amos	3		2		
Arnold, Rufus	1	4	4		
Arnold, Abab	1	3	2		
Arnold, Enoch	1	2	3		
Walcott, Benjamin	2	3	3		
Walcott, John	1	4	2		
Walcott, Mary	1		1		
Bishop, John	1		1		
Bishop, John, Junr	2	2	4		
Fuller, Ezekiel	1	2	2		
Whipple, Eleazar	2	1	2		
Whipple, Joseph	1	1	2		
Whipple, Anna			3		
Mowrey, James	1	2	3		
Follet, Abraham	2	1	2		
Martin, Isaac	1	3	3		
Peck, Joel	1	2	3		
Brown, Nicholas	3	2	5		
Davis, Jemima			2		
Metcalf, Ebenezar	1	6	1		
Davis, Hannah			2		
Wilkinson, Simon	3		4		
Wilkinson, Joab	1	1	3		
Wilkinson, Anna	2		5		
Streeter, Nathan	1	3	3		
Staples, Stephen	2	3	7		
Razy, Joseph	1	2	3		
Razy, Anthony	1	1	2		
Razy, Isaac	1	2	2		
Wetherhead, Enoch	2		1		

PROVIDENCE COUNTY—Continued.

NAME OF HEAD OF FAMILY.	Free white males of 16 years and upward, including heads of families.	Free white males under 16 years.	Free white females, including heads of families.	All other free persons.	Slaves.
CUMBERLAND TOWN—continued.					
Wetherhead, Nathan	1	5	2		
Hill, Roger	3	1	6		
Bowen, William	1	1	4		
Whipple, John, Junr	2	3	4		
Whipple, Ibrook	1	1	4		
Whipple, Mary			1		
Blanding, Ephraim	1		3		
Blanding, Samuel	2		2		
Grant, Jabez	1		1		
Tower, Benjamin	1	1	3		
Jackson, Morris	2	1	1		
Bennett, Timothy	2	1	5		
Otis, Isaac	4	3	3		
Walliott, Ebenezar	1	1	1		
Tate, Betsey		1	2		
Cargill, James	7	4	3		
Hardin, Seth	1		2		
Carpenter, Asa	3	3	7		
Jilson, Amaziah	1	3	3		
Burlingam, Molly	1		1		
Aldrish, Jonathan	1	1	2		
Aldrish	1	1	4		
Harris, Asa	1	1	1		
Chace, Joseph	1	1	3		
Brown, Ichabod	1	2	2		
Miller, Daniel	1	2	8		
Miller, Josiah	4	3	4		
Burlingham, Betsey		1	3		
Brown, Abiel	4		5		
King, Reuben	2	1	5		
Wilkinson, Nedebiah	1	1	3		
Howard, John	1	1	2		
Miller, Daniel, Junr	1	1	3		
Fairbrother, Thomas	1	2	4		
Howard, Samuel	3	1	4		
Staples, Nathan	1	1	4		
Cesar (Negro)				3	
Amsberry, Jeremiah	2	1	2		
Amsberry, Jeremiah	1	3	2		
Whipple, John	1	1	3		
Whipple, Daniel P	2	1	2		
Whipple, Christopher	2	2	5		
Wilkinson, Benjamin	2	3	4		
Baker, Abiel	1	4	3		
Bishop, Gideon	1	1	3		
Wilkinson, William	3	1	3		
Fuller, John	1		6		
Lee, Joseph	4	2	5		
Lee, Levi	1	1	4		
Smith, Jonathan	1	1	2		
Waterman, Elisha	5	3	4		
Smith, Daniel	1	1	3		
Mosher, Luthan	1	3	3		
Brown, Christopher	2		4		
Dexter, David	1	2	4		
Dexter, Mary			2		
Kent, William	3	1	1		
Carpenter, William	1	2	1		
Carpenter, Ebenezar	1	1	4		
Dexter, James	2	1	5		
Fowler, Ichabod	1	3	5		
Miller, Peter	3	3	6		
Chaffee, William	4		5		
Grant, John	2	1	4		
Grant, Gilbert	1	1	2		
Wilmarth, Mary		1	3		
Dexter, John	1	3	3		
Dexter, Sarah		1	4		
Dexter, Daniel	1	1	1		
FOSTER TOWN.					
Collins, Thomas	2	1	1		
Rounds, Bartram	3	4	4		
Rounds, Joseph	1	3	2		
Colwell, John	1	5	2		
Colwell, William	2	1	9		
Colwell, Christopher	3	7	2		
Colwell, Daniel	2	2	4		
Merithew, William	1		1		
Anderson, Amasa	1	1			
Potter, Hannah	1	2	2		
Hopkins, Timothy	3	4	6		
Smith, John	2	2	4		
Parker, Paul	1	4	4		
Hopkins, Thomas	1	2	1		
Hopkins, Padden	1	1	3		
Hopkins, Joseph	3	3	3		
Hopkins, Zebediah	2		2		
Hopkins, Jonah	1	1	1		
Tucker, Joseph, Junr	1	1	4		
Davis, Joseph	2	2	4		
Davis, Simon	1		2		
Arnold, Oliver	1		2		

NAME OF HEAD OF FAMILY.	Free white males of 16 years and upward, including heads of families.	Free white males under 16 years.	Free white females, including heads of families.	All other free persons.	Slaves.
FOSTER TOWN—con.					
Hopkins, Jeptha	1	2	4		
Hopkins, Barnet	1	2	1		
Hopkins, Ephraim	1	4	7		
Davis, Mason	1	1	2		
Hopkins, Jonathan	2	2	6		
Arnold, Caleb			3		
Hunter, Elisha	1		5		
Bucklin, Squire	3	1	7		
Cole, Richard	3	1	6		
Potter, William	1	1	2		
Hopkins, John	1	2	1		
Hopkins, Jonathan	4	3	7		
Hopkins, Rial	1	3	7		
Mowrey, Andrew	2	3	4		
Arnold, Oliver	1		2		
Wade, Gideon	1	1	3		
Salisbury, Joseph	1	1	6		
Green, William	4	2	2	1	
Hopkins, Sabin	2	1	1		
Pray, Jason	2	1	3		
Pray, Hugh	4	2	4		
Pray, Jonathan	2	2	3		
Pray, Jeremiah	1		1		
Saunders, Robert	5		1		
Baker, William	1	2	3		
Smith, Charles		5	2		
Smith, Samuel		1	2		
Smith, Samuel, Junr	1	1	5		
Simmonds, Jonathan	4		2		
Allen, Joshua	1	1	1		
Wetherhead, Joseph	2	1	2		
Wood, Charles		3	3		
Potter, Sprague	2		1		
Barrows, Nehemiah	1	3	1		
Wade, Simon, Junr	1		1		
Wade, Nehemiah	1		2		
Wade, Levi	2	2	3		
Wade, Simon	1		3		
Westcoat, George	2	1	3		
Horton, Nathaniel	1	2	4		
Stone, Oliver	3	1	1		
Hammond, Amos	3	2	5		
Bullock, Daniel	1	1	3		
Miller, Samuel	1		4		
Miller, Noah	1	2	3		
Bosworth, Jonathan	3	5	6		
Jones, Joshua	2	2	7		
Shippey, Solomon	1	3	5		
Shippey, Eseak	1	2			
Shippey, Hannah	2		1		
Shippey, Job	1	3	2		
Shippey, Hosea	1		1		
Mitchel, Daniel	1	1	6		
Horton, Nathaniel, Junr	1	1	3		
Hopkins, Ezekiel	1		2		
Frazier, William	1	1	4		
Hopkins, Ezekiel, Junr	1	1	2		
Philips, Luke	1	2	2		
Smith, John	1	1	3		
Brown, John	1	1			
Brown, Patrick	1	1	1		
Wallen, Emos	1	1	2		
Ballou, Peter	1	4	2		
Burgis, Gideon	1	4	3		
Hopkins, Peleg	1		4		
Gibbs, Bristol				3	
Dexter, Benjamin	1	1	2		
Tift, Martha			4		
Slaughter, John	1		3		
Fuller, Jonathan		3	3		
Adams, Hizah		2	3		
Slaughter, Silas	1	5	5		
Colegrove, Stephen	1	2	3		
Colegrove, Caleb	1		1		
Taylor, William	3	2	6		
Baker, Abijah	2	2	3		
Baker, George	3	1	3		
Slaughter, Abiel	1	3	4		
Simmonds, Caleb, Junr	1	1	1		
Simmonds, Josiah	1	1	2		
Simmonds, Caleb	1	4	3		
Hopkins, Joseph	1	1	4		
Wood, Nathan	1	1	2		
Toogood, Jonathan	1	1	3		
Dailey, Sylvester				8	
Ballou, Asa	1	1	5		
Crossman, Asahel	1	1	2		
Capron, Benjamin	1	2	2		
Green, Richard	1	2	2		
Paine, Riel	1	1	2		
Walker, Jacob	1		2		
Simmonds, Simon	1	2	2		
Burrough, James	1	3	7		2

NAME OF HEAD OF FAMILY.	Free white males of 16 years and upward, including heads of families.	Free white males under 16 years.	Free white females, including heads of families.	All other free persons.	Slaves.
FOSTER TOWN—con.					
Broadway, William	3	2	5		
Bowen, Jabez	5		3		
Simmonds, Thomas	2	3	3		
Cooke, Wanton	1		2		
Goodpaid, Stephen	2	2	4		
Tucker, Joseph	1		2		
Tucker, Nathaniel	2		2		
Brown, Fleet	2	2	4		
Hopkins, Oliver	1	5	2		
Hopkins, Holly	1		2		
Simmonds, Ezra	1		1		
Cole, James	1	3	5		
Paine, Isaac	2	4	3		
Paine, Isaac, Junr	1	1	1		
Hopkins, Peter	1	1	2		
Hopkins, Jeremiah	1	1	3		
Cole, Samuel	2	1	2		
Esten, Henry	1	1	2		
Esten, King	1	1	1		
Esten, Obadiah	1	2	6		
Simmonds, Hezekiah	1	1	2		
Esten, Theophilus	1	2	5		
Hopkins, Daniel	1	2	3		
Davis, Robert, Junr	1	1	5		
Whitman, Robert	2		3		
Rounds, William	2	1	2		
Rounds, John	2	2	5		
Rounds, Benjamin	1	3	1		
Sheldon, William	1	1	8		
Austin, Joseph	1	7	2		
Williams, Jeremiah	1	1	2		
Anthony, Jonathan	4	3	8		
Walker, Philip	1	3	5		
Whitman, Darius	1	2	3		
Smith, Benjamin	1	3	2		
Place, Nathan	2		1		
Philips, Nathaniel	1		2		
Philips, Nathaniel, Junr	1	2	2		
Westcoat, John	3	3	2		
Whitman, Benjamin	1		2		
Whitman, Stephen	2	3	7		
Howland, Asahel	2	1	3		
Howland, Samuel	1	1	4		
Davis, Stephen	1	2	4		
Davis, William	1	4	2		
Blackmore, William	1	3	3		
Randal, William	2	4	3		
Cole, Abraham	1	2	2		
Cole, Robert	1		1		
Davis, Robert	1	1	2		
Cole, Hugh	3	1	1		
Cole, Pabodie	2	4	4		
Pettis, James	1	3	2		
Little, Jessee	1	1	1		
Parker, John	2	1	3		
Salisbury, Henry	1	1	4		
Salisbury, Henry, Junr	1		2		
Walker, Abraham	1	3	3		
Hill, Nehemiah	1	2	4		
Irons, Samuel	1	4	5		
Rounds, Simeon	1	2	3		
Round, Levi	1	3	5		
Round, Peleg	2	1	2		
Round, Peleg, Junr	2	2	4		
Round, John	1	4	4	1	
Walker, William	1	4	4		
Eddy, John	2	3	3		
Hopkins, Nicholas	2	1	8		
Hopkins, Stephen	1	1	8		
Hopkins, William	2	1	3		
Davenport, William	1	1	4		
Hopkins, Noah	1	1	3		
Hopkins, Mathewson	1	2	3		
Bennett, Benjamin	1	2	4		
Bennett, Thomas	1	1	2		
Walker, George	1	1	2		
Philips, Abraham	2	2	3		
Simmonds, James, Junr	1		3		
Wood, Reuben	1	3	3		
Harrington, Jenckes	1	3	3		
Harrington, Randal	1	2	3		
Bennett, Arthur	2	2	4		
Williams, John	2	8	3		
Potter, Simeon	1	3	5		
Hammond, John	1	2	3		
Randal, John	1	2	3		
Bennett, Daniel	2		4		
Hammond, Thomas	2	2	3		
Soal, David	1	5	2		
Wilcox, Abraham	3	1	1		1
Soal, Jonathan	1	2	3		
Young, Zadock	1	1	3		
Bennett, Stephen	1	2	3		

PROVIDENCE COUNTY—Continued.

FOSTER TOWN—con.

NAME OF HEAD OF FAMILY.	Free white males of 16 years and upward, including heads of families.	Free white males under 16 years.	Free white females, including heads of families.	All other free persons.	Slaves.
Baker, John	1	4	4		
Baker, Amos	1	2	2		
Baker, James	1	2	3		
Bennett, Josiah	1	2	4		
Russell, Abraham	1	2	2		
Philips, Jacob	2	2	5		
Stone, Nathaniel	1	2	2		
Potter, Peter	1	3	4		
Tillinghast, Samuel	2	2	5		
Parker, Peter	2	2	6		
Philips, Ezekiel	2	4	3		
Colwell, Richard	1	1	2		
Potter, Rowse	1	1	7		
Mathewson, Resolved	1	4	5		
Hill, William	3		2		
Hill, Benjamin	3	4	4		
Peter, Joseph				2	
Merithew, Philip	1	1	1		
Perkins, Elias	2		2		
Manchester, Nathaniel	1	1	4		
Wells, Benjamin	1	1	2		
Angel, Benjamin	1	1	2		
Perkins, Samuel, Junr	2	2	5		
Perkins, Samuel	1		2		
Angel, Nehemiah	1	2	6		
Moss, James	1	2	3		
Megee, George	1		2		
Meccoon, James	1	1	4		
Fuller, Francis	3	3	8		
Cole, David	1	3	5		
Cole, Daniel	1	1	2		
Young, Nathan	2	1	3		
Young, Asa	1	5	2		
Dyar, Abijah	3		4		
Wood, Daniel	3	2	5		
Wood, William	1		2		
Carver, Oliver	1	1	4		
Herrington, Ephraim	2	1	3		
Herrington, William	1	3	5		
Bennett, Nathan, Junr	2	4	3		
Bennett, Nathan	2	1	3		
Philips, Zephanius	1		1		
Bennett, Laban	1		1		
Clarke, Caleb	1	1	1		
Hopkins, Jonah, Junr	1	2	4		
Herrington, John	3	1	2		
Herrington, Amos	1	2	3		
Absworth, Peleg	1	3	4		
Potter, Caleb	1	5	3		
Wilcox, Jeremiah	2		8		
Sweet, Angel	2	1	5		
Weaver, Reuben	1	1	3		
Yaw, Philip	2	1	3		
Herrington, Josiah, Junr	1	2	3		
Herrington, Josiah	3		1		
Read, Reuben	1	2	5		
Herrington, Stephen	1	1	2		
Mitchel, Richard	1	1	4		
Hatch, David	1	1	6		
Stone, John	1	2	3		
Potter, Thomas	2	3	2		
Potter, Anthony	1	1	2		
Kennedy, Alexander	2	5	7		
Randal, Jathan	1	2	1		
Randal, John	1	2	3		
Saunders Joseph	1		1		
Randal, Silas	1	2	3		
Bosworth, William	1	2	3		
Tripp, Abiel	2		3		
Tripp, Benjamin	2	3	3		
Pratt Job	1	3	3		
Pratt, Amasa	1	3	4		
White, Benjamin	1	1	3		
Herrington, Simon	2	2	6		
Herrington, Nathaniel	1		2		
Herrington, Nathaniel, Junr	1	1	4		
Herrington, John, Junr	1	3	1		
Herrington, Rufus	2	6	3		
Johnston, George	1	1	2		
Johnston, Job	1	1	1		
Blanchard, William	1	3	1		
Brayton, Thomas	1	1	4		
Johnston, John	3	1	3		
Griffith, Southwood	1		2		
Dorrence, George, Junr	3	1	3		
Dorrance, Alexander	1	2	3		
Dorrance, James	3		1		
Dorrance, William	1		2		
Dorrance, Samuel	1	5	5		1
Pierce, Benjamin	1		2		
Strannahan, James	1		1		
Brown, Benjamin	2		6		
King, Joshua	3	4	2		

FOSTER TOWN—con.

NAME OF HEAD OF FAMILY.	Free white males of 16 years and upward, including heads of families.	Free white males under 16 years.	Free white females, including heads of families.	All other free persons.	Slaves.
Cranston, James	1		2		
Parker, Thomas	1	3	5		
Tyler, James	3	3	3		
Blanchard, Reuben	2	3	5		
Smith, Benjamin, Junr	1	2	1		
Tyler, John	2		2		
Tyler, James, Junr	1	3	2		
Tyler, Isaih	1		2		
Tyler, William	2	2	1		
Blanchard, Isaac	3	1	4		
Foster, Lemuel	1	1	1		
Foster, Samuel	1	2	1		
Green, Oliver	1	3	2		
Plane, Benajah	1		6		
Place, John	1	1	1		
Plane, Stephen	3	4	4		
Plane, Enoch	2	2	2		
Plane, Job	1	1	3		
Plane, Rufus	1	6	3		
Brown, Nathaniel	2	1	2		
Brown, Elisha	1		1		
Fenner, Obadiah	2	2	2		
Howard, William	2	2	3		
Howard, Daniel	1	3	4		
Howard, John	2		2		
Howard, Thomas	1	3	4		
Howard, James	1	3	6		
Smith, Daniel	1	2	2		
Foster, Stephen, Junr	2	3	3		
Cooke, Constant	1	1	6		
Cooke, Peter, Junr	1	1	1		
Wells, James	3	2	6		
Wells, Caleb	1	1	1		
Fry, Jeffry A	1	2	3		
Lyon, John	3	1	3		
Herrington, Obadiah	1		1		
Lyon, John, Junr	1	1	1		
Simmonds, Stephen	1	1	2		
Fry, Benjamin	2	1	3		
Carpenter, Syril	5	1	4		
Parker, Jacob	1		3		
Brown, John	1	3	2		
Brown, James	2		3		
Brown, Jonathan	2	1	4		
Philips, James	1		2		
Philips, Asa	1	1	2		
Cranston, Samuel	1	3	5		
Cranston, John	1	2	2		
Cranston, Peleg	3		2		
Cranston, Peleg, Junr	1		4		
Bates, Asa	1	1	3		
Brownwell, Benjamin	3		3		
Fish, Silas	1	3	6		
Fish, Artemus	1	5	6		
Fish, Elisha	1	1	3		
Shearman, Job	1	3	5		
Albro, Job	1	2	5		
Rice, John	2	1	2		
Parker, William	1	2	3		
Hopkins, Samuel	2	3	5		
Bowen, Jacob	1	3	3		
Rice, James	1	1	5		

GLOCESTER TOWN.

NAME OF HEAD OF FAMILY.	Free white males of 16 years and upward, including heads of families.	Free white males under 16 years.	Free white females, including heads of families.	All other free persons.	Slaves.
Mathewson, John	1		2		
Sprague, Ruth	2		2		
Salisbury, Stephen	1		2		
Mitchel, Thomas	1	1	4		
Dyer, Anthony	1		4		
Mitchel, Joseph	1		2		
Bowen, Joseph	1		1		
Andrews, Squire	1	3	4		
Bishop, William	1	1	3		
Bishop, Zepheniah	1	1	3		
Sprague, Peter	3		1		
Hicks, Barnet	2		3		
Russy, William	3	1	4		
Lewis, Obadiah	2		2		
Lewis, Obadiah, Junr	3	1	1		
Lewis, James	1	1	3		
Tinkum, Hezekiah	4		1		
Winsor, Jessee	3	1	6		
Warner, Mary	2	1	2		
Warner, Elihu	1		1		
Warner, Daniel	1	2	3		
Cole, James	2	3	1		
Bowen, Hezekiah	1		1		
Caldwell, Stephen	1	2	2		
Bowen, Azael	1	4	1		
Bowen, Simon	1	4	2		
Bowen, Ezra	3	1	3		
Winsor, Thomas	1	1	5		
Staples, Nathan	1	2	3		
Gross, John	2	1	4		

GLOCESTER TOWN—con.

NAME OF HEAD OF FAMILY.	Free white males of 16 years and upward, including heads of families.	Free white males under 16 years.	Free white females, including heads of families.	All other free persons.	Slaves.
Blanchard, Reubin	2	1	6		
Walker, Elijah	1		1		
Winsor, Ira	2		3	1	
Steere, Jeremiah	3	1	3		
Steere, Jonah	2		4		
Steere, Jeremiah, Junr	1		1		
Medberry, Benjamin	2	2	3		
Potter, Christopher	2	1	2		
Sax, John	1	1	4		
Brown, Chad	2		3		
Brown, Eseck	1	2	3		
Hicks, Daniel	1		3		
Sprague, Elisha	1	1	4		
Cole, Ebenezar	1	2	2		
Inches, Ishmael	1	2	6		
Bowen, Sally		1	4		
Burlingham, David	3	1	5		
Burlingham, Benedict	2	1	3		
Brown, Hannah	3		3		
Burlingham, Richard	1		2		
Place, Peter	1	2	7		
Place, John	5	1	3		
McNamara, Mrs Esther			4		
Hunt, Seth	1	3	4		
Bump, Wanton	1		2		
Plane, Reubin	1	1			
Steere, Noah	1	4	3		
Smith, Elizabeth			3		
Place, Joseph	1		1		
Steer, Elisha	1		2		
Steer, John	1		1		
Henry, Benjamin	1	1	7		
Steere, Enoch	4		3		
Place, Daniel	2	4	3		
Steer, Caleb	2	4	3		
Ross, Stephen	1	3	2		
Evans, Richard	1	2	5		
Hawkes, Susama	1	1	3		
Evans, Edward	1		2		
Evens, Daniel	1	2	2		
Eddy, Jonathan	2	3	3		
Smith, Dorius	1		5		
Eddy, Olney	1	3	5		
Hawkins, Stephen	1	3	5		
Smith, Simon	6	1	6		
Green, John	1		2		
Smith, William	1	3	3		
Burlingame, Thomas	2	1	3		
Baker, Abraham	2	4	4		
Baker, Levi	1		4		
Arnold, Daniel	1	2	3		
Whiting, William	1	1	4		
Steere, William	1	2	2		
Steere, Richard	4	1	3		
Bellows, Hezekiah	3	1	2		
Bellows, Eleazer	1	1	2		
Pettiface, Mrs Sybel	1		2		
Morrey, Richard	1	1	2		
Pettiface, Eleakin	1	2	4		
Olney, Joseph	2	1	3		
Keech, Zephaniah	1	2	5		
Philips, John	1	2	4		
Armstrong, Jesse	2	2	4		
Olney, John	1	2	3		
Pettiface, Samuel	3		4		
Smith, Stephen	1	3	3		
Colwill, Carles	3		1		
Colwill, William	1	1	2		
Colwill, John	1	4	5		
Caldwell, David	2	1	2		
Smith, Chad	1	2	4		
Pettiface, Job	2	1	2		
Pettiface, Hosea	1	5	4		
Smith, Rufus	1	2	3		
Brown, Elisha	1	2	6		
Philips, John	1		1		
Goodale, Moses	1	1	1		
Smith, John (son of Benjamin)	4	2	5		
Burlingame, Eseck	1	2	5		
Crosby, Benjamin	1	3	5		
Steer, Enoch	1	2	7		
Mann, Abel	1	1	4		
Crossman, Daniel	2	3	4		
Hopkins, Zebediah	1	1	4		
Hopkins, Jeremiah	1	2	1		
Hopkins, Thomas	1		2		
Peckham, Seth	1	3	5	1	
Philips, Jeremiah	3	1	4		
Winsor, Amos	1	3	4		
Aldrich, Benjamin	1		2		
Winsor, Joseph	3	3	4		
Winsor, Samuel	1	3	3		
Colwell, Benjamin	1	2	9		
Hawkins, William	1		3		

PROVIDENCE COUNTY—Continued.

GLOCESTER TOWN—con.

NAME OF HEAD OF FAMILY.	Free white males of 16 years and upward, including heads of families.	Free white males under 16 years.	Free white females, including heads of families.	All other free persons.	Slaves.
Hawkins, William	1	2	4		
Hawkins, Moses	1	2	3		
Wheeler, Henry	3	2	4		
Hawkins, Joseph	1	2	3		
Olney, Stephen	2	3	3		
Mowrey, David	2		4		
Kimball, Dean	3	1	3		
Williams, Silas	2	1	4		
Fenner, John	4	1	5	1	
Bowen, Eleazer	1		2		
Keech, Stephen	3		2		
Ford, Joseph	1	1	3		
Williams, John	2	3	3		
Luther, Abiel	2		1		
Luther, Brightman	1	2	2		
Wright, Samuel	3		2		
Page, William	2	1	6		
Smith, Stephen	4		5		
Smith, Eseck	2	1	3		
Hawkins, Elijah	2	1	4		
Steer, Samuel	4	2	3		
Hawkins, Benjamin	1		1		
Hawkins, Elizabeth	1		3		
Aldrich, Ebenezer	1		2		
Aldrich, Stephen	3		4		
Steer, Rufus	2	3	2		
Philips, Aaron	1	3	1		
Briggs, Aaron	1		6		
Mowrey, Gideon	2	1	5		
Mowrey, Uriah	2	1	5		
Wright, Benjamin	1	1	1		
Philips, John	1	3	6		
Pearce, Benoni	1	2	3		
Page, Joseph	3		4		
Irons, Samuel	3	2	6		
Pierce, George	1	1	4		
Irons, Resolved	1	2	3		
Steer, Job	1	1	2		
Aldrich, Joseph	1		1		
Aldrich, Joseph, Junr	1	4	4		
Aldrich, Jessee	1		4		
Blackmore, Nathaniel	3		5		
Andrews, John	3		1		
Andrews, John, Junr	1	3	3		
Barns, Mathew	1		2		
Vallet, David	1	5	2		
Steer, Asa	2	2	4		
Potter, Jessee	2	1	4		
Paine, Stephen	2	1	4		
Field, Charles	3	3	3		
Brown, Elisha	2	3	7		1
Irons, Stephen	2	1	3		
Turtelott, William	2	1	10		
Smith, Obed	1	1	3		
Cooman, William	3	1	3		
Hawkins, Stephen	1	4	5		
Vallett, Jonathan	2	3	5		
Tinkum, Nehemiah	1	1	4		
Winsor, Joshua	3	2	4		
Hicks, Luther	1	1	2		
Hawkins, Uriah	2	2	3		
Martin, William	1		1		
Martin, Levi	1	1	2		
Durfee, Robert	1		2		
Mason, Hannah	1	3	3		
Armstrong, Elijah	2	2	6		
Mason, Joseph	1	1	2		
Smith, John	3	1	7		
Smith, Zadock	1		2		
Smith, Aria	1		3		
Mathewson, Daniel	1	2	5		
Wallen, Joshua	1	1	1		
Buckstone, Aaron	1		2		
Wallen, Ishmael	1		2		
Wallen, Martha	1		2		
Wallen, Isaac	3	2	3		
Wallen, Jacob	1	3	3		
Pigsley, Welcome	1	3	4		
Pettiface, Ezekiel	1	2	3		
Smith, Mrs Lydia		2	3		
Salisbury, Richard	1	3	3		
Cooper, Moses	3		3		
Whipple, Stephen	2	2	3		
Cooper, Stephen	3	3	5		
Smith, Daniel	1	1	5		1
Salisbury, David	2		2		
Ballou, Eleazer	3	1	5		
Kelley, Isaih	1		3		
Baker, Abraham, Junr	1		3		
Whipple, Jonathan	3		2		
Philips, David, 3d	1		1		
Thornton, Jeremiah	2	2	5		
Jenckes, Peter	1	2	3		
Page, William	2	3	4		
Durfee, John	1	2	2		
Page, Daniel	2		2		
Clemmons, Richard	2	3	2		
Wallen, Prescilla			2		
Stephens, Squire	1		1		
Young, David	1	4	5		
Andrews, Jonathan	2	4	1		
Gladcomb, William	3	2	4		
Bowen, Joseph	1	3	3	1	
Wilmoth, Timothy	3	2	8		
Knapp, Jonathan	2		2		
Saunders, Jeremiah	2	3	2		
Brown, Peleg	1	3	3		
Owen, Thomas	4	2	3		
Owen, Solomon, Junr	3	2	6		
Owen, Solomon	3	1	5		
Owen, Thomas, Junr	2	2	4		
Kimball, Asa	2	3	4		
Kelly, David	1	1	3		
Paine, Nathan	3	3	5		
Potter, Sarah	1		2		
Potter, James	2	1	5		
Corey, Thomas	1		2		
Smith, William	1	1	2		
Smith, Jessee	2	2	2		
Smith, Obed	1	2	3		
Mason, Aaron	1	1	1		
Eddy, Amosa	1	4	3		
Machintine, Rufus	1	2	2		
Hill, Isaac	1	1	3		
Eddy, Jessee	1	3	1		
Heldrich, Martha			2	1	
Wells, John	1	1	3		
Sayles, Ezekiel	1	1	7		
Sayles, Eseck	2	2	3		
Sayles, Israel	1		2		
Sayles, Abad	2	1	3		
Ross, Asa	1	3	4		
Pettiface, Jonathan	1		3		
Paine, Latto	1	2	2		
Smith, Wait	1		1		
Ross, John	1	3	5		
Cooke, Joshua	1	3	4		
Ballord, Benjamin	5	3	4		
Fairfield, Abraham	2	3	5		
Burlingame, Elisha	1	4	3		
Mitchel, Uriel	1	4	4		
Mackintire, Simon	1	3	2		
Watson, Abraham	1	3	4		
Darling, Ebenezar	2		2		
Smith, James	2		4		
Smith, Asa	1	3	2		
Cooke, Michael	1	4	3		
Richardson, David	1	2	6		
Philips, Adam	2	2	1		
Bowdish, David	2	1	4		
Darling, Sarah			2	7	
Salisbury, John	1	3	4		
Sprague, Richard	1	1	2		
Herrington, Andrew	3	1	4		
Blackmore, Stephen	1	3	6		
Mowrey, Uriah	1	3	3		
Mowrey, Asahel	1	1	2		
Baker, Rufus	1	1	1		
Cooke, Samuel	1	1	5		
Cooke, Zepheniah	1	2	3		
Barns, Thomas	1		3		
Barns, Stephen	1	1	5		
Barns, Daniel	1	2	6		
Walden, John	1	2	2		
Barns, Benjamin	1	1	2		
Ballou, Joseph	1	2	6		
Mathewson, Joshua	1	3	5		
Cooke, Elijah	2		7		
Cooke, Benjamin	1	1	2		
Philips, Andrew	2	4	9		
Gorey, Daniel	1	4	3		
Brown, Stephen	1	2	2		
Sayles, Elisha	2	1	2		
Hamilton, Francis	2		8		
Balton, Sylvanus	2		3		
Harris, Jonathan	2		4		
Harris, Amaziah	1	1	2		
Ballard, Jeremiah	1		2		
Ballard, Jeremiah	2		1		
Ballard, Andrew	1	3	4		
Harris, Eleazar	1	3	5		
Harris, Eseck	2	2	3		
Harris, Mrs Marthaw			2		
Harris, Joseph	1		1		
Sweet, James	1	4	6		
Shippey, John	1	2	2		
Herrenden, Preserved	1	3	2		
Smith, James	1	5	2		
Cooper, Moses, Junr	3	1	2		
Ballou, Seth	1		3		
Ballou, Asa	2	2	4		
Logee, Aaron	1	4	3	1	
Mitchel, Elisha	2		2		
Cooke, Stephen	3	1	3		
Mitchel, John	5		2		
Batley, Jessee	1	2	2		
Ross, Isaac	3	2	5		
Cooke, Sylvanus	3	1	3		
Cooke, Gideon	2	5	5		
Eddy, Zephenius	1	3	6		
Sly, William	3		4		
Pettiface, William	1	1	2		
Kelly, James	1		3		
Raymond, William	1	2	2		
Steer, Simon	1	2	5		
Putnam, Jockthan	4	1	7		
Taft, Mijaman	2	3	1		
Curtis, Thomas	2	1	2		
Herrenden, Benjamin	1	1	2		
Lapham, William	2	2	3		
Lapham, Solomon	3		5		
Mathewson, John	2	3	4		
Aldrich, Richard	1	1	2		
Ballard, Jeremiah	1	2	4		
Wood, James	2	1	2		
Herrenden, Solomon	2	1	2		
Brown, Josiah	2	1	5		
Ballou, Jeremiah	2	1	6		
Inman, David	1		2		
Inman, William	2		4		
Inman, John	1	1	4		
Smith, Arnold	1		2		
Raymond, Israel	2	2	2		
Handy, Ebenezar	3	2	8		
Salisbury, Edward	1	3	2		
Bundy, Mark	1		2		
Baker, John	1		2		
Inman, John, Junr	1	2	2		
Inman, Asa	4		3		
Wallen, Rebecca	1				
Ballou, David	2	6	3		
Comstock, Samuel	3	1	2		
Page, William	2	3	4		
Buckstone, Charles	1	1	4		
Bacon, Ephraim	1	1	4		
Arnold, William	1	1	6		
Inman, Israel	1		2		
Inman, Elisha	1	2	3		
Inman, Samuel	3	3	3		
Bartlet, Caleb	2	2	6		
Philips, David	2		4		
Bishop, Gideon	1	1	4		
Benson, Elihu	1	2	4		
Arnold, Benedict	2	2	5		
Mann, Israel	1	2	2		
Wall, Thomas	3	3	5		
Bishop, Thomas	2		8		
Wheelock, Daniel	2	2	4		
Inman, Adam	1	1	2		
Cooke, Israel	3	5	4		
Bowen, William	4	1	5		
Chilson, Israel	2	1	3		
Chilson, Abner	1	1	2		
Esten, John	3	1	4		
Esten, Joseph	1	3	5		
Esten, John, Junr	1	2	2		
Mowrey, Jeremiah	2	1	4		
Arnold, Noah	2	3	3		
Weirs, Robert	1				
Whipple, John	1	1	1		
Comstock, Eseck	3	2	4		
Thayer, Silas	2	2	2		
Brown, Daniel	2	1	3		
Thayer, Ephraim	2		3		
Smith, Abner	1		3		
Shearman, Alkeaney	4		4		
Arnold, Noah, Junr	2	1			
Arnold, Abor	1		1		
Salisbury, William	4	1	4		
Aldrich, Zachaus	1	1	4		
Arnold, Aaran	2		4		
Aldrich, Gira	1	2	4		
Arnold, Eleazer	2	1	1		
Clemmens, Wright	1	1	3		
Hunt, George	1	1	4		
Hunt, John	2		1		
Anthony, James				7	
Harris, John	1	2	3		
Woodward, Stephen	2	2	6		
Curtis, Daniel	1		3		
Pettiface, John	3		3		
Pettiface, Seth	1	1	2		
Pain, Paszala	1	2	2		
Aldrich, Peter	2		4		
Shippey, Thomas	2	4	4		

PROVIDENCE COUNTY—Continued.

GLOCESTER TOWN—con.

NAME OF HEAD OF FAMILY.	Free white males of 16 years and upward, including heads of families.	Free white males under 16 years.	Free white females, including heads of families.	All other free persons.	Slaves.
Shippey, Joseph	2	2	3		
Smith, Martin	3		5		
Brown, Jeremiah	1		1		
Brown, David	1	1	1		
Brown, Israel	1	1	3		
Humes, Moses	1	1	2		
Paine, Benjamin	1		2		
Paine, Abden	1	1	2		
Paine, Nathan	3		2		
Paine, Nathan, the 3d	1	2	5		
Paine, Moab	1	1	1		
King, James	2	1	3		
Eddy, Enoch	1	1	1		
King, James, Junr	1	1	1		
Ross, John, Junr	1	1	2		
Williams, Abner	1	4	4		
Logee, Caleb	1	4	3		
Burlingame, Asa	1	2	3		
Wilcox, Jira	3	2	4		
Lapham, Jethro	1		2		
Lapham, Jessee	1	1	1		
Wilcox, William	1		1		
Lapham, Levi	1	1	2		
Crany, Stephen	1		1		
Chace, Joseph	1	4	2		
Eddy, Willard	1	2	3		
Eddy, Zachariah	1	2	3		
Stone, James	1		1		
Mowrey, Stephen	1	1	2		
Stone, John	1	2	6		
Stone, George	1		1		
Mann, Amos	1	1	4*		
Mann, Arnold	1	1	2		
Stone, Asabel	1	2	3		
Eddy, Lippet	2	1	4		
Batho, Jacob	2	1	4		
Howland, John	3	1	8		
Howland, Thomas	2	1	5		
Aldrich, Jessee	1		2		
Howland, James	1		1		
Kimball, John	1		1		
Jenny, Timothy	1	7	1		
Jenny, Seth	3		5		
Kimball, Howland	1	2	2		
Pollock, Henry	2	2	3		
Short, John	2	4	5		
Tucker, John	1	4	3		
Short, Asa	1	3	5		
Cutler, Knight	1	2	2		
Pollock, Mingo				7	
Sheldon, John	1	2	3		
Irons, Jeremiah, Junr	2	4	4		
Eddy, Samuel	2	3	6		
Eddy, Eseck	1	2	2		
Lashuers, Joseph	1	2	6		
Blois, Sarah	1	2	3		
Hill, Levi	1	2	4		
Keech, Joseph	2	2	4		
Smith, Jonathan	2	1	2		
Moffatt, Eli	1	1	3		
Salisberry, Benjamin	1	2	3		
Hopkins, Aziel	1		1		
Chace, Stephen	1	1	4		
Brown, Joseph	1		2		
Brown, Ezekiel	1	3	1		
Batty, Benjamin	3		4		
Ross, Seth	2	1	6	1	
Cooper, Nathan	1	1	6		
Taft, Moses	1	3	2		
Cowen, James, Junr	1		2		
Ross, William	2	1	4		
Brown, George	1	1	8		
Brown, Israel, Junr	1	3	2		
Sayles, Christopher	2	2	5		
Winsor, Stephen	3	4	3		
McIntire, Pelatiah	1	1	1		
Curtis, Mrs Alice		1	2		
Sayles, Ishmael	2		3		
Short, Samuel	1		3		
Trask, John	1	2	2		
Cutler, Samuel	1		2		
Harrenden, Reubin	2	2	3		
Drake, Ishua	1		2		
Green, Edward	2	2	6		
Tucker, Jessee	1	1	1		
Sprague, Boomer	2		2		
Clarke, Abraham	1	1	3		
Clarke, Eleazer	1	2	4		
Bowdish, Nathaniel	3	3	4		
Hill, David	2	3	3		
Reynolds, James	1	2	3		
Richmond, David	3	5	6		
White, Asa	1	1	2		
Keech, Jessee	1	4	6		
Arons, William	1	4	6		

GLOCESTER TOWN—con.

NAME OF HEAD OF FAMILY.	Free white males of 16 years and upward, including heads of families.	Free white males under 16 years.	Free white females, including heads of families.	All other free persons.	Slaves.
Brown, Nedabiah	3		6		
Durfey, John	1	5	2		
Brown, Benjamin	1	2	4		
Brown, Simon	1	1	1		
Eddy, Gideon	1	2	5		
Smith, Job	2		3		
Moffatt, Enoch			1	3	
Chace, Levi	3	3	7		
Colegrove, Asa	1	3	4		
Burringham, Stephen	1	2	4		
Mitchel, John	1	1	1		
Ide, John	1	3	4		
Tucker, John	1	2	3		
Smith, Reubin	1		1		
Smith, Jeremiah	1		2		
Pray, John	4		2		
Arnold, Jabez	1	3	3		
Arnold, Caleb	1	5	2		
Arnold, William	2	3	5		
Wilkinson, William	3	2	5		
Pettiface, Samuel	5	2	3		
Churchill, Joseph	2	2	4		
Cornel, Oliver	2	4	2		
Turner, Stently	2	1	4		
Dexter, Burzilla	1	3	4		
Turner, Jshua	1	1	1		
Turner, William	1	1	2		
Aldrich, Elisha	3	2	4		
Place, Stephen	2	4	6		
Westcoat, Oliver	1	1	1		
Green, Peter	1	2	3		
Hammond, Gideon	1	5	2		
Cobb, Thomas	1	2	2		
Bowen, Isreal	1	1	2		
Ballard, Jacob	1	2	4		
Steer, William	1	1	5		
Plan, Simon	1	1	3		
Bowen, Elkanah	2		3		
Davis, Jabez	3	3	3		
Bowen, Obadiah	1	1	1		
Davis, John	1	4	4		
Page, Joseph	2	1	2		
Tucker, Robert	1	2	5		
Durfee, James	1	3	3		
Aldrich, Timothy	2	2	2		
Davis, John	3	1	5		
Saunders, Robert	3	2	3		
Philips, Joseph	2	3	6		
Wilkinson, Benjamin	1	1	1	1	
Wheeler, Hezekiah	2	1	5		
Wilder, Asaph	1	5	2		
Wood, William	1	1	2		
Wood, Thomas	4		2		
Pray, Richard	1	2	2		
Prentice, Thomas	1	2	2		
Ballou, William			3		
Steer, Stephen	2	7	4		
Arnold, Stephen	2	3	3		
Darling, Ebinezar, Junr	1	3	3		
Richardson, Joseph	1	2	6		
Sprague, Jedadiah, Junr	2	2	2		
Sprague, John	1	2	1		
Cowen, Joseph	2	2	2		
Smith, Thomas	1	2	3		
Cowen, John	2	2	6		
Paine, Benjamin	3	1	2		
Sprague, Jedadiah	3	5	4		
Paine, Stephen	3	6	4		
Peters, Mark	3	3	3		
Mowrey, Jacob	2	2	3		
Walter, Daniel	2		3		
Cowen, Benjamin	1	1	4		
Luther, Abiel, Junr	4	2	5		
Bowen, George	3	3	6		
Brown, Elisha	2		3		
Brown, Eseck		4	3		
Brown, Jessee	1	1	2		
Tripp, Jessee	2		2		
Keech, Nicholas	2		2		
Keech, Jeremiah	1		2		
Owens, Daniel	2	2	4		
Boyden, Asa	1		1		
Sayles, Thomas	2	4	6		
Owens, Thomas	1		5		
Hinds, Philamon	1	3	2		
Woods, John	1		2		
Stephens, Justice	2	4	2		
Cowen, James	1	1	2		
Cowen, John	2	2	5		
Winsor, Anan	1	5	4		
Cowen, David	1	2	2		
Winsor, Abraham	3	4	8		
Wade, William	2	3	6		
Saunders, Henry	2	4	3		
Wade, Mary	1	2	6		

GLOCESTER TOWN—con.

NAME OF HEAD OF FAMILY.	Free white males of 16 years and upward, including heads of families.	Free white males under 16 years.	Free white females, including heads of families.	All other free persons.	Slaves.
Wade, Williard	1	2	3		
Wade, Mary		1	4		
Saunders, Rufus	1	3	3		
Keech, Sylvanus	1	2	6		
Saunders, Abram	1		2		
Sweet, Jeremiah	2	2	5		
Saunders, Stephen	3	2	4		
Tinkum, John	1		2		
Ballou, David	2	2	7		
Potter, Sprague	3	3	4		
Inman, Obadiah	1	5	5		
Saunders, Othniel	3	1	4		
Wells, John	4	3	7		
Wade, Nathaniel	3	2	4		
Mitchel, Reubin	1	3	6		
Smith, Sylvanus	1	1	2		
Wood, Charles	1	2	3		
Mitchel, Daniel	1		2		
Williams, Squire	1	3	6		
Williams, Amos	2	1	2		
Whipple, Benajah	3	1	2		

JOHNSTON TOWN.

NAME OF HEAD OF FAMILY.	Free white males of 16 years and upward, including heads of families.	Free white males under 16 years.	Free white females, including heads of families.	All other free persons.	Slaves.
Vincent, Caleb	1	1	4		
Waterman, Labon	3	1	4		
Latham, William	3	2	5		
Roome, Cesar (Negro)				2	
Clifford, John	2	2	5		
King, William B.	2	3	3	1	
Burden, William	1	3	2		
Williams, Jeremiah	1	2	2		
Thornton, Elisha	1	1	3		
King, Josiah	2	1	2		
Thornton, Richard	3	3	7		
Smith, Lydia			1		
Sheldon, Ezekiel	1	1	1		
Borden, Richard	1	1	2		
Waterman, Benjamin	3		2		1
Clarke, Jonathan	1		2		
Greene, Joshua	1		2		
Greene, Samuel	2	2	2		
Burden, Joseph	2	1	4		
Hawkins, Hope	2	1	3		
Perrige, Samuel	2	1	2	1	
Pierce, Samuel	3		2		
Robinson, Hannah		1	3		
Woodmansey, George	1	3	3		
Olney, Ezeck	1	2	3		
Childs, William, Junr	1		1		
Briggs, Peter	2		3		
DeBloss, Stephen	1		7		
Mornton, Edward	2	1	7		
Angell, Joshua	1		2	1	
Sprange, Reuben	3	1	4		
Olney, Isaac	1		2	1	
Cezar, Joseph				8	
Cezar, John				11	
Angell, Daniel	2	1	4		
Angell, William	1	1	6		
Waterman, Nathaniel	1		1		
Sweet, Philip	2	5	3		
Brown, Reuben	2	3	6		
Belknap, Jacob	1		1		
Belknap, Abram	3	3	6		
Barnes, John	1		1		
Pain, Squire	1	1	1		
Day, Nathaniel	1	1	2		
Pain, William	1		4		
Boyd, James	1	2	2		
Brown, Charles	1	1	5		
Hammond, Stephen	3	1	4		
Arnold, Jonathan	1	2	2		
Horton, Samuel	1	1	2		
Horton, Amos	3	2	3		
Williams, Peleg	1	4	5		
Edey, Daniel	1	1	2		
Waterman, Job	2	1	2		
Waterman, David	1	3	2		
Saunders, Samuel	2		2		
Hawkins, Rufus	2	1	1		
Hawkins, Nehemiah	3	1	1		
Thornton, Robert	1	3	2		
King, Meriba			2		
Winsor, James	2	2	3		
Baxter, William	1		2		
Windsor, Samuel	3		5		
Mathewson, Noah	6	1	5		
Mathewson, John	1		5		
Windsor, Isaac	3	5	5		
Thornton, Jonathan	1	1	5		
Olney, Emos	3	3	3		1
Smith, David	1		1		
Kimbol, Joshua	2	2	9		
Bullock, Christopher	1	3	4		

PROVIDENCE COUNTY—Continued.

JOHNSTON TOWN—con.

NAME OF HEAD OF FAMILY.	Free white males of 16 years and upward, including heads of families.	Free white males under 16 years.	Free white females, including heads of families.	All other free persons.	Slaves.
Randal, Jos'hp	2		2		
Randal, Caleb	1	3	3		
Gray, William	1		1		
Rhodes, William	1	1	1		
Sheldon, Asa	1	2	3		
Rhodes, John	1	2	3		
Mathewson, Jonathan	1	1	9		
Thornton, Ephraim	1	7	2		
Thatcher, Nathaniel	1	1	1		
King, Isaih	1	1	4		
Frank, Andrew(Negro)				8	
Steere, Samuel	1	4	4		
Waterman, Charles	3	5	4		
Brown, Gideon	2	1	2		
Kimbol, Benjamin	1	2	3		
Lewis, Prince (Negro)				8	
McDonnald, Allice			3		
McDonnald, John	1	1	3		
Waterman, Daniel	2	1	5		
McDonnald, Jeremiah	1	1	1		
Frank, William (Negro)				2	
Keech, Joel	3	1	3		
Tripp, Seth	4		4		
Smith, Susannah	1	2	6		
Thornton, Stephen	2	1	3		
Sweet, James	2	1	3		
Mathewson, William	3	2	7		
Sweet, Valatine	1	2	5		
Sweet, Anna		1	1		
Patt, Jonathan	1	4	4		
Olney, Job	1		2		
Mornton, Jeremiah	3	3	5		
Burlingham, Roger	1	2	3		
Austin, Phebe			1	1	
Mornton, Daniel	3	4	5		
Greene, Benjamin	1	3	3		
Pain, Benjamin	1	1	2		
Pain, John	1	1	1		
Harris, Cesar (Negro)				2	
Dailey, Peter (Negro)				5	
Fisk, Fisher			2	1	
Latham, Stephen	1	2	2		
Arnold, Thomas	1	3	2		
Waterman, William	2	4	4	1	
Thornton, Daniel	2	2	2	1	
Thornton, Solomon	1	3	2	1	
Waterman, John	2		2		
Waterman, Job	2	2	5		
Sprange, Daniel	2	2	3		
Sheldon, Jeremiah	2	1	2		
Chilson, Reubin	1	2	3		
Sheldon, John	1	4	2		
Jennings, Francis	2		3		
Smith, Benjamin	1	3	4		
Arnold, Philip	1	2	3		
Harris, Abigail		1	3		
Brown, John	3		3		
Brown, Obidiah	3	1	4		
Brown, Christopher	1	2	2		
Cobb, John (Negro)				4	
Peck, Jacob	1	1	4		
Philimore, Isachar				5	
Frank, Bettey & Toby				2	
Ladd, Jeremiah	1		3		
Sprange, Ebenezar	4	1	4		
Mann, Thomas	1	2	6		
Pierce, Amiel	1	2	4		
Strivens, Henry	1	3	3		
Strivens, Nathaniel & Brother	2				
Lewis, David		1	1	2	
Williams, Robert	5		4		
Harris, Benjamin	1	3	2		
Harris, Seth & Jos	2				
Carpenter, Nicholas	4		2		
Sheldon, John	1	4	2		
Harrison, Robert	1	1	5		
Busey, Nicholas	1		2		
Randal, Henry	2	1	8		
Rutenburg, John	1	1	1		
Williams, Oliver	3	1	6		
Williams, Daniel	4	1	5		
Usher, John	1	3	2		
Angell, Isreal	3	3	7		
Luther, Consider	4	2	3		
Luther, Benjamin	1	4	2		
Fish, Isaac	1	5	5		
Fish, Joseph	1	2	2		
Hazzard, James	1		2		
Hills, James	1	2	5		
Fenner, Arnold	1	1	3		
Richards, John	1	1	2		
Fenner, Richard	1	2	2		
Angell, Daniel	1		2		

JOHNSTON TOWN—con.

NAME OF HEAD OF FAMILY.	Free white males of 16 years and upward, including heads of families.	Free white males under 16 years.	Free white females, including heads of families.	All other free persons.	Slaves.
Babcock, Joseph	3		3		
Burden, Oliver	1	1	2		
Stephens, Simeon	1		3		
Waterman, John	3	1	4		
Waterman, Joseph	3	1	3		
Randal, James	3		3		
Thornton, Joseph	3		3		
Forster, Spencer	1	1	2		
Fenner, Arthur	2		3		
Fenner, Pardon	1	1	3		
Rhodes, Peleg	1		1		
Thornton, Christopher	2	1	1		
Arnold, Isaac	1		2		
Mathewson, James	1	3	4		
Pogue, John	2	1	4		
Remmington, Joshua	2	3	4		
Remmington, Caleb	2	4	4		
Atwood, Athanias	2	1	4		
Harris, Andrew	2	3	4		
Harris, Olney	1	1	1		
Albertson, Caleb	2	1	4		
Clemments, Thomas	1		2		
Alberson, Joseph	1	1	2		
Alaverson, Elizabeth			4		
Kelton, Samuel	2	1	2		
Atwood, Benjamin	2		2		
Angell, Nedebiah	1	1	6		
Latham, Abram	1	1	1		
Latham, Leban	1	1	2		
Millet, Benjamin	1		4		
Beverley, Sheldon	1	1	5		
Waterman, Benjamin	2	3	7		
Williams, Peleg	1		1		
Burden, Abram	4	5	4		
Alverson, John	2	1	3		
Thomas, Sally					1
Thornton, Christopher	1	2	6		1
Harris, Caleb	4	2	5		1
Harris, John	1		5		
Smith, John	2		4		1
Smith, Alpheus	1		1		
Demon, Peleg	1		2		
Dyre, John	3	1	2		
Thornton, Solomon	3	1	6		
Fenner, Edward	3	1	5		
Wilbore, Joseph	2		2		
Whipple, Benjamin	1	1	1		
Edwards, John	1		2		
Mathewson, Patience		1	1		
Brown, Gideon	2	1	3		
Brown, David	1		2		
Viol, John	1	1	2		
Dyar, Thomas	1	1	4		
Williams, Jeremiah	1		1		

NORTH PROVIDENCE TOWN.

NAME OF HEAD OF FAMILY.	Free white males of 16 years and upward, including heads of families.	Free white males under 16 years.	Free white females, including heads of families.	All other free persons.	Slaves.
Dexter, Jeremiah	1		5		1
Brown, Cudgo (Negro)				5	
Davis, Moses	4	3	5		1
Cumstock, James	1		1		
Cumstock, Woodbury	1		3		
Harkness, Robert	1		2		
Bowers, Charles	1	2	4		
Jenkes, Levi	1	1	3		
Nightingale, Bristol				7	
Holbrook, Felix					1
Walker, Nathaniel	2		3		
Walker, Nathaniel, Junr	2	2	2		
Pitcher, John	1	3	3		
Bishop, Nathaniel	2				
Armington, George	1	1	3		
Harris, Benjamin	1				
Jenkes, Stephen	1		1		
Jenkes, Jerathmiel	1	1	3		
Jenkes, Stephen	1	3	3		
Haley, Samuel	1		2		
Harris, Benjamin, Junr	1	2	2		
Jenkes, David	1		2		
Armington, Josiah	3	1	3		
Greene, Timothy	4	1	3	1	
Wilkerson, Oziel	6	2	3		
Croad, Nathaniel	2		2		
Tolar, Daniel	1	1	3		
Brown, Sysvanous	1		4		
Jenkes, Comfort	1	1	1		
Bolten, Richard	1	2	2		
Arnold, Benjamin	2	1	3	1	
Kingsley, Benjamin	1	2	4		
Durfee, James			2		
Jenkes, Benjamin	1	2	4		
Ballou, David	1	1	2		
Bagley, Joseph	1		2		
Jenkes, Moses	1	4	2		

NORTH PROVIDENCE TOWN—continued.

NAME OF HEAD OF FAMILY.	Free white males of 16 years and upward, including heads of families.	Free white males under 16 years.	Free white females, including heads of families.	All other free persons.	Slaves.
Scott, Martha			1		
Bagley, William	3		3		
Bussey, Jeseniah	2				
Sweetland, Erast'us	2	3	1		
Field, John	1	1	2		
Sheldon, James	2		6		
Arnold, David	2	3	4		
Jenkes, George	2	3	2		
Jenkes, Esek	1	5	1		
Jenkes, Elezar	2	2	7		
Spears, Thomas	1		3		
Pitcher, Samuel	1	2	2	1	
Palmer, Jabez	2	1	2		
Jenkes, Experience					
Thorp, Reuben	3	1	5		
Barras, Nehemiah	2	2	3		
Martin, Constant	1	1	3		
Hicks, Comfort	1	1	3		
Jenkes, Ichabod	3	2	5		
Hastings, Peter	1	3	3		
McCish, Thomas	1	1	1		
Cumstock, John	2	2	5		
Maxwell, William	5	1	5		
Sheldon, Nehemiah	1	3	7		
Lango, Ishmael(Negro)				4	
Pyke, Peter	2	1	2		
White, William	1		2		
Tucker, John	2	3	4	1	
Dexter, Christopher	3		5		
Eston, Esek	1	3	4		
Bump, Susannah			1		
Law, Roger	1	1	1		
Eston, Cesar (Negro)				2	
Scoctt, Job	2	2	6		
Saler, Jeremiah	1	1	3		
Anthony, Daniel	5	2	7		
Winslow, Jacob	2	4	3		
Randal, Peter	1	2	5		
Randal, William	1	3	4		
Randal, John	2	3	3		
Randal, Joseph	2	3	3	1	
Hawkins, Joseph	1	2	7		
Hopkins, James	1	1	4		
Woodard, Ruth	1	1	3		
Carroll, Lawrence	1		1		
Peck, Mary			2		
Hopkins, Daniel	1	2	2		
Angell, James	1		2		
Whipple, George	1	2	1		
Pain, Martha		1	1		
Whipple, Joseph	2		3		
Hopkins, Esek	2		5	1	
Dexter, Marecy	1	1	4		
Smith, Jeremiah	1	2	4		
Atlin, Thomas (Negro)				2	
Brown, Elisha	2	1	1		
Olney, Thomas	1		3		1
Olney, Thomas, Junr	2	3	5		
Olney, Stephen	2	3	5		1
Olney, Ithamer	1	2	2		
Anthony, Peleg	4	1	4	2	
Smith, Edward	4	1	2		1
Hutchins, Jesse	1		2		
Plank, Justice	1		2		
Whipple, Jonathan	1	1	1		
Angell, Enoch	3	2	3		
Olney, Hezekiah	2	2	4		
Hawkins, Hezebiah	1	3	3		
Whipple, Thomas	1		2		
Angell, George	1	1	3		
Sweet, Daniel	1	2	3		
Whipple, Ezekiel	1	2	5		
Chamberlain, Walter	1	2	2		
Angell, Rufus	1	2	2		
Whipple, Elezar	2	1	2		
Hawkins, David	1	2	3		
Angell, Elisha	1	1	4		
Angell, Hope	1	4	6		
Angell, Oliver	1		2		
Brown, Stephen	3	2	6		
Angell, Solomon	2	2	4		
Tift, Rufus	1	2	6		
Edwards, Thomas	1	1	2		
Smith, Nehemiah	2	2	5		2
Chilson, John	1		2		
Smith, Jesse	1	3	2		
Young, Othoniel	1	5	2		
Angell, James	3	4	3		
Baker, Seth	1		2		
Olney, Samuel	3		3	3	
Bushee, William	1				
Congdon, Ephraim	1	2			
Olney, James	1		4		
Olney, Gideon, Junr	1	3	3		

PROVIDENCE COUNTY—Continued.

NORTH PROVIDENCE TOWN—continued.

NAME OF HEAD OF FAMILY.	Free white males of 16 years and upward, including heads of families.	Free white males under 16 years.	Free white females, including heads of families.	All other free persons.	Slaves.
Olney, Gideon	5		4		
Wescoat, Mr	2		1	1	
Olney, Charles	1		2		
Oley, Charles, Junr	2	4	3		
Whipple, Ephraim	2	3	3		
Olney, Epinetus	2	1	3		
Olney, Ezra	3	2	3		
Smith, Esek	2		5		
Annis, Obidiah	1	4	2		
Whipple, Jabez	2	2	3		
Whipple, John	1	3	5	1	
Randal, Henry	1	2	5		
Whipple, Daniel	3		3	1	
Whittle, Benjamin	2	3	4		
Currie, George	1	1	2		
Williams, Stephen	1	2	2		
Thornton, Rufus	1	1	2		
Jenkes, Caleb	1	1	2		
Latham, Benjamin	3				
Axtell, Henry	1	1	1		
Corps, Elizabeth			1		
Thursfield, Thomas	2	1	2		
Beanmond, John	1		2		
Ladd, Joy	1	2	3		
Tripp, John	2	2	5		
Pain Anna			1		
King, Abner	2	1	3		
Trueman, Jonathan	1		5		
Harvey, Nathan	1	1	3		
Waterman, John	1		2		
Read, Simeon	2		2		
Brown, Andrew	1	4	6	1	
Brown, Elisha	2	2	7		
Thornton, Charles	1	2	4		
Stone, John	2	1	3		
Rutenburg, Jenkes	1	2	1		
Atwood, David	1		1		
Olney, Anna			1		
Rhodes, James	1	1	3		
Hawkins, Mary	1	1	3		
Randall, Dolly			2		
Salsberry, Abner	1	1	4		
Patten, Moses	1	1	2		
Abbitt, Stephen	9	2	6		
Nash, Robert Wright	1		1		
Angell, Jessee	2	3	6		
Wamsley, Forller				5	
Angell, Thomas	1		2		
Rutenburg, Innocent			1		
Wamsley, James				7	
Patterson, Hezekiah	1	2	3		
Potter, Susannah	1	1	2		

PROVIDENCE TOWN.

NAME OF HEAD OF FAMILY.	Free white males of 16 years and upward, including heads of families.	Free white males under 16 years.	Free white females, including heads of families.	All other free persons.	Slaves.
Brown, Phineas	2	1	5		
Brown, Dexter	2	1	2	1	
Brown, Daniel	1	3	5		
Brown, Morris	1	1	2		
Corps, Esther	1		1		
Brown, Richard	1	1	4		
Brown, Susannah			1	1	
Carnall, Jessee	1	3	3		
Sharp, Samuel (Negro)				4	
Tabor, Harry (Negro)				2	
Brown, Peter (Negro)				3	
Martin, William	1		2		
Hopkins, Uriah	2	2	5		
Edey, Comfort	1	4	4		
Luther, Uriel	1				
Cozzens, Benjamin	1	1	1		
Cozzens, Benjamin, Junr	3	1	4		
Cozzens, Andrew	1	2	1		
Bradford, Talloman	1		3		
Holder, James	1	2	5		
Lord, Roger	1	1	1		
Field, Joseph	1	4	4		
Luther, John	1	1	5		
Slocum, John	1	3	3		
Dickey, Ruth	2		3		
Drown, John	1	3	2		
Drown, Esther		2	2		
Thayre, Uriah	1	1	3		
Chace, Jonathan	1	1	1		
Gray, Amasey	7	4	7		
Thurber, Samuel	2	3	4		
M'Leannen, Plato (Negro)				3	
Barras, Peter	1		3		
Robilliard, James	1		1		
Smith, David	1	2	2		
Thomas, George Christiana	1	2	2		
Bazil, Jonathan	1	2	1		

PROVIDENCE TOWN—continued.

NAME OF HEAD OF FAMILY.	Free white males of 16 years and upward, including heads of families.	Free white males under 16 years.	Free white females, including heads of families.	All other free persons.	Slaves.
Mason, Aaron	3	1	5		
Yeats, Hannah			1		
Tripp, Auther	1	2	1		
Earle, John	1		4		
Aplin, Benjamin	1		2		
Pain, Thomas	1	4	2	1	
Waterman, Cesar (Negro)				2	
Aplin, Ruth			2		
Sanford, Martha			1		
Bowen, Calib	1		3		
White, Phebe	1		1		
Shalden, Timothy	2	1	2		
Luther, Thomas	1	2	4		
Knowles, Jonathan	1	2	2		
Smith, John	2		2		
Martin, Sylvanus	1	4	5		
Penniman, Elias	1	6	2		
Fuller, Robert	1	1	1		
Lindsey, Weltha			3		
Lybbey, David	2		2	1	
Howell, David	3		5		
Randall, Stephen	1	2	2		
Turpin, Benjamin	1	1	4		
Human, Bazil (Negro)				5	
Hopkins, Primus (Negro)				4	
Fuller, Anna	1		2		
Robinson, Keziah			2		
Fuller, Polly		2	1		
Philson, David	1	2	2		
Vezia, Benjamin	1	3	4		
Cesar, William (Negro)				6	
Smith, Jack (Negro)				4	
Read, Abijah				3	
Hopkins, Sant (Negro)				6	
Albro, Josiah	1	1	2		
Simmons, Jeremiah	1		3		
Simmons, Josiah	1	2	2		
Stephens, Lydia			2		
Allen, Betsey			2		
Stray, Michael	1	2	3		
Simmons, John	1	3	1		
Witaker, Mr	1				
Smith, Jeher	4	2	4		
Orms, John	4	1	4		
Salsberry, Joseph	1	1	5		
Smith, Charles	1	4	4		
Greene, Jonathan	2	4	5		
Brown, Smith	3	1	3		
Pegan, Thomas (Negro)				4	
Saltonston, Brittain (Negro)				4	
Hawkins, Joseph	1	2	3		
Holden, John			2		
Newell, Robert	2	3	5		
Burns, James	1		3		
Gonsolve, John	1	3	3		
Fowle, Jonathan	1	1	4		
Teal, John	3		3		
Lippit, James (Negro)				3	
Jenks, Prince (Negro)				3	
Nash, Robert W.	1		1		
Salsberry, Jessee	3		2		
Smith, Nedebiah	1	1	2		
Vincent, Laban	1	4	3		
Angell, Fenner	1	2	2		
Bastow, William	1		2		
Bowen, Oliver	3	1	2	2	
Smith, Job	3	1	4	1	
Field, Thomas	4		2		
Tabor, Benedict	1		3		
Wheaton, Ephraim	4	1	3		
Hewes, Joseph	2		1		
Lyon, Jacob	1	4	1		
Brown, London (Negro)				2	
Drown, Samuel	2	2	2		
Butler, Abner	3	1	3		
Salsberry, Archibald	2		3		
Esterbrooks, Charles	1				
Martin, Philip	1	2	3		
Allen, William	1	2			
Thurston, Elizabeth			1		
Chaffee, Amos	1	4	4		
Healey, John	1	1	1		
Westcott, James	3	3	3		
Hamlin, Samuel	2		2		
Callender, Mary	1		4		
Smith, Noah	3	2	4		
Brown, Bonno (Negro)				2	
Brown, Primus (Negro)				3	
Weeden, George	2	2	4		
Angell, Isaac	2	2	4		
Walter, James	1	3	1		

PROVIDENCE TOWN—continued.

NAME OF HEAD OF FAMILY.	Free white males of 16 years and upward, including heads of families.	Free white males under 16 years.	Free white females, including heads of families.	All other free persons.	Slaves.
Burr, David	1	1	5		
Olney, George	1	1	4	1	
Olney, Deborah			3		
Skinner, Maria				1	
Graves, Hannah	1		7		
Olney, Bristol				10	
Marshall, Benjamin	1	1	3		
Hicks, Pleasant (Negro)				5	
Smith, Samuel	3	2	4		
Whipple, Amey			2		
Sweet, Nemiah	2	2	5		
Burr, Ezekiel	2	1	3		
Dunn, Esther			2		
Stephens, Isabella			2		
Brown, George	1	4	2		
Burr, Joshua	1	2	4		
Loring, Simeon	1	1	3		
Scranton, Sarah		1	3		
Whipple, Azariah	2		2		
Currie, James	1	2	3		
Currie, Elizabeth	2		2		
Currie, Robert	1		2		
Smith, Benjamin	1	1	1		
Frink, Isaac	1	1	1		
Burr, Levi	2	1	4		
Burr, James	4	1	4	1	
Sprange, Obadiah	3	1	4		
Saunders, Hepzabeth		1	5		
Healey, Samuel	1		2		
Bordine, Comfort	1	1	6		
McClain, David	1		3		
Draper, Paul	1		1		
Nightingale, Quam				2	
Esterbrooks, Cuff				2	
Balch, Sarah	2		2		
Crandall, Joseph	1	2	2		
Simmons, Quam				7	
Covell, Silas	1	1	3		
Thurber, Squire	2	1	1		
Smith, Bridget		2	1		
Keen, Charles	3	4	7		
Giles, Abigeil	1		1		
Dexter, Molly			1		
Thurber, Samuel	1		2		
Thurber, Edward, Junr	1	3	3		
Alger, Benjamin	1	2	4		
Hill, Samuel	1		1		
Thurber, Edward	1	1	5		
Hammond, Jonathan	2	1	3		
Wheaton, Comfort	3		2		
Sterrey, Nathan	1		1		
Earle, Ralph	1		1		
Whipple, Joseph	1	1	8	1	
Jestram, John	1	4	1	1	
Colegrove, William	1		4		
Francis, Joseph	1	3	3		
Lawton, John	1		2		
Wheaton, James	1		5		
Wheaton, Benjamin	1	2	1		
Marsh, Jonathan	3		1		
Ephraim, Comfort				3	
Siscoe, Mode				10	
Whipple, John	1		1		
Hopkins, Ruth			2		
Healey, Recompence	1	1	2		
Clarke, Samuel	1		1		
Brayton, Daniel	1		1		
Metcalf, Joel	1	1	6		
Keen, Medford				3	
Steel, Benjamin	1		4		
Hill, John	1	2	4		
Macomber, Ebinezor	1	3	4		
Hunt, Abijah			2		
Burr, Joseph	3	2	2		
Hawks, Susannah			3		
Jones, Benjamin	1	4	5		
Jackson, Samuel	2		2		
Earle, Abigail	2		2		
Anthony, Michael	1	2	1		
Howland, John	2	1	2		
Russell, John, Junr	1		1		
Snow, William	1	4	5		
Cumstock, Joseph	1	1	1		
Reynolds, John	2		2		
Reynolds, Grindal	2		2		
Arnold, Thomas	2	1	3	2	
Wheaton, Seth	2	1	5		
Lee, John	2	3	2		
Hubberd, Ezra	2	3	3		
Brown, Mary			4		
Metcalf, Michael	2	4	7		
Russell, John	1	3	5		
Packard, Melzar	1	3	3		
Miller, Nathan	1		4		

PROVIDENCE COUNTY—Continued.

PROVIDENCE TOWN—continued.

NAME OF HEAD OF FAMILY.	Free white males of 16 years and upward, including heads of families.	Free white males under 16 years.	Free white females, including heads of families.	All other free persons.	Slaves.
Laurence, Joseph	2	4	2		
Hitchcock, Enos	1		2	2	
Young, Samuel	1		4	1	
Tyler, William	3	1	6		
Allen, Amos	2	1	4		
Smith, William	1	1	3	1	4
Cumstock, Benjamin	2	4	4		
Snow, Josiah	1	3	5		
Anthony, Reubin	1	3	1		
Tew, Newport				4	
Sessions, William	2		1		1
Whipple, Molly			4		
Remmington, Stephen	2	4	2		
Whitemore, Jessee	2		2		
Wheaton, Nathaniel	2	1	2		
Crawford, Gideon	3		2		
Rutinburgh, David	1		1		
Crawford, Gideon, Junr	2		2	2	
Bowen, Henry	1	1	3		
Hill, Christopher	1	1	3		
Fisher, Nathan	2	1	1		
Hall, Sarah	3	5	6		
Nightingale, Samuel	1	1	5		2
Throop, Amos	1		2		2
Allen, Benjamin	5		2		
Olney, Simeon	1	2	2		
Olney, Hannah			1		
Allen, Philip	2		1	2	
Packard, Nathaniel	2		4		
Peck, Aaron	1	3	4		
Thurber, Benjamin	1	2	2		
Salsberry, Joshua	2	2	4		
Otis, Jacobs	1	4	4		
Thurber, William	3	1	2		
Hunt, Levi	1		1		
Easton, Nicholas	2	2	5		
Greene, Caleb	5		4	1	
Greene, Thomas	1	1	2		
Allen, Zacheriah	4	1	5	2	
Sessions, Darius	2		5		
Bradshaw, Mr	1		2		
Brown, Eseck	2	1	2		
Russell, Jeremiah	2	2	2		
Goreham, Jabez	3	2	4		
Mawney, John	1	1	4		
Pitman, Saunders	2		3	1	
Olney, Richard	1	1	3	1	
Richmond, Nathaniel	1		1		
Cushing, Nathaniel	2	3	3	1	
Cushing, Hannah	1		3		
Bowler, Mr	1		5		
Kitton, Stephen	3		6		
Arnold, Mary			3		
Green, James	3		2		
Martin, Wheeler	1		1		
Sheldon, Job	2	2	4		
Lyndon, Danforth P	1		1		
Williams, Elizabeth			3	1	
Thayre, Simeon	2	3	4	1	
Sprange, Rufus	5	5	7		
Hazliff, Robert	1		1		
Treadwell, Jonathan	3	1	4		
Harris, Stephen	1	1	2		
Rice, Henry	7	1	3	2	1
Daggett, Abner	1	1	4	1	
Daggett, Thomas	2		1		
Wilkerson, David	1		3		
Bastow, Samuel	1	1	2		
Fenner, Yockey				2	
Bowen, Primus				8	
White, John	1		4		
Frost, Ebenezer	2	2	2		
Peck, Penelope			4		
Welsh, Elizabeth		1	2		
Carter, John	5	3	7		1
Wheaton, Caleb	2	3	4		
Page, William	2	2	3		
Danna, Nathaniel	3	2	1		
Goodwin, Elizabeth	1	2			
Pool, Samuel	1		1		
Page, Primus				3	
Page, Ambrose	4	1	3	1	
Lippett, Moses	1	1	4		
Updike, John	3	1	6		
Russull, Joseph	2		5	3	
Taylor, Benjamin	2	2	1		
Taylor, Edward	2	1	3		
Luther, Oliver	3	1	6		
Stoves, William				5	
Congdon, Joseph	2	1	3		
Springer, Richmond	1	3	3		
Congdon, Jonathan	1	1	1		
Tabor, Ichabod	1	2	4		
McClune, William	1	2	3		
Almey, William	4	2	3	1	
Shackleford, Magg	2		5		
Knowles, Edward	3	1	5		
Hoppin, Nicholas	1	2	4		
Power, Mary			4		
Holden, Charles	1	7	3		
Hall, Sarah			2		
Edmonds, Lemuel	2	1	3		
Law, Isreal	1		4		
Teal, Calib	1	1	1		
Whipple, Sarah			2		
Lewis, John	1	1	2		
Farster, William	2		1		
Fenner, Martha	1	1	2		
Devall, James	1	1	1		
Hopkins, Pamp (Negro)				4	
Riggs, Comfort	10	1	5		
Dodge, Seril	3	3	2		
Bradford, George	2	3	3		
Rhodes, Lavinus	1	1	2		
Atkinson, Stephen	1	1	2		
Mann, Aaran	1		2		
Dexter, Knight	3	1	2	2	
Allen, William	1	2	2	1	
Learned, William	1	4	5	1	
Pierce, Isaac	1	2	3		
Dailey, Daniel	2	1	5		
Sterry, Patience				1	
Waterman, Rufus	3	3	4	2	
Angell, Nathan	2	1	3	1	1
Tellinghast, Jonathan	1	1	1		
Bliven, Sarah		1	2		
Test, Alexis	1		2		
Hull, Gideon	2	2	4		
Wainwood, Robert				3	
Hudson, Robert	1	4	1		
Barker, William	1		3		
Cornell, Richard	3		3		
Sheldon, John	1		1		
Lyndon, Cesar				5	
Lippett, John	1	2	2		
Anthony, David	3		1		
Fuller, Olney	1		4		
Spencer, Daniel	1	1	7		
Lasell, John	1	3	5		
Owens, William	3	2	3		
Peck, Nathaniel	1	1	2		
Nichols, John	1	1	4		
Hammond, John	1	1	5		
Jackson, Richard	6	1	5		
Forster, John	1		2	1	
Donnizon, Catharine			2		
Jefford, Caleb	3		2		
Thompson, Ebenezar	3	3	6	2	2
Jenks, John	4	2	4	2	1
Pitman, Isaac	1		3		
Laroche, Banrit	1		1		
Williams, John	2		4		
Cooper, Isaac (Negro)				6	
Bickford, Betsey	4	1	4		
Addison, Benjamin	1	3	2		
Fenner, Arthur	4		5	2	
Bowen, Jabez	2	2	2	2	
Jenks, Joseph	1	1	3	1	
Sabin, Dolly		1	5		
Long, Thomas	2	1	4		
Baker, William	2	4	3		
Miller, Thomas	3	1	4		
Bowman, Charles	1	7	4		
Waterhouse, John	1	3	2		
Burn, Jacob	1	2	3		
McKinsey, James	1			4	
Stoker, Christopher	1		2		
Holden, John	1		1		
Sears, John	1				
Allen, George	2	5	2		
Tolman, Thomas	1	1	2		
Manning, James	60	1	3	2	
Ray, Uriel	1	2	5	4	
Wescott, Samuel	2		2		
Healey, Sally			2		
Linguist, Andrew	3				
Bradford, Sarah		2	2		
Bowen, Ephraim	1	2	5	1	
Chace, Samuel	2	2	3		3
Bowen, William	2	1	5	1	1
Brown, Hope			3		
Chace, John	1	1	3	1	
Simmonds, Nathan	1	2	2		
Simmonds, Aaron	1	1	2		
Tillinghast, Daniel	4	1	3	4	
Brown, Nicholas	5	1	4	3	
Francis, John	1	1	4	1	
Halsey, Thomas L	4	1	3	1	2
Brown, Samuel	2		7		
Brown, Isaac	2	1	5	1	
Hopkins, Stephen	2	3	2		
Hopkins, Ruth			2	2	
Bowen, Susannah	1		2	1	
Gardner, Polly			3		
Alexander, George	2				
Field, Betsey		2	3		
Stoddard, Sarah	2	1	2		
Lindley, Joshua	1	3	6		
Winkley, Isaac			3		
Simmonds, Martin	2		4		
Clapp, Deborah			2		
Dring, Thomas	2		2		
Sterling, Henry	2	1	2		
Allin, Samuel	1		1		
Sweet, Content			1	1	
Field, Jemima			1		
Simmonds, Obed	1		1		
Edey, Caleb			1		
Holloway, Keziah	2		1		
Collin, Daniel			2		
Ross, Elizabeth	5		3		
Ross, George	1	1	2		
Hawkins, Jabez	1	2	2		
Cushing, Prime				2	
Ruggles, Baston				2	
Brown, Elizabeth	3	2	2		
Smith, Simon	2		7		
Rogers, John	5	1	5	1	
Hopkins, Sarah	1		4	2	
Duplissee, Peter	1		2		
Johnson, Mary	1		1		
Reily, Thomas	1		1		
Crawford, Joseph	1	1	1		
Nixon, Nelly	2		3		
Boyd, Samuel	1		1		
Coleman, Mrs			1		
Thurber, Relief	1		1		
Pease, Jerusha	1		3	1	
Coats, Catharine			1		
Tyler, Ann			3		
Brown, Elisha	3	4	5		
Whiting, John	3		3		1
Brown, Liverpool				7	
Brown, Providence				3	
Johnson, Cato				2	
Newfield, Mary				4	
Brown, Waitstill	1		3	3	
Inman, Richard	1	2	2		
Young, James		1	3		1
Frederickson, Nicholas	1		3		
Tyler, Mary	2		2		
Page, Thomas	4	4	3		
Gardiner, James	2	4	2		
Freeman, Charles	1	2	2		
Sabin, Thomas	3		8		1
Vent, John	1	1	3		
Wiseman, John	5		1		
Arnold, Welcome	5	2	6	2	
Bishop, Demus	2	1	4		
Ramsey, Stocbridge	1		4		
Coggshall, Charles	4	3	2		
Gifford, Sarah			2		
Brown, Ichabod	3	1	6		
Cross, Freelove	1		1		
Burgis, John	1		3		
Dodge, Mr	1		2		
Spelman, Elhin	1	3	4		
Cozens, Elizabeth			5		1
Pitman, John	3	5	6	2	
Brown, William	1	5	2		
Spear, London				7	
Earle, Cudge				3	
Gardner, Cato				9	
Champlin, York				3	
Arrow, Newport				3	
Coggeshall, Gould					
Wilbore, Uriel	1	2	3		
Fisher, Patience		1	1		
Cozens, Dick				4	
Johnson, Quaco				5	
Hazzard, Sampson				6	
Bowen, Isaac	3	3	5		
Ingraham, Simeon	1	4	3		
Peck, William	1	1	3	2	
Downer, Sarah			3		
Carlis, John	1		3		
Sterry, Cyprian	2	1	6	3	4
Nightingale, Joseph	2	3	5	4	2
Cook, Hannah	4	1	4		
Wilkie, Samuel	1		2		
Carpenter, Gershom	2	3	3		
Bucklin, Daniel	6	1	3		
Whipple, Stephen	1		3		
Cook, Nicholas	1	3	3	1	
Cook, Daniel	1	1	7		

PROVIDENCE COUNTY—Continued.

NAME OF HEAD OF FAMILY.	Free white males of 16 years and upward, including heads of families.	Free white males under 16 years.	Free white females, including heads of families.	All other free persons.	Slaves.
PROVIDENCE TOWN—con.					
Lassell, Charles	1		3		
Brown, Moses	5	2	1	1	
Daggett, William	1	2	3		
Brown, John	2		4	2	
Butler, David	2		2		
Hacker, Joshua	5	3	4		
Peck, Joseph	2		6		
Smith, Joshua	2	1	2		
Allen, Joseph	2	5	3		
Olney, Daniel	1	1	3		
Weeden, Samuel	2	1	3		
Coats, Daniel	1		1		
Sheldon, Isreal	3	2	4		
Bailey, Nathaniel	1		1		
Carlile, John	5	2	2		
Preston, John	1	1	3		
Barney, Cromell	2	1	3		
Berry, Sarah			3		
Trowbridge, Benjamin	1	1	1		
Hunt, John	1	1	2		
Ingraham, Patience	1	1	3		
Tillinghast, John	1	2	7		
Beverley, Stephen	1	2	2		
Farrier, Arthur	2	2	3		
Gardner, Patience				2	
Yamma, Bristol				7	
Stafford, Fortune				2	
Power, Nancy & Molly			2		
Fisk, William	1		3		
Luther, Thomas Sweet	1		1		
Harding, William	5	2	2		
Jenkins, Jonathan	1		1	1	
Fossey, Elizabeth			1		
Swain, Batchelor	1		3		
Devol, Simon	3	1	2		
Bacon, Iraih	1		3		
Holroyd, William	3	5	4		
Smith, James	5	2	1		
Weeden, Jonathan	2	1	2		
Williams, Rebeckah			2		
Arnold, Joseph	1		1		
Arnold, Joseph, Junr	1	1	2		
Clarke, Parker	1	1	1		
Carr, Robert	2	2	2		
Cozens, William	1	3	1		
Earl, William	5	1	3		
Sabin, John	2	1	5		
Sabins, Jessee	1	1	2		
Ashton, William	4		3		
Sweet, Abigail		1	2		
Godfrey, Christopher	2		2		
Arnold, Christopher	2	1	2		
Gifford, Josiah	4	3	6		
Manchester, John	1		2		
Warner, Samuel	2		2		
Bucklin, Jabez	3	1	2		
Davis, Job	1	2	3		
Aplin, Stephen	1	3	1		
Sheldon, Christopher	2		1		
Brown, Daniel	1		2		
Cole, Lillis	1		1		
Godfrey, Samuel	1		8		
Pettingale, Leonard	1		1		
Doyle, John	5		2		
Arnold, James	3		2		
Davis, Seth	4		1		
Alverson, William	2	3	5		
Haywood, Dilla		1	4		
Tillinghast, Joseph	1	4	4		
Packard, Samuel	1		2		
Sheldon, Pardon	3	1	3		
Jenks, Jeremiah	2	1	7		
Ethforth, Samuel	1	2	3		
Davenport, Samuel	4	1	6		
Jenkes, Deborah			2		
Gibbs, John	1	3	7		
Gladding, Jonathan	2	1	4		
Spurr, John	1	1	2		
Tillinghast, William	1	5	3		
Brown, John	1		2		
Burrough, John	3	2	4		
Clann, Nancy		1			
Bennett, William	1		2		
Chatty, John	1	1	2		
Davis, John	3		4		
Davis, Isreal	3		2		
Davis, Benjamin	2		1	6	
Power, Nicholas	5	3	6	3	
Nava, Member				3	
Dickins, Edward	2		1		
Almey, William	1	2	3		
Burkit, John	1		3		
Ormsbry, Caleb	1	2	3		
Woodard, Jacob	1	1	5		
Freeze, Jacob	1	2	4		
PROVIDENCE TOWN—con.					
Dwyre, Patrick	2		2		
Crooker, Robert	1		4		
Penniman, William	2		2		
Daspre, Peter	1		1		
Winslow, Reubin	3	3	1		
Knight, Samuel	1	1	3		
Mitchell, Thomas	1	3	1		
Wilson, Joseph	1	1	3		
Bishop, Lemuel	1	2	4	1	
Coleman, Ebor	3		5		
Coleman, John	3	1	1		
Spooner, Thomas	1	1	2		
Pitcher, Lemuel	2	3	5		
Crapron, Christopher	1	2	3		
Mitchel, Anna	1		4		
Godfrey, Caleb	1		1		
Arnold, David	2	1	4		
Barton, Asa	1		2		
Baker, Joshua	1		2		
Bullock, John	2	3	4		
Gladding, Charles	1	4	2		
Sheldon, John	2	1	2		
Stratton, Philip	3		2		
Ross, Sanford	1	3	3		
Viol, John	1		4		
Perrin, Daniel	1	4	3		
Irish, Benjamin	1	1	2		
Gay, Luther	1	1	3		
Grafton, Benjamin	2	2	4		
Grafton, Nathaniel	1	3	2		
Teal, Calib	1	2	1		
Andrews, Peleg	1	2	1		
Simmons, Josiah	3	1	3		
Simmons, Molly	1		1		
Wescott, Sally	2		3		
Sweetland, Nathaniel	3	3	3		
Jones, Mary	1		2		
Greene, John	1	2	1		
Hunt, Edward	2	3	4		
Ormsbey, Calib	2	1	3		
Walker, Calvin	1		3		
Pitcher, James	3	1	3		
Blinn, Robert	3	2	4		
Ormsbey, Josiah	1	1	3		
Ormsbey, James	2		1		
Stillwell, Daniel	2	5	2		
Dexter, Esek	1		1		
Ethforth, John	1	1	3		
Crapon, Samuel	3	1	2		
Sheldon, John	1		3		
Bennett, Thomas	2	1	2		
Holden, Randall	1		2		
Dexter, Benjamin	1		2		
Thayre, Thomas	1	3	5		
Church, Nathaniel	1	1	1		
Chaffee, William	1	1	2		
McClain, Hector	1	1	1		
Pierce, Daniel	3		4		
Earle, William, Junr	1	3	2		
Sinkins, Barsheba	1		1		
Warner, Amas	1	1	2		
Warner, John	1		5		
Griffiths, John	2		3		
Clarke, John Innis	3	1	4	5	
Short, Samuel	2	2	2		
Tarp, John	3		5		
Thomas, Lewis	1	2	3		
Wood, John	1	1	2		
Pitts, John	1		3		
Molloy, John	1		2		
Carder, John	1		1		
Wetherington, Mr	1		1		
Cumstock, Daniel	1	2	4		
Pitman, Thomas	2	2	2		
Cole, Mary	1		3		
Bowers, Lemuel	5	3	4		
Piles, Martha			1		
Martin, Asa	5	1	4		
Pitts, Ignatius	24	2	2		
Olney, Christopher	7	1	6	1	
Willey, John	1	2	2		
Williams, Waterman	1		3		
Humphreys, Rufus	1		3		
Freeman, Cato					5
Gorham, Samuel	1		1		
Merrow, Timothy	1		2		
Waterman, John	3	1	5	1	
Hardenburg, Jacob	1		2		
Potter, Mary			2		
Row, Calib	1	2	2		
Rogers, Molly	1		1		
Warner, Henry	1	1	4		
Williams, Thomas	4	1	4		
Olney, Elisha	1		2		
Briggs, Randall	2		3		
PROVIDENCE TOWN—con.					
Carey, John	3	2	2		
Leadenburger, John	1	1	4		
Carpenter, Waterman	1	2	5		
Hargill, William	1	2	3		
West, Amy			1	1	
Hoyle, Joseph	2	6	3		
Ebinezar, Mr	1		7		
Wheaton, William	2	1	1		
Hannover, York				6	
Olney, Cabez	1	2	2		
Valintine, William	1	2	1		
Randall, Mm			1	2	
Jacobs, Nathaniel	2	1	4		
Durfee, Ezekiel	2	1	6		
Drowne, Solomon	1		5		
Drowne, Sally			4		
Potter, Lydia	2	1	5		
Whitemore, Joseph	1	2	2		
Graves, James	4	1	4	1	
Robinson, Christopher	1	2	4		
Dean, Calvin	4		4		
Hoffman, Henry	2	3	3		
Jones, John	1		1	1	
Miller, Josiah	1	1	4		
Pettis, Daniel	1	1	3		
Whipple, Christopher	2	4	2		
Whiting, Nathaniel	1		2		
Gridley, John	4	1	3		
Williams, Hannah			2		
Gorden, George	2		2		1
Field, Martha	2	1	3		
Manchester, Isaac	1	1	1		
Randal, Benjamin	3	2	6		
Patten, David	1	1	3		
Carpenter, Oliver	4	1	4		
Gilmore, Nathaniel	3	3	6		
Brownell, William	2	2	3		
Waterman, William	1	1	2		
Wescott, Anthony	1	1	2		
Mason, Pardon	1	2	1		
Woodard, William	1	1	1		
Lee, Charles	1	1	3	1	
Carpenter, Ephraim	1		1		
Wescott, Jacob	1	1	2		
Branch, Ahollab	1	2	3		
Fenner, Daniel	1		2		
Cahoon, Isaiah	2		6		
Ingraham, Samuel	8	1	3		
Allen, Nathan	1	1	2		
Brown, Chad	1	2	1		
Pettice, John	1		3		
Williams, Joshua	1		3		
Edey, Joseph	4	2	5		
Tolman, Benjamin	2	3	3		
Edey, William	2	2	3		
Edey, Barnett	2	1			
Edey, Jeremiah	3		5		
Carpenter, Jonathan	1	6	1		
Tabor, Thomas	1		4		
Walker, Peleg	1		1		
Haswill, Ephraim	1	1	1		
Field, John	1	2	3		
Field, Daniel	1	1	2		
Gardner, Calib	1		2		
Field, Lemuel	1	4	2		
Hoppin, Benjamin	2	5	4		
Wallen, Jonathan	2	1	3		
Allen, Paul	1	6	3	1	
Talbott, Benjamin, Junr	1		4		
Pierce, Oliver	1		2		
West, Benjamin	2		2		
States, Peter	2	2	6		
Potter, George	1	1	3		
Miller, Benjamin	1		4		
Beverley, John	1		4		
Stephens, Nancy		1	1		
Pierce, John	1	3	1		
Howland, Benjamin	1	1	1		
Ruttenburg, Thomas	2	1	4		
Turner, Amas	1	3	2		
Dyre, Anthony	1	2	8		
Butler, Quaco	1			5	
Munroe, James	4	2	7		
Snow, Samuel	2	2	4		
Wright, Aaron	2		4		
Warner, Hollimon	1	2	3		
Parker, Abijah	1	5	2		
Aborn, James	3	1	2	1	2
Freeman, Jacob			2	1	
Jones, John	4	1	3		
Chace, Amos	1	5	5		
Whiting, Joshua	2	1	5		
Merrow, Ralph	1	5	5		
Hopkins, Ebar				6	
Walker, Ephraim	3		3		

PROVIDENCE COUNTY—Continued

PROVIDENCE TOWN—con.

NAME OF HEAD OF FAMILY.	Free white males of 16 years and upward, including heads of families.	Free white males under 16 years.	Free white females, including heads of families.	All other free persons.	Slaves.
Coles, Thomas	1		1		
Fuller, Joseph	2		2		
Spooner, Samuel	1		4		
Sherman, James	1	2	2		
Fenner, Richard	2	2	5		
Craige, John	1	1	6		
Thurber, John	1	1	4		
Knight, Polly			3		
Turtelott, Daniel	1	2	2		
Potter, Ebijah	1	2	2		
Potter, William	3	1	4		
Stevenson, Daniel	1	1	2		
King, Calib	1	2	5		
Smith, Phebe			4		
Tripp, Othenial	2		1		
Keen, John	3	8	4		
Chamberlain, Joseph	1				
Peck, Elihu	1	3	3		
Edey, Esek	1		1		
Brown, Elisha	2	1	4		
Searles, John	1		1		
Arnold, Nehemiah		4	3		
Thurston, Richard	1		2		
Box, Daniel	1		3		
Lewis, Nancy		1	2		
Grinman, Jeremiah	1	1	3		
Talman, Elizabeth	1		2		
Edey, Esek	2	1	5		
French, Jonathan	1	3	3		
Carpenter, William	1	1	1		
Potter, Reubin	3	2	4		
Nobles, Isaac	2	2	3		
Field, James	1		4		
James, Mrs	1		2		
Furlong, Edward	1		1		
Warner, Nathan	1	2	1		
Germain, John	1	4	4		
Anthony, Rachel			2		
Field, William	1	4	3		
Kennedy, Mary		1	2		
Hammond, James	1	2	2		
Wheaton, Calvin	2		3		
Holden, Oliver	1		1		
Manchester, Mathew	4	1	2	1	
Manchester, William	1	1	2	1	
Masury, Joseph	1	1	3		
Ingraham, Thomas	1		3		
Anthony, Daniel	1	1	1		
Williams, Nathan	2		3		
Noble, Mark	1	1	2		
Greatreax, John	2		3		
McCluer, James	1		2		
Miller, Consider	2	2	2		
Miller, John	1				
Smith, Jabitha			3		
Sisco, Ebin				2	
Marvin, Richard	2		1		
Branch, Nicholas	1	2	2		
Branch, Daniel	1		2		
Ralph, David	1	1	4		
Penno, Peter	1	2	3		
Edey, Peleg	1	1	3		
Healey, Martha			2		
Card, Potter	1	1	3		
Arnold, Calib	1		4		
Savers, Hannah			3		
Lawrence, Daniel	1	3	3		
Frothingham, Nathaniel	2		3		
Sheldon, Edward	1	1	1		
Tift, David	2		2		
Proud, Samuel	3	1	3		
Snow, Daniel	1	1	3		
Snow, James	1	3	3		
Billings, William	2	2	3		
Remmington, Amey			1		
Hardwell, Stephen	1		3		
Thurston, Daniel	1	1	1		
Snow, James	2	2	3		
Snow, Sarah			1	6	
Snow, Joseph	1	2	1		
Searle, Sollomon	1		2		
Jones, Barney	1	1	2		
Munroe, John Lindney	2	2	4		
Johnson, John	1		5		
Carder, Francis			2		
Searle, Solomon			5		
Field, John	4	1	2		
Howe, Sally			3		
Richmond, Barzilla	1		3		
Richmond, William	3	2	5		
Wheeler, Bennett	4	4	3		
Field, Joseph	2	2	3		
Gladding, Benjamin	1		7		
Fenner, Arthur, Junr	1		3		

PROVIDENCE TOWN—con.

NAME OF HEAD OF FAMILY	Free white males of 16 years and upward, including heads of families.	Free white males under 16 years.	Free white females, including heads of families.	All other free persons.	Slaves.
Ross, Edward	1	3	1		
Hawkins, Edward	2	1	3		
Brown, William	1		2		
McGuire, Francis	2		3		
Brown, Zepheniah	2	1	4		
Pettice, John	2	1	3		
Pettice, James	2	1	1		
Hill, Jonathan	2		1		
Harris, Tobey				3	
Larkins, Joseph	1		3		
Potter, Sarah			3		
Finch, Ruth				2	
Prentice, Thomas	2		2		
Church, Deborah				3	
Wescott, John	1	2	3		
Pyke, William	1	1	1		
Tift, Daniel	3	1	1		
Tift, Daniel, Junr	1		1		
Tift, Mary		1	2		
Carpenter, John	2		2		
Bowers, James	1	3	2		
Snow, Joseph	1		2		
Jackson, Daniel	3	2	3		
Perrin, John	2		5		
Smith, Ann			2		
Pyke, Sanford	1	2	2		
Jacobs, Ebinezar	1	1	2		
Bailey, Gideon	1		3		
Dwyre, Benjamin	2	1	3		
Arnold, Nathan	1		1		
Manchester, Mrs			3		
Tolbott, Benjamin	3		5	1	
Kimball, Mr	1		1		
Bacon, Henry	1		2		
Bacon, William	2		1		
Crapron, Penelope	1	3	5		
Ward, Henry	2	1	5	2	
Nightingale, Abigail	1		4		1
Grammon, James	1		5		
Munroe, Thomas	2	1	3		
Taylor, William	2		2		
Hicks, David	2	2	1		
Dexter, Stephen	1		2		
Mann, Benjamin	2		1		
Paul, William	2	1	2		
Corey, William	1	6	3		
Peckham, James	1	1	3		
Hull, Peleg	1		2		
Crapron, Benjamin	1	2	2		
Brown, Polly		1	1		
Potter, Phineas	1		3		
Potter, Joseph	1	5	3		
Sweeting, Job	3		2	1	
Young, Thomas	1	1	4		
Taylor, Robert	1		3		
Mumford, John	1	2	4		
Bacon, Elijah	7	1	5	1	1
Haswell, Philip	1	3	3		
Giddens, Mrs			1		
Bowler, Metcalf	1		2		
Vaughn, Boon	1	1	2		
Smith, Turpin	1	2	3		
Mallin, William	1		3		
Johnson, Samuel	2	2	3		
Wood, John	1		3		
Ager, John	1	1	3		
Jones, William	3		1	3	
Rawson, Joseph	2	3	2		
Pyke, John	1	2	1		
Sears, Mrs			2		
Smart, Thomas	1		2	1	
Thurber, Stephen	3		3		
Thurber, Samuel	1	4	2		
Thurber, Darius	1	1	5		
Hammond, Cesar				4	
Aborn, Prudy				4	
Hargill, Charles				3	
Grafton, William	4	2	3		
Gladding, Nathaniel, Junr	1	2	4		
Mirithrew, Richard	1	1	2		
Dollis, Michael	1	1	3		
Esterbrooks, John	1	2	2		
Cowens, Ward	4		3		
Alexander, Henry	2	3	1		
Tripp, Abiel	1		2		
Barton, John	1	2	6		
Gladding, Nathaniel	1	3	4		
Carpenter, Oliver	2	1	4		
Shedal, John	1	2	3		
Taylor, Peter	3		3		
Franklin, Asa	2	2	5	1	
Franklin, Benjamin	1	1	1		
Rice, Mrs			2		
White, William	1		1		

PROVIDENCE TOWN—con.

NAME OF HEAD OF FAMILY.	Free white males of 16 years and upward, including heads of families.	Free white males under 16 years.	Free white females, including heads of families.	All other free persons.	Slaves.
Mumford, Nancy			2		
Forster, Theodore	1	1	2		
Clapp, Isaac			2		
Molton, Thomas	1	1	1		
Jones, Gersham	4	4	6		
Lawrence, John	1	1	2		
Mac Neil, Hopestill	1	1	1		
Sisson, Benjamin	1		3		
Edey, Benjamin	2	1	3	1	
French, Timothy	1		1		
Bay, Disimbo				3	
Ham, Levi	2		4		
Clarke, Samuel	1	2	7		
Spencer, Giles	1	2	3		
Larcher, John	2	1	2		
Larcher, William	1	2	2		
Givens, William	1		2		
Carlile, John, Junr	2		1	1	
Billings, William	1		3		
Tabor, Benjamin	1		2		
Dexter, Andrew	1	3	3		
Danforth, Joseph	3	3	3		
Field, John	1		3		
Gladding, Timothy	3	2	5		
Burrill, James	3		2	1	
Williams, Andrew	3	2	3		
Waterman, Duke	4	1	6		
Gibson, John	2	3	4		
Potter, Reuben	2	3	4		
Viol, John	3		1		
Cooke, Joseph	1		1	1	
Mathewson, John	2	2	2	1	2
Allen, Gabriel	1	1	3		
Mathewson, Elizabeth			1		
Clements, Ephraim	1		3		
Fuller, Sylvester	1	2	3		
Spencer, William	1	1	2		
Badger, Moses	3	2	2		
Martin, John	1	2	3		
Young, William	1	1	3		
Rhodes, William	5	3	2		
Kelton, Harris	1		1		
Parker, Freelove			1		
Roan, Mrs	1		1		
Johnson, Betsey			4		
Beverley, George	3		3		
Greene, Josiah	3		4		
Dougherty, James	1		3		
Black, James	1		3		
Price, Edward		2	2		
Sheppardson, Mary		2	4		
Rice, Betsey		2	2		
Vincent, Noel	1	2	1		
Sissell, Lydia			2		
James, Samuel	1	2	2		
Ewing, John	2		1		
Gardner, Sanford	1		2		
Bradford, Joseph	1	2	3		
Hacker, Ebenezar	1	1	2		
Ayres, Mrs			2		
Moss, James	1	2	1		
Ham, Phebe		1	3		
Edey, Benjamin	2	1	2		
Brown, Davis	1		2		
Wheat, William	1		3		
Pitts, Michael	2	3	3		
Stokes, John	1		3		
Wheeler, Joseph	1	2	2		
Ham, Jonathan	2	2	2		
Clarke, Patrick	1		2		
Dunwell, Samuel	1	2	6		
Peabodie, Jane			2		
Atwell, Amos	4	1	4	2	
Williams, Benons	1	2	2		
Harding, Eleazar	3		7		
Warner, Amos	1	1	3		
Wilkerson, William	2	1	3		
Lippitt, Charles	1	3	4		
Gladding, Warren	1		2		
Peck, Lewis	1	3	2		
Tyler, William	3	1	3		
Soule, Mrs			4		
Ady, John	1		2		
Paul, Wilbore	1		2		
Young, Gideon	2	2	4		
Butler, Samuel	2	1	2		1
Butler, Samuel, Junr	1	1	2		
Coy, Jonathan W	3	2	2		
Andrews, Zepheriah	3	2	2		
Andrews, Benjamin	1	1	3		
Grinnell, Peter	1	3	2		
Farnum, Mary		2	4		
Gladding, Nathaniel	2		3		
Peckham, William	2	3	3		
Martin, David	3		4		

PROVIDENCE COUNTY—Continued.

PROVIDENCE TOWN—con.

NAME OF HEAD OF FAMILY.	Free white males of 16 years and upward, including heads of families.	Free white males under 16 years.	Free white females, including heads of families.	All other free persons.	Slaves.
Wescott, Ford	1	2	3		
Lee, William	2	1	4		
Holland, Mary		1	1		
Black, Samuel	2	2	6		
Sales, David	1	1	4	2	
Smith, Abiel	1		3		
Jenkins, Sarah	3	1	5		
Aborn, Samuel	1	1	3		
Rhodes, Joseph	1		2		
Cushing, Indrira			3		
Lansford, Holbort	1		2		
Barton, William	4	4	3	1	1
Bourne, Benjamin	1	1	3	2	
Walker, Susannah		2	2		
Whitman, Jacob	1		2	1	1
Dorrance, John	2	1	1	1	
Whitman, Jacob, Junr	1		4	1	
Lee, Samuel	1	3	1		
Philbrooks, Thomas	1		3		
Mason, John	2	2	2		
Aldridch, Eseck	2	3	2	1	
Jackson, Thomas	1	2	4		
Brown, James	1		1		
Wilson, William	1	4	3		
Harvey, James	1	1	6		
Scovell, Peter	1		1		
Gibson, John	1		5		
Field, Edward	1		1		
Delliberry, Philip	1		3		
Dunwell, Esther			4		
Dunwell, Martha	2	3	1		
Maloney, John	1		1		
Sprig, Mary			2		
Eams, David			2		
Shields, William	1	1	4		
Stewart, Archibald	3	1	2		
Butler, Mrs		1	3	1	
Hill, Jonathan	1		3		
Jenkins, Jeremiah F	2	4	4	1	
Jones, Thomas	2	3	5		
Reiley, Terrence	2		4		
Sabins, James	1	3	4		
Sabins, James, Junr	1	1	1		
Atwood, James	1	1	1		
Thurber, John	1	1	4		
Coggeshall, Cato				5	
Manning, Lewis				3	
Donnison, Jonathan	1	2	4		
Bucklin, Joseph	1	2	5		
Tritten, John	2		3		
Davis, Robert	1	2	4		
Davis, Mr	1	1	2		
Martain, Joseph	8	1	3		
Hodges, Benjamin	1		1		

SCITUATE TOWN.

NAME OF HEAD OF FAMILY.	Free white males of 16 years and upward, including heads of families.	Free white males under 16 years.	Free white females, including heads of families.	All other free persons.	Slaves.
Williams, Benjamin	1		2		
Williams, Abigail	1		2		
Smith, Eseck	1	4	3		
Smith, Solomon	1	2	3		
Aldrich, James	2	1	6		
Wescoat, Oliver	2		2		
Mowrey, Thomas	3	2	4		
Westcoat, Caleb	1	2	3		
Cornell, Gideon	2	4	8		
Aldrich, Caleb	1	2	2		
Potter, Ezra	3		5		
Smith, Resolved	2		5		
Ide, Joseph	2		2		
Fortelot, Jonathan	4		2		
West, Charles	1	1	1		
Wilkinson, John	2	1	3	1	
Peckham, Stephen	3	3	3		
Angel, Jabel	1	3	5		
Aldrich, Welcome	2	1	1		
West, William, Junr	2	2	3		
Burgis, Benjamin	1	4	5		
Joeling, Joseph	1	2	2		
Kimbol, Jarvis	1	2	3		
Wheeler, Henry	1		3		
Wescoat, Stentle	1		2		
Sprague, Peleg	1	3	3		
Wood, Thomas	2		3		
Salsberry, William, 3d	2	2	5		
Comel, Nathaniel	2		3		
Harris, Stephen	1	3	6		
Knowlton, Lydia			2		
Salsberry, Thomas	2	1	4		
Borden, Asa	1	6	2		
Hicks, Dan	2		6		
Brown, Samuel	2	3	4		
Brown, Jessee	1	5	4	1	
Cole, Abner	1	3	1		
Mathewson, John (Son of Israel)	2	3	2		

SCITUATE TOWN—con.

NAME OF HEAD OF FAMILY.	Free white males of 16 years and upward, including heads of families.	Free white males under 16 years.	Free white females, including heads of families.	All other free persons.	Slaves.
Cole, Jessee	1	1	6		
Salsberry, William	1		1		
Salsberry, Joseph	1	3	3		
Boss, Benjamin	1		1		
Elliott, John	1	1	2		
Slack, Miss Wait	1		1		
Bowen, Elisha	3		4		
Aldrich, Moses	1	1	2		
Aldrich, John	2		3		
William, James	4	6	7		
Slack, Benjamin	4	3	6		
Cole, Rufus	2	2	3		
Aldrich, William	1		2		
Harris, John	2	3	7		
Cole, Jessee	1	1	5		
Harris, Charles	3	2	3		
Harris, Thomas	3	2	7		
Mathewson, Thomas, Junr	3	2	4		
Bowen, Elisha, Junr	1	2	6		
Merrow, Samuel	1	6	5		
Steer, Reuben	1	1	2		
Smith, John	1	1	3		
Luther, James	1		4		
Harris, Mrs Naonni		2	1		
Salsberry, Charles	1	3	3		
Mathewson, Thomas	2	1	3		
Mitchel, Joseph	1	1	1		
Smith, Coomer	1	3	5		
Packer, John	1	2	3		
Whitaker, Joseph	1		3		
Kimball, James	1	1	2		
Kimball, Joseph	3	1	1		
Whitaker, Seril	1		2		
Kimball, Stephen	3	2	3		
Bunn, Henry	1	2	4		
Perry, Samuel	1	2	1		
Whitten, Samuel	3		3		
Aldrich, Noah	2	3	6		
Taylor, Richard	1	3	3		
Slack, Mrs Barbary		1	3		
Smith, Stephen	5	3	8		
Grayson, Richard	1		3		
Potter, Robert	1		1		
Taylor, Elisha	1		3		
Angel, Ezekiel	1		2		1
Bullock, Christopher	1		2		
Taylor, Benjamin	4	1	2		
Taylor, Thomas	1		1		
Taylor, Knight	4	2	7		
Atwood, John	1		6		
Kimball, Noah	1	1	4		
Adwood, Abraham	1	1	2		
Keech, Job	1	1	2		
Boss, Benjamin, Junr	2	2	2		
Fisk, Noah	1	1	4		
Fenner, Samuel	2	1	4		
King, George	1	4	5		
Potter, Caleb	2		2		
Salsberry, William	3	2	2		
Taylor, Benjamin, Junr	1	3	5		
Burlingham, David	2	1	3		
Rhodes, Richard	2	1	2		
Blackman, John	1		2		
Medberry, Joseph	1	2	4		
Fuller, Peleg	2		3		
White, Eleazer	1	3	2		
Bosworth, Benajah	1	3	4		
Potter, Winsor	1	3	5		
Corps, Abraham	1	1	4		
Potters, John	1	2	5		
Taylor, Job	1	1	1		
Burlingham, Abraham	1	2	3		
Waterman, Richard	3	3	3		
Burlingham, Sarah		2	3		
Pratt, Abner	1	1	3		
Angel, Abraham	2	2	7		
Colegrove, William	1	2	3		
Medberry, Nathaniel	1	2	3		
Medberry, Isaac, Junr	1	4	3		
Medberry, Isaac	3		3		
Andrews, Jeremiah	2	2	6		
Sayles, Thomas	2	1	3		
Peck, Peleg	3	1	5		
Peck, Peter	1		3		
Tift, Robert	1		3		
Tift, Samuel	1	4	3		
Mann, John	1	2	2		
Fenner, James	1	3	2		
Angel, Samuel	4	2	3		
Howard, Nathan	1	2	2		
Steer, Mrs Trifina			4		
Rutenborough, William	1	1	2		
Lovel, Nathaniel	1	4	2		
Hammell, Caleb	1		2		

SCITUATE TOWN—con.

NAME OF HEAD OF FAMILY.	Free white males of 16 years and upward, including heads of families.	Free white males under 16 years.	Free white females, including heads of families.	All other free persons.	Slaves.
Sylvester, Amos	1	2	6		
Coon, Nathaniel	1		4		
Philips, Elisha	2	3	3		
Jefferds, William	1		2		
Leech, Stephen	2		5		
Leech, Betty		1	3		
Searle, Edward	2	2	4		
Philips, William	1		2		
Leech, Asa	1	2	4		
Leech, Oliver	2		6		
Leech, Lewis	1	3	1		
Mathewson, James	3	1	1		
Lovel, Alexander	1	4	4		
Bates, John	1	3	3		
Bates, Reubin	1	2	3		
Bates, Thomas	1	1	3		
Barns, Elisha	1	1	3		
Barns, William	1	3	6		
Andrews, James	1	3	6		
Dorr, Aaron	3		1		
Westcoat, Peleg	1		2		
Henry, Thomas	1	1	2		
Potter, William	2		4		
Patty, William	2	4	1		
Mathewson, James, Junr	1	1	1		
Mathewson, John	2	1	3		
Guile, Mary		2	3		
Angel, Abel	1	4	4		
Manchester, John	1	4	4		
Guile, Mary	1	1	4		
Batty, Joshua	2	3	5		
Wood, Barnet	1		2		
Batty, John	2	1	2		
Batty, Caleb	1		3		
Hackstom, William	1	2	3		
King, Elisha	1	1	3		
Wood, Aomas	1		1		
Wood, Thomas	1	1	2		
Wood, Abraham	1	1	2		
Prosper, Bill				10	
Prosper, Pop				4	
Batty, Ruth			4		
Smith, Richard	4		3		
West, Thomas	1	1	5		
Ralph, Obadiah	1		3		
Blackman, Amagiah	1	1	4		
Manchester, Baize	2		3		
Eddy, Caleb	1		3		
Eddy, Elkanah		1	4		
Thomas, Nicholas	1	2	5		
Thomas, Mary			2		
Harris, Mary		2	3		
Harris, Gideon	1	5	2		
Harris, Stephen	1		4		
Harris, Stephen	1		2		
Angel, Tabathy		1	2		
Angel, Pardon	3	3	6		
Field, Thomas	2		5		
Walker, Charles	3		2		
Yaw, John	2		2		
Carver, Joseph	1	1	1		
Davis, William	2	3	4		
Potter, Jabez	1	3	1		
Mathewson, Aaron	2	1	2		
Simmons, William	1		2		
Simmons, Daniel	3	2	6		
Smith, Jonathan	1	5	4		
Arnold, Simon	2	5	5		
Bishop, Ezekiel	1	2	3		
Sprague, Betty			2		
Sprague, Ebenezer	1	1	3		
Simmonds, Levi	1	2	3		
Randal, Job	2	3	2		
Simmonds, James	2	2	3		
Borden, John	2		3		
Piskett, John	1		2		
Williams, Ephraim	1	2	3		
Place, David	1	2	2		
Ballou, Jeremiah	1	2	3		
Jenckes, Samuel	1	5	4		
Young, Joseph	1		2		
Potter, Christopher	1	1	2		
Potter, Nicholas	1	2	4		
Webb, John	1		4		
Philips, John	1	3	4		
Aldrich, Samuel	1	1	6		
Aldrich, Stephen	1	1	2		
Vaugh, John	1	1	3		
Franklin, Samuel	1		3		
Hill, Mathew	1		2		
Hill, Nathaniel	1		6		
Hill, John	3	2	6		
Smith, Christopher	1		5		
Turner, Palmer	3		3		
Smith, Stephen, Junr	1	1	3		
Smith, Stephen	1		3		

PROVIDENCE COUNTY—Continued.

NAME OF HEAD OF FAMILY.	Free white males of 16 years and upward, including heads of families.	Free white males under 16 years.	Free white females, including heads of families.	All other free persons.	Slaves.
SCITUATE TOWN—con.					
Knight, William	1		3		
Coon, Martin M	1	1	1		
Smith, Nathan	1	6	1		
Austin, Gideon, Junr	3	2	3		
Austin, Gideon	3		3		
Potter, William	4	1	5		
Wilbore, Simeon	1	3	5		
King, Samuel	3	2	6		
Philips, David	1	1	7		
Carpenter, John	3	1	5		
Potter, Christopher	1	1	1		
Knight, Joseph	1	1	1		
Wilbore, Samuel	1	2	4		
Potter, Thurber	1	1	1		
Parker, James	4	2	2	2	
Wilbore, John	2	2	5	1	
Potter, Gideon	1	2	2		
Young, John	1	1	3		
Fish, Elihu	1		2		
Williams, Ephraim	4		4		
Knight, David	2		2		
Blackmar, Theophilus	1	1	8		
Potter, Jeremiah	2	2	2		
Youngs, Stephen	2		1		
Youngs, William	1	1	1		
Horton, Benjamin	1	2	6		
Youngs, Stephen, Junr	2	3	5		
Carpenter, Joseph	2	2	3		
Whipple, Benedict	4		5		
King, Ralph	2	3	4		
Wood, Benjamin	1		2		
Wood, Nathan	1	1	2		
Wilbore, Job	1	2	1		
Wilbore, Keney	1		2		
Angel, Betty	1		2		
Young, Daniel	2	1	3		
Yaw, Abraham	1	3	2		
Yaw, David	1	2	2		
Roberts, Thomas	2	1	3		
Potter, Russell	1		1		
Knight, Jonathan	1	1	2		
Wood, Ezekiel	1	2	3		
Knight, Robert	1		3		
Knight, Israel	3	1	3		
Knight, Darius	1	1	1		
Profit, Peter				8	
Walton, Thomas	1	2	3		
Wilbore, Stephen	1	1	1		
Edwards, John	2		1		
Angell, Joseph	1	1	1		
Weaver, Thomas	1	2	3		
Parker, Thomas	2	3	5		
Franklin, Squire	1	1	3		
Knight, Richard	1	1	4		
Taylor, John	1	1	2		
Fisk, Johnson	1	1	2		
Bennett, John	2	3	3		
Colvin, Philip	1	1	8		
Knight, Francis	1		1		
Colvin, Pleg	3	3	3		
Stone, Charles	1	2	3		
Stone, Jeremiah	1		5		
Stone, Henry	1	2	2		
Edwards, Richards	1	1	2		
Edwards, Ephraim	2	2	3		
Edwards, Christopher	1	3	4		
Edwards, Nicholas	1		2		
Edwards, Nicholas, Junr	1	1	7		
Potter, Nehemiah	2	4	3		
Pardon, John	1		1		
Corey, William	3	1	3		
Pettis, Benjamin	3	1	3		
Pierce, Mrs Lunciney		1	2		
West, William	2	1	6	1	3
West, Samuel	1	1	1		
West, Hyram	1		2		
Aylenton, Roger	1	1	1		
West, John	2	5	5		
Hopkins, Thomas	1	2	1		
Sprague, Jeremiah	2		5		
Breyton, Francis	1		1		
Hopkins, Charles	1		2	1	
Walker, Obadiah	1	2	2		
Drew, Sylvanus	1	1	2		
Wilkinson, Joseph	2	2	5		
Hopkins, Timothy	2	1	5		
Hopkins, Lycha			3		
Randal, Stephen	2	1	5		
Hopkins, Hanan	3		4		
Molly, Mrs	2	1	6		
Hopkins, Reubin	2	2	3		
Hopkins, Reubin, Junr	2	4	3		
Davis, Stephen	1		3		
Hopkins, Isaac	1	1	2		
Ralph, Christopher	1	1	2		

NAME OF HEAD OF FAMILY.	Free white males of 16 years and upward, including heads of families.	Free white males under 16 years.	Free white females, including heads of families.	All other free persons.	Slaves.
SCITUATE TOWN—con.					
White, William	1	1	2		
Colvin, Noah	1	1	2		
Fenner, Arthur	3	1	4		
White, John	1	1	3		
White, Aaron	1	2	2		
White, David	1	2	5		
Ralph, Jabes	2		3		
White, Susannah		1	3		
Colvin, Mathew	1		2		
Potter, Samuel	4	1	5		
Potter, John	3	1	5		
Potter, Thomas	1	2	1		
Frankling, James	1		1		
Frankling, John	2	3	5		
Knight, Benajah	1	1	2		
Colvin, Aaron	1	2	1		
Potter, Cornel	1	1	2		
Ralph, Thomas	1	2	3		
Ralph, David	1		1		
Ralph, Nathan	2	1	2		
Colvin, Benoni	1	1	5		
Bates, James	1	1	2		
Kent, Samuel	1	2	4		
Colvin, John	1	1	1		
Field, Chad	1	1	2		
Fisk, Daniel	2	2	5		
Collins, Lydia			2		
Westcoat, Daniel	1	3	5		
Baker, Jeremiah	1	1	6		
Randal, Nehemiah	1		3		
Graves, Constant	1	3	4		
Bates, Oliver	2	2	4		
Fisk, Caleb	6	1	7		
Bossett, William	1	1	1		
Bates, Nathan	1	1	2		
Fisk, Peleg	2	2	4		
Fisk, Moses	1	4	7		
Fisk, Job	1		1		
Fisk, Job, Junr	2	3	4		
Fisk, Peleg, Junr	1		2		
Randal, Hnry	1	1	2		
Knight, Israel	1		1		
Knight, James	1	1	7		
Collins, Eleazer	2	4	3		
Collins, Azakel	1	5	2		
Young, Robert	1	1	1		
Smith, Samuel	1		1		
Remmington, Joseph	1		1		
Remmington, Joseph, Junr	1	3	3		
Watson, Thomas	1	2	4		
Hopkins, Rufus	6		3		2
Colvin, Josiah	2	1	3		
Colvin, David	1	1	2		
Colvin, Andrew	1	1	2		
Johnston, William	1	2	2		
Burlingham, David	1		2		
Snow, Zebadiah	1	3	2		
Remmington, Jonathan	1	1	3		
SMITHFIELD TOWN.					
Pearce, Benjamin	1	2	5		
Burden, Timothy	1		2		
Jenckes, Primus (Negro)				2	
Bowman, Cain (Negro)				7	
Jenckes, Joseph	3	1	10		
Arnold, Isaac	2	3	4		
Arnold, Zebadiah	1	3	3		
Jenckes, Nicholas	1	3	1		
Arnold, Christopher	1		1		
Scott, Jeremiah	2	3	10		
Dexter, Andrew	2		3		
Dexter, Waterman	1	5	2		
Alexander, Roger	1	2	4		
Spaulding, Aholiab	2	1	3		
Spaulding, Joseph	1		1		
Spaulding, Nathaniel	1		2		
Wilkinson, Mrs Abgail	3		2		
Wilkinson, Joseph	1	2	1		
Whipple, Benjamin	1		5		
Whipple, Jeremiah	1	1	3		
Dexter, Jonathan	3	1	5		
Dexter, Nathan	1	2	6	1	
Harris, Uriah	1		1		
Harris, George	1		2		
Arnold, Levi	2	5	2		
Arnold, Benjamin	1	1	3		
Bensley, Arnold	1	2	6		
Arnold, Enoch	2	2	3		
Cumstock, Ichabod	3	3	6		
Ballou, Peter	4		2		
Ballou, William	2	3	1		
Busklin, Jeremiah	2	2	2		
Wood, John	1	2	1		

NAME OF HEAD OF FAMILY.	Free white males of 16 years and upward, including heads of families.	Free white males under 16 years.	Free white females, including heads of families.	All other free persons.	Slaves.
SMITHFIELD TOWN—con.					
Arnold, Joshua	1		2		
Arnold, Israel	1	3	5		
Arnold, Mrs Eleithem	1	2	4	1	
Arnold, Samuel	2	1	5	1	
Arnold, Abraham	1		3		2
Tucker, Samuel	3		3		
Arnold, Job	2	1	4		1
Harris, Israel	1		1		
Smith, John	1	1	2		
Smith, Benjamin	2	6	6		
Jenckes, John	5	2	4		
Jenckes, Joseph	3		4		
Jenckes, Mrs Ispersion			2	1	
Arnold, Luke	1	3	4		
Arnold, Nathaniel	2	1	4	1	
Whipple, John	1	1	3		
Smith, Abraham	1	1	4		
Jenckes, Ishua	4	1	4		
Jenckes, Adam	1	2	2		
Harris, Preserved	3	1	4		
Harris, Rufus	1	5	5		
Harris, David, the 2d	2	1	4		
Whipple, William	2		2		
Aldrich, Simon	2	2	4		
Smith, George	1		3		
Mowrey, Elisha	5		5		
Tucker, Morris	1	2	3		
Streeter, Rufus	2	1	4		
Wright, Charles	1	2	1		
Newman, Thomas	2	1	1		
Newman, Nathaniel	1		4		
Whipple, Stephen	5	2	7		
Coe, John	1	4	2		
Clarke, Samuel	2	3	6	1	
Ballou, Aaron	2	4	5		
Ballou, Moses	3	3	5		
Hill, Samuel	4	1	8		
Hill, Samuel, Junr	2		3		
Walker, John	1	1	2		
Lapham, Augustus	2	2	7		
Lapham, Nancy		1	2		
Gulley, William	2	6	5		
Gulley, Jonathan	2	2	6		
Smith, Clad	1	3	2		
Wing, Benjamin	3	4	4		
Wilkinson, Israel	3	2	7		
Shrefe, Ishua	3		2		
Wilkinson, Mary	2	1	4		
Sprague, Nehemiah	2	2	3		
Sprague, Elias	2	3	4		
Allen, Walter	2	3	5		
Lee, James	1	1	1		
Green, William	1	1	1		
Aldrich, William	1	3	4		
Arnold, Seth	4	1	4		
Arnold, Elisha	2		4		
Arnold, George	1	4	5		
Arnold, Ezekiel	1	1	5		
Paine, Arnold	3		3		
Paine, John	3	1	6		
Staples, Sarah			1	4	
Arnold, Peleg	3	3	4		
Cumstock, Ezekiel	1		1	2	
Arnold, Caleb	2		3		
Arnold, Miss Phila			2		
Arnold, Daniel	6	2	16		
Rogers, Mrs Plain			2		
Brayton, James (Melatto)				7	
Cumstock, George	2		4		
Cumstock, Hezidiah	1	1	2		
Southwick, Zacheus	1	1	3		
Comstock, Henry	1	2	5	1	
Sprague, Enoch	2		1	2	
Rhodes, Asa	1		3		
Boice, John	1		3		
Mann, Joseph	1	1	3		
Bartlet, Elisha	3	3	4	1	
White, Mrs Alice		1	3		
Hill, Jacob	1		4		
Cumstock, Mrs Rachel		1	1		
Aldrich, Mary		1	1		
Arnold, Joseph	1	2	4		
Trask, Ebinezar	1	1	5		
Trask, Frederich	1	1	2		
Green, Jebes	1	2	2		
Tucker, Nathan	1	2	4		
Arnold, Elijah	1	2	6		
Buffum, William	2	3	8		
Cruff, Joel	3	2	2		
Buffum, David	3	2	5		
Mann, Joab	3	1	2		
Mann, Oliver	2		3		
Harkness, Adam	2		3		
Mosher, Jonathan	1	1	1		

PROVIDENCE COUNTY—Continued.

SMITHFIELD TOWN—con.

NAME OF HEAD OF FAMILY.	Free white males of 16 years and upward, including heads of families.	Free white males under 16 years.	Free white females, including heads of families.	All other free persons.	Slaves.
Mosher, Welcome	1	1	2		
Cumstock, Anthony	1		2		
Harkness, Samuel	1		3		
Shippy, David	1	3	2		
Wilson, Alexander	1	2	3		
Goldthwait, John	4	2	3		
Holbrook, Micah	3	1	4		
Buffum, Benjamin	1		2		
Northup, John	1	3	2		
Sweat, Hannah			3		
Buxton, James	2	3	4		
Buxton, Henry	1	1	3		
Buxton, Daniel	1	1	2		
Ballou, Daniel	1		1		
Buxton, Celeb	1		3		
Ashley, Freeman	2	5	3		
Buffum, Stephen	1	1	1		
Buffum, Joshua	1	1	2		
Buffum, Joseph	2	1	2		
Carroll, Joseph	1	1	2		
Dow, Samuel	1		1		
Read, John	2	2	4		
Read, David	1		1		
Thornton, Elisha	1	4	4		
Capron, Joseph	1	1	3		
Cumstock, Stephen	2	2	5		
Ballou, Abraham	3	2	6		
Tift, Israel	2	1	3		
Eddey, Stephen	1		1		
Aldrich, Israel	1	1	2		
Carroll, Jesse	1	1	2		
Crood, William (Negro)				5	
Buffum, Richard	1	3	2		
Peane, Benjamin	2	1	3		
Kelly, Joseph	1		2		
Kelly, Eliphalet	1	1	1		
Trask, Ebinezar, Junr	1	2	3		
Inman, Elisha	1	5	3		
Randal, Edward	1	2	3		
Hull, John	1	2	3		
Tift, Peter	2		2		
Tift, James	2	2	3		
Mowrey, Ezekiel	2	3	3		
Sayles, Eseck	2	3	5		
Philips, Reubin	1	3	2		
Mathewson, Daniel	3		2		
Mowrey, Zebediah	1	4	2		
Cooke, Eli	1		3		
Cass, Ebinezar	1	2	4		
Thornton, Simon	1	1	1		
Cass, Amos	1	2	2		
Staples, Ebinezar	2	1	3		
Mann, David	2		6		
Arnold, Ruth	3	1	2		
Mann, Moses	1	1	4		
Morton, James	2	1	6		
Cumstock, Joseph	2		1		
Cooke, Samuel	2	1	3		
Cumstock, Laban	1		3		
Aldrich, Samuel	2		1		
Aldrich, Samuel	2	1	4		
Allen, Daniel	2	1	4		
Bellows, Elijah	1	1	3		
Spears, Elkanoh	1	2	3		
Arnold, William	3		4		
Mawney, Cato				2	
Mowrey, Philip	4	1	5		
Mowrey, David	4		4		
Arnold, Stephen	2		2		
Aldrich, Thomas	3	2	9		
Chilson, Miss Mary	2	1	3		
Homes, Oliver	1		4		
Smith, Thomas	1	1	4		
Aldrich, Joel	1	2	3		
Cumstock, Ruth	1	2	4		
Mowrey, Stephen	1	4			
Eddy, David	2		3		
Mowrey, Jonathan	2	1	7	1	
Mowrey, Uriah	1	1	2		
Jaxo, Jacob (Negro)				7	
Sayles, Thomas	1	1	2		
Smith, Mary		1	6		
Staples, William	1		2		
Aldrich, Reuben	1	2	2		
Aldrich, Reuben, Junr	1		2		
Aldrich, Nathan	2	2	1	1	
Aldrich, Levi	2		2		
Aldrich, Naman	1	4	4		
Herrington, Freelove	3	2	6		
Aldrich, Caleb	3	1	4		
Aldrich, Prime				2	
Aldrich, Ishmael	1	1	3		
Wilkinson, Lydia		1	3		
Howe, Samuel	3	1	2		
Chace, Barnabas	2	2	4		

SMITHFIELD TOWN—con.

NAME OF HEAD OF FAMILY.	Free white males of 16 years and upward, including heads of families.	Free white males under 16 years.	Free white females, including heads of families.	All other free persons.	Slaves.
Hall, Asa	1		2		
Capron, Welcome	1	4	3		
Aldrich, Augustus	1	3	4		
Paine, Benoni	1	3	4		
Mann, John	3	1	5		
Streeter, George	1	4	8		
Sayles, Daniel	1	3	4		
Buckling, Syvanus	1		2		
Sayles, Stephen	1	1	4		
Jenckes, Jessee, Junr	1	1	1		
Arnold, Gideon	1		1		
Sayles, Gideon	1		3		
Sayles, Jonathan	4	1	3		
Sayles, Smith	2	2	5		
Newell, Benjamin	1	4	5		
Joslin, John	3	2	5		
Angel, Abiah	1	2	3		
Ballou, Benjamin	1	1	4		
Ballou, John	1		2		
Aldrich, William	2	1	3		
Sayles, Sylvanus	1	1	1		
Alverron, David	1	1	4		
Shippey, John	1	1	4		
Whitman, John	1	1	4		
Sayles, Richard	1	3	2		
Sayles, John, the 2d	2		8		
Sayles, Stentley	2	4	3		
Mowrey, John	3	4	2		
Mowrey, Eseck	3		2		
Harris, David	3	1	3		
Harris, Ann	2	2	4		
Harris, Robert	2	2	4		
Harris, Jeremiah	3	1	4		
Jenckes, George	3	1	2	1	1
Young, Zebediah	2	3	4		
Olney, Obadiah	2		3		
Olney, Elisha	3	4	8		
Arnold, Asa	3	1	2	1	
Muzzy, James	3	1	5		
Wilkinson, John	2		2		
Williams, George	1	1	3		
Olney, Jeremiah	1	1	3		
Olney, Benjamin	1	2	1		
Olney, James	1	1	2		
Bensley, William	2		2		
Jenckes, Henry	4	1	3		
Arnold, Stephen	3	1	4	1	
Arnold, Jonathan	4		4	1	
McLellen, Samuel	2	1	3		
Jenckes, Thomas	2	3	5		
Twist, Stephen	1	1	5		
Jenckes, John	1	1	5		
Smith, Welcome	1		2		
Clark, Aaron	1		5		
Wilbore, Daniel	4		2		
Wilbore, Christopher	2	2	2		
Angel, Charles	3	1	3		
Medbury, Benjamin	2	1	3		
Angel, John	3	1	3		
Keech, Abraham	2	2	3		
Whitman, Valantine	1	1	7		
Angel, Gideon	2		3		
Arnold, Silas	2	1	4		
Angel, Isaac	1	1	2		
Young, James	2		1		
Trip, Edward	1	1	2		
Angel, Benjamin	1	3	2		
Hawkens, Stephen	1	1	2		
Brown, Eleazer	1	2	3		
Pitcher, Mr	1	2	2		
Angel, Ezekiel	3	2			
Philips, John	1		1		
Philips, Gideon	1	1	3		
Reanup, Daniel	1	1	5		
Keech, Samuel	3	3	5		
Young, Andrew	1	1	2		
Whitman, Stephen	1	2	3		
Keech, Amos	2	4			
Smith, Emor	2		3		
Fomun, Stephen	2		9		
Brittain, Abeal	1	1	1		
Angell, Ruth	1		3	1	
Stead, Daniel	3	3	5		
Angel, Mary	1		3		
Smith, Jeremiah	4	3	7		
Angell, Joseph	2	2	3		
Angel, John	1	1	2		
Angel, Abram	1	2	2		
Smith, Rufus	2	2	2		
Smith, Jacob	1		5		
Wilbore, Daniel, Junr	1	1	5		
Young, Nathan	1	1	2		
Kimson, Joram	1		2		
Smith, Jesse	1		2		

SMITHFIELD TOWN—con.

NAME OF HEAD OF FAMILY.	Free white males of 16 years and upward, including heads of families.	Free white males under 16 years.	Free white females, including heads of families.	All other free persons.	Slaves.
Angel, Jonathan	1		2		
Kimson, Nathan	1	1	1		
Brayton, Isaac	1	1	5		
Angel, Job	3	1	5		
Medberry, Edward	2	3	5		
Smith, John	3	2	9		
Sprague, Joseph	3	2	4		
Harris, David	1		1		
Harris, Jonathan	1		3		
Harris, William	2	1	4		
Harris, Amey	1	1	4		
Harris, Jabez	2		4		
Brayton, Stephen	3	3	4		
Aldrich, Samuel	1	3	5		
Sayles, Benjamin	1		3		
Jenckes, Jesse	3		4		
Huchinson, Daniel	1	1	2		
Smith, Jacob	1		1		
Shippay, Samuel	2	1	4		
Medbury, Nathaniel	2	2	15		
Medbury, Nathan	1	3	5		
Cumstock, Gideon	1		2		
Sayles, Oziel		4	3		
Paine, Mrs Jemima	1	1	4		
Paine, Ladan	1	1	4		
Paine, Belah	2	2	2		
Paine, Obed	1	2	2		
Smith, Elijah	1		1		
Capron, Comfort	1	1	3		
Capron, Labon	1	1	1		
Paine, Joseph	1		2		
Paine, Jonathan	1	1	4		
Smith, Joshuah	1	1	3		
Smith, Eseck	1	1	2		
East, John	1		2		
Herrington, Moses	1	2	4		
Brown, Simon	1		2		
Newell, Jonathan	1	1	2		
Baker, George	2		3		
Harrenden, Warton	1	2	1		
Brown, Benjamin	1		3		
Brown, Mrs Alice	1		3		
Ballard, Jonathan	1		3		
Smith, Oliver	2	1	5		
Herrenden, Elijah	2		3		
Herrenden, Ebenezer	2		2		
Mowrey, Abel	1	2	3		
Wing, Benjamin, Junr	2	2	3		
Wing, Jebez	2	1	3	1	
Walker, Walter	1	1	4		
Sayles, Charles	1	2	2		
Cody, Elias	1	1	1		
Steere, Anthony	1	1	4		
Steere, John	2		2		
Smith, Daniel, Junr	2	2	4	1	
Mowrey, Annanias	2		2		
Mowrey, Enas	2	2	3		
Mowrey, David, Junr	2		1		
Mathewson, Othniel	1		1		
Inman, Joseph, Junr	1	3	1		
Mathewson, Sarah		1	2		
Mathewson, Joseph	2	2	7		
Harrington, Abraham		2	2		
Sayles, John	2	1	3		
Mowrey, Joseph	2	1	4		
Mowrey, Richard	2	6			
Mowrey, Mrs Zerviah			2		
Mowrey, Jonathan, Junr	1	1	2		
Mowrey, Nathaniel	1	2	2		
Sheldon, Benjamin	1	5	5		
Newfield, Elisha	1	3	2		
Miller, Jonathan	2	7	2		
Inman, Joseph	1	4	2		
Inman, Rufus	1	6	3		
Caldwell, John	1	6	3		
Waterman, Benjamin	2	1	2		
Paine, John	3	1	6	9	5
Aldrich, Samuel	4		6		
Aldrich, Samuel	1	3	9	5	
Bartlet, Noah	2	1	4		
Aldrich, Stephen	2	4	6		
Aldrich, Gardiner	2		1		
Holden, Gersham	1		3		
Jenckes, Jessee	1	1	5	3	
Jenckes, Margaret			3		
Latham, Benoni	1		4		
Mowrey, Daniel, Junr	2	1	4		
Mann, Daniel	2	1	7		
Mowrey, Eleazer	2	2	2		
Herrenden, Ezekiel	2	2	4		
Sayles, Sylvanus	2	1	4		
Appleby, James, Junr	3	1	3		
Mowrey, Job, Junr	2	1	3		
Appleby, John	2		4		

PROVIDENCE COUNTY—Continued.

SMITHFIELD TOWN—con.

NAME OF HEAD OF FAMILY.	Free white males of 16 years and upward, including heads of families.	Free white males under 16 years.	Free white females, including heads of families.	All other free persons.	Slaves.
Mowrey, Daniel	2	1	4		
Mowrey, Daniel, 3d	3	7	8		
Aldrich, Job	4	3	3		
King, Isaac	1	3	4		
Mowrey, Sylvester	2		2		
Olney, Freelove		1	1		
Smith, Daniel	7	1	4		
Aldrich, Ann	4	2	4		
Appleby, Thomas	2	2	3		
Balcomb, Joseph	1	1	3		
Balcomb, Jesse	2	2	4		
Mowrey, Job	2	3	3		
Olney, Aaron (Negro)				8	
Wamsley, Thomas				7	
Bishop, Abner	1		1		
Smith, James	3	1	5		
Smith, Elisha (Melatto)				7	
Evans, Elisha	1	3	2		
Evans, David	4	3	9		
Mowrey, William	1	1	4		
Aldrich, Joshua	1	4	5		
Place, Joseph	1	1	1		
Tucker, Abigail	3	1	4		
Windsor, Nancy		1	3		
Foster, Jessee	2	3	6		
Winsor, Abraham	3		3		
Waterman, William	3	1	6	1	
Smith, John	3	2	2		
Winsor, Zenus	2	3	5		
Winsor, Augustus	1	1	5		
Freeman, David	1		2		
Brittain, David	1		2		
Smith, William	3		2		
Smith, Resolved	1	3	2		
Smith, Rebecca			1		
Mitchel, Edwarard	1		2		
Latham, Arthur	1	2	4		
Latham, Robert	1	1	2		
Carpenter, John	4	1	4		
Latham, Joseph	4	1	4		
Place, Joseph, Junr	1	3	2		
Barnes, Enoch	3	2	7		
Winsor, Jeremiah	2	1	3		
Otis, Nicholas	1	1	1		
Russell, John	1		4		
Smith, Thomas	1	4	3		
Dyer, Oliver	1	2	2		
Waterman, Andrew	3	2	8	1	
Poke, Edward	1	1	3		
Cozzens, John	1	2	4		
Sweet, Benajah	1	1	3		
Sweet, Jeremiah	3	1	3		
Dean, Timothy	2	2	5		
Mathewson, Abraham	3	1	5		
Peck, Peleg	1	4	3		
Mathewson, David	3	2	5		
Potter, William	4	2	7		
Holmes, Samuel	2	2	4		
Smith, Elisha	1	1	4		
Seavers, Obed	1		3		
Slack, Joseph	1	2	4		
Waterman, Mary		1	2	1	1
Eddy, Thomas	4		2		
Angel, Christopher	2		4		
Angel, David	3	2	4		
Winsor, Samuel	1		2		
Winsor, Duty	3	2	2		
Winsor, John	3	2	3		
Steere, Elisha	2	2	6		
Steere, David	3	1	3		
Tunmore, William	1	1	4		
Smith, Juni	1	3	4		
Kelly, Elisha	1	1	5		
Farnum, Noah	1	2	5		
Comstock, Jacob	1	2	1		
Sweet, Philip	1	1	8		
Farnum, Joseph	3	2	5		
Wood, Patty			3		
Stephens, Ebinezar	1	1	2		
Hawkins, John	2	3	4		
Smith, Emor	2		4		
Drake, James	1	1	3		
Mowrey, Abiel	1		3		

WASHINGTON COUNTY.

CHARLESTOWN TOWN.

NAME OF HEAD OF FAMILY.	Free white males of 16 years and upward.	Free white males under 16 years.	Free white females.	All other free persons.	Slaves.
Taylor, Nathan	2	3	6		
Park, Hannah Hanson	6		3		
Hazard, George Wanton	1	2	3		
Lewis, Nathan	1	2	3		
Congdon, Robert	2		2	2	
Sheffield, Thomas	3	6	5		
Sheffield, Phebe (Widow)			3		
Hoxie, Thomas	1	1	2		
Babcock, Christopher, Esqr	4		4	3	1
Hall, Thomas	1	2	3		
Hoxie, Benjamin	1		1	2	
Wilcox, Joseph	1	1	3		
Gavit, John	1	2	2		
Lewis, Nathaniel	1	2	2		
Saunders, Nathan	1	1	1	1	
Lazil, Abner	1	1	1	1	
Crandal, Simeon	1	1	4		
Saunders, Joshua	1	5	6		
Saunders, Daniel	1	1	2		
Crandal, Caleb	1	2	3		
Knowles, Thomas	1	2			
Lewis, Peleg	2		3		
Babcock, Primus				5	
Wilcox, Edward	2		2	2	
Stanton, Samuel	2	1	4	1	
Utter, Josias	1		5		
Stanton, Daniel	1	4	2		
Stanton, Mercy (Widow)	1		6		
Sherman, Daniel	1	1	2		
Stanton, Lodowick	4	4	6	1	
Crandal, Simeon, ye 2d	1		1		
Potter, James	1	1	3		
Macomber, Jonathan	2	3	5		
Hoxie, Benjamin, Esqr	1	2	5		
Greene, Edward	1	3	3		
Putnam, John	1	1	1		
Crandal, Simeon, Junr	1	1	3		
Sheffield, Stanton	1	1	3		
Crandal, Jesse	2	3	3		
Clark, Simeon	1		2		
Hall, Hannah			2		
Hall, George	1		3		
Crandal, Enoch	2	3	3		
Greene, Rathbun	1	2	3		
Studson, Thomas	1	1	2		
Thomson, Lodowick	1		1		
Stanton, Stephen	1	1	4		
Crandal, Gideon	1	1	2		
Stanton, Samuel, 2d	1		7		
Burdick, Jonathan	1	2	5		
Davis, Joseph, Junr	1	2	5		
Burdick, Epharim	2	2	5		
Kinyon, Joshua	2		7	1	
Saunders, Isaac	1	2	4		
Davis, Joshua, Junr	1		3		
Dinah (Indian)				1	
Johnson, Theodate	1		4		
Johnson, Daniel	1	1	2		
Burdick, Ichabod	1	6	4		
Peckham, James	1	2	4		
Hoxie, Edward	1				
Hoxie, Stephen	1	3	2		
Edwards, Daniel	1	2	2		
Peirce, Nathan	1	1	1		
Saunders, Tobias	3		4		
Greene, Henry	1	2	6		
Clossen, Ichabod	1	2	6		
Clossen, John	1				
Taylor, Joseph	3	4	4		
Taylor, Dennis	2	2	2		
Young, Thomas	1	2	2		
Kinyon, Lodowick	1	4	5		
Kinyon, Mumford	1	1	1		
Austin, Joshua	1	1	1		
Larkin, Kinyon	2	2	4	2	
Worden, Christopher	1	1	5		
Prosser, Arnold	1	2	3		
Taylor, Jeremiah	1	2	2		
Crandal, James	1		2		
Adams, Henry	1		1		
Lewis, Thomas	1			6	
Austin, Steven	1	3	3		
Peirce, Daniel	1	2	5		
Hoxie, Peleg	1	2	4		
Wilbore, John	1	2	2		
Harvey, Joseph	1		2		
Johnson, John	1	1	4		
Colvin, Levi	1		3	1	
Young (Widow)			4		
Austin, George	1	2	3		
Crandal, Ethan	1	7	4		
Hall, Rhodes	1	1	6		
Peckham, Braddick	1	2	6		
Johnson, Gideon	4	3	3		
Putman, John	1	1	3		
Peckham, Abel	1		3		
Harvey, William	2		6		
Cooper, George (Indian)				4	
Dick, Thomas (Indian)				8	
Hoxie, Peleg, Jun	1	2	4		
Goodbody (Widow)			2		
Kinyon, Nathan, Jun	1		1		
Kinyon, Nathan, Sen	1	2	3		
Welch, John	2	9	4		
Grinnell, Steven	1	1	1	1	
Adams, Thomas	1	5	2		
Johnson, John	1	1	2		
Collier, John, Esq	1				
Niles, Jerusha (Indian)				4	
Hammock, Hanah (Indian)				2	
Secater,* David (Indian)				250	
Greene, Amos	2	6	6		
Cross, Peleg	1		3	2	3
Kinyon, William	1	1	5		
Kinyon, Roger	1				
Hoxie, Coll. Gideon	1	1	3	1	
Congdon, Robert	1	1	2	1	
Welch, Henry	4	6	4		
Champlin, John	2	1	7	2	
Kinyon, Samuel	1	2	3	1	
Cross, Peleg, Jun	3	2	6	1	
Hill, Martha	1	2	4		
Macomber, Jonathan	2	1	5		
Allen, James	3	2	3		
Allen, James	1	1	2		
Carey, Elias	1	1	2		
Gardner, William	1		3	1	
Stanton, Henry	1		6	1	
York, William	2		3		
Stanton, Genl Joseph	2	2	2	1	
Greene, Rathbun	1	2	2		
Clerk, Simeon	1	4	3		
Noyce, Coll. Peleg	4	2	4	3	
Noyce, Peleg, Jun	1		1		
Congdon, Benjamin	2	2	3		
Harvey, Joseph, Jun	1	2	1	1	
Hall, George	1		3		
Kinyon, Joshua	2	2			
Potter, Sarah (widow)			3		
Burdick, Samuel	3	2	5		
olney, Amos (Negro)				10	
Burdick, Sylvester	1	3	2		
Jaques, Nathan	1	1	6		
Burdick, Isaiah	1	3	2		
Harry, John (Black)				3	
Perry, John	1	5	3		
Perry, Edward	1	2	3	2	
Congdon, James	3	3	4		
Clerk, Joseph	1	2	3		
Perry, Samuel	1	2	3		
Burdick, Gideon	3	2	5		
Hall, Augustus	1	1	2		
Hoxie, Judge Joseph	3		2	6	6
Church, Sylvester	1	1	2		
Shumbark, Thomas	1	2	3		
Lewis, Amos	1				
Kinyon, James	2		4		
Kinyon, Daniel	1	10			
Kinyon, Amos	1	1	4		
Hall, James	1	2	4		
Church, Isaac	1	4	5		
Church, Susanna (widow)	2	4	4		
Congdon, Deborah					
L'loyd, John	1	3	4		
Hazard, Richard (Negro)				5	

*Head of the Indian Tribe in Charleston and head of the Indian Council. Reports to me that there is according to the best Estimate taken in March last by the Indian Council of men, Women, & Children 250.

WASHINGTON COUNTY—Continued.

NAME OF HEAD OF FAMILY.	Free white males of 16 years and upward, including heads of families.	Free white males under 16 years.	Free white females, including heads of families.	All other free persons.	Slaves.
CHARLESTOWN TOWN—continued.					
Jaques, Stafford	1		3	1	
Cross, Gideon	1	3	5		
Perry, Simeon	1	3	3	1	
Congdon, James, Esqʳ	1	4	4		
Congdon, James, yᵉ 3ᵈ	1		1		
Nigh, James	1	3	2		
Nigh, Dinah (widow)			2		
Nigh, Caleb	1		1		
Nigh, Joshua	1	1	2		
Nigh, Stephen	4		3		
Perry, Peter (Negro)				6	
Lewis, Augustus Johnson	1	2	4	1	
Hazard, Dick (Negro)				5	
Church, Isaac	1	1	6		
Tucker, Nathan	2		2		
Tucker, Benjamin	1	1	2		
Allen, Christopher	1	3	1		
Tucker, John	2	5	3		
Tucker, Tabatha (widow)	4		1		
Clerk, Caleb	1	1	2		
Greene, Benjamin	2		8		
Healy, John	1	2	2		
Tucker, Numan	1		1		
Clerk, Timothy	1	1	2		
Clerk, Jonathan	2	3	2		
Clerk, William	1	2	6		
Card, Joshua, Jun	1	1	5		
Browning, John	1	2	3		
Kinyon, Joseph	1		1		
Clerk, George	1	1	1		
Wilcox, David	1	4	3		
Card, Elijah	1	2	2		
Card, Shadrick	1	1	3	1	
Johnson, Stephen	1	1	1		
Clerk, Oliver	1	3	5		
Clerk Samuel	1				
Clerk, William	1	1	2		
Clerk, Rowland	1	4	4		
Browning, William	1	2	5		
Hall Silas	1	2	3		
Dick, Isaac				2	
Dick, Daniel				4	
Brown, John				7	
Larkin, Roger	1	1	2		
Peekin, William	1	3	4		
Webster, Joseph	1	1	2		
Kinyon, James	1	1	2	1	
Jones, Robert	1	3	4		
Hall (Widow)			3		
Clerk, Joseph	1		1		
Greene, Clerk	1		1		
Clerk, George	1	1	2		
Clerk, Job (Joiner)	1	3	3		
Greene, Amy (widow)			1		
Johnson, John (Indian)				5	
Carey, Elias	1		2		
Hazard, Robert	1	2	3		
Littlefield, Daniel (Negro)				6	
Hall, James	1	1	2		
Iuion, Benjamin (Indian)				1	
Hanon (Widow)		2	2		
Welch, Henry	1				
Hanon, Gusty	1	2	3		
Welch, John	1	3	4		
Hall, Augustus	1	1	2		
Wappy (Indian)				5	
Hoy, George (Indian)				3	
Johnson, John (Indian)				6	
Jones, Robert	1	3	4		
Clerk, Job	1	2	5		
Clerk, Stephen	1		2		
Card, John	1	2	6		
Card, John, Jun	2	1	5		
Ely, Paul	2	4	4		
Holloway, Gideon	1	3	1		
Card, Joshua	1	1	4		
Card, William	1	2	2		
Card, Akus	1	3	5		
Card, Augustus	1	2	2		
Lawton, James	1	1	2		
Pettes, Joseph	1	1	2		
Cross, Samuel	3	1	8		
Hazard, Robert	1	2	3		
Mowry, Edward	1		1		
Greene, Thomas	1		1	1	
Greene, John	1	1	5		
Greene, Allen	1	3	4		
Lewis, Augustus	1	3	3		
Woodmary, David	1	3	3		
Worden, Jeremiah	1		1		

NAME OF HEAD OF FAMILY.	Free white males of 16 years and upward, including heads of families.	Free white males under 16 years.	Free white females, including heads of families.	All other free persons.	Slaves.
CHARLESTOWN TOWN—continued.					
Worden, Samuel	1	2	5		
Worden, Benjamin	2				
Jones, Robert	1	3	4		
Blevin, Samuel	1	2	3		
Browning, Ephraim	1	3	5		
Browning, Hazard	1	1	3		
Baker, Thomas	1	2	3		
Targee, Colentine	1	2	4		
Hall, Abel	1	1	1	4	
Holloway, Joseph	1	1	2		
Greene, Reuben	1	2	3		
Greene, Jeofry	1				
Greene, Henry	1	1	1		
Lawton, James	1	1	3		
Babcock, Simeon	1	4	3	2	
Worden, Benjamin	1	1	5		
Worden, Samuel	1	2	5		
Clerk, Jonathan	1	3	1		
Kinyon, Joseph	1		1	2	
Kinyon, Joseph, Jun	2	1	5		
Kinyon, Caleb	1	1	1	1	
Kinyon, John	1	1	6	1	
Hall, Jonathan	1		3	1	
Barber, Peleg	2	3	4		
Clerk, Jabez	1	4	3		
Crandal, Elijah	1	2	3		
Larkin, Roger	1	1	1	1	
Clerk, Caleb	1	1	1		
Clerk, Nathan	1	2	1	1	
Tucker, Tabathy (widow)	2	2	2		
Greene, Browning	1	1	1		
Greene, Braddock	1	1	2		
Browning, Ephraim	2	3	5		
Johnson, Stephen	1	1	4		
Wilcox, David	1	2	2		
Clerk, Jonathan, Jun	1	3	2		
Ely, John	1	1	3		
Clerk, Timothy	1	1	2		
Clerk, William, Jun	1	2	4		
Clerk, William	1	2	5		
Browning, Ann (widow)			2		
EXETER TOWN.					
Wilcox, Mary (widow)		1	4		
Smith, Joseph	1		6		
Wilcox, Nathan	2	2	5		
Dawly, Desire		3	4		
Wilcox, Hopson	3	2	5		
Wilcox, Robert	2	5	3		
Trip, Charles	1		2		
Sprague, Solomon	4	2	4		
Sweet, John	1	2	4		
Chapel, Frederick	1	4	1		
Harvey, Wait	2	2	4		
Sunderland, George	1	1	6		
Reynolds, James	2	1	3		
Whitford, Ezeikel	1		2		
Gardner, Zebulon	2	1	4		
Nigh, John	2	1	4		
Strange, William	1	1	3		
Reynolds, Joseph (Cooper)	3		3		
Reynolds, Great Joseph	4	1	5		
Littlefield, Daniel	2		2		
Arnold, Caleb	1	1	4		
Congdon (Widow)		3	2		
Northup, Benjamin, Jun	1	2	2		
Brown, Jonathan	1	2	2		
Reynolds, Robert	3	3	8		
Peirce, George	2	3	4	1	
Gardner, Francis	1	3	1		
Bates, James	1	4	2		
Reynolds, Benjamin	3	1	3	4	
Wait, Fortune				4	
Reynolds, Jonathan	5		5		
Arnold, Joseph	3		3		
Reynolds, Henry	1	3	4		
Congdon, William	1		3		
Tillinghast, Daniel	2	1	4		
Tillinghast, Samuel	2	1	1		
Bently, Benidick	1		2		
Tillinghast, Pardon	1	2	3	1	
Peirce, Paul (Negro)				6	
Dawly, Nathan	1		2		
Dawly, Shebnah	1	2	4		
Dawly, Elizabeth (widow)			2		
Reynolds, George	1	2	2		
Gardner, Nicholas, Esqʳ	1	2	1		7
Gardner, William	1	2		1	
Gardner, Nicholas, Jun	5		5		

NAME OF HEAD OF FAMILY.	Free white males of 16 years and upward, including heads of families.	Free white males under 16 years.	Free white females, including heads of families.	All other free persons.	Slaves.
EXETER TOWN—con.					
Gardner, Vincent	1		2		1
Gardner, James (of Nicholas)	1	2	3		
Gardner, Hanah		1	2		1
Sweet, John, Jun	1	1	4		
Chapel, Frederick	1	4	1		
Harvey, Hanah		1	1		
Sunderland, Daniel, Esqʳ	2	1	3		1
Sunderland, Augustus	1		2		
Sunderland, Daniel, Jun	1	1	5		
Sweet, Jonathan	1	3	5		1
Smith, Jeremiah	1	2	3		
Smith, Ebenezer	1		2		
Hammond, Joseph	1	3	6		3
Hammond, John	2		5		
Albro, William	4	1	6		
Enos, Ichabod	3	1	5		
Holloway, William	5		2		
Browning, Isaac	4		3		
Potter, Pero				2	
Potter, William (Yako)	4		3	1	
Bates, David	3	4	4	1	
Bently, Abigail			3		
Whitford, David	1	1	3		
Bramin, James	1	3	2		
Champlin, Elisha	1	1	2		
Babcock, Jonathan	2	1	2		
Rathbun, Obadiah	1	1			
Dawly, Peleg	1	3	4		
Burchill, Thomas (Indian)				6	
Arnold, Oliver	1		5		
Arnold, Caleb	4		3	1	
Money, Joseph	1	2	5		
Money, Samuel	1	3	3		
Card, John	1	3	4		
Austin, Thomas	1		2		
Arnold, Josias	3	4	3		
Herrington, William	1	2	2		
Sherman, Moses	2	1	3		
Sherman, Moses, Jun	2	1	3		
Mowry, Joseph	2	3	3		
Bramin, Content (widow)	2	1	3		
Bramin, William	1	3	4		
Eldridge, Sylvester	1	1	1		
Sunderland, Augustus, Jun	1				
Armstrong, Edward	1	3	4		
Weeden, Benjamin	1		2		
Champlin, Freelove		4	5		1
Trip, Charles	1	1	2		
Albro, William	1	3	2		
Sunderland, Daniel, yᵉ 3ᵈ	1	1	6		
Dawly, Nicholas	1	1	2		
Dawly, David	1	3	3		
Dawly, William	1	3	5		
Champlin, John	2		3		
Champlin, Samuel	1	2	4		
Champlin, Thomas	1	2	3		
Dawly, Benjamin	2	3	7		
Dawly, Oliver	2	4	7		
Trip, Martha (widow)			3		
Dawly, Ephraim	1	1	2		
Gardner, Nicholas (of George)	3	2	2		
Trip, Perigrine	2		3		
Sherman, Reynolds	1	1	3		
Young, Caleb	3		3		
Gardner, Rowland	1	3	1		
Gardner, Stephen	1	4	3		
Mowry, John	2	2	5		
Tillinghast, Braddock				4	
Potter, Freeman	1		2		
Ginidore, Peter	1	1	2		
Freeborne, Gideon	1	1	1		
Josylin, Henry	1	2	3		
Herrington, William	1		2		
Mowry, Christopher	1	1	1		
Hitt, Sweet	1	1	1		
Austin, Amos	1	1	2		
Whitford, Ezeikel	1		2		2
Rathbun, Mary & Sarah Austin			2		
Chapman, Isaac	1		2		3
Brown, Sherman	1	2	2		
Herrington, Henry	4	1	7	1	1
Hamilton, Othniel	1	2	5		1
Greene, Benjamin	2		2		
Reynolds, George	1	2	1		
Reynolds, Abigail	1		1		
Gardner, Abel	1	2	3		
Whitman, Daniel	4	1	5		

WASHINGTON COUNTY—Continued.

EXETER TOWN—con.

Name of head of family.	Free white males of 16 years and upward, including heads of families.	Free white males under 16 years.	Free white females, including heads of families.	All other free persons.	Slaves.
Congdon, Desire			1		
Reynolds, Ceasar				7	
Bates, Jonathan	2		1		
Champlin, Christopher	2	2	5		1
Peirce, Christopher	3	1	3		1
Whitman, Stephen	1		3		2
Greene, William	2		1		
Reynolds, John	1	1	2		
Coggeshall, Christopher	1	1	1		
Gardner, Mary	1		2		
Brown, Alexander	2		3		
Hall, Daniel	1	1	3		
Holloway, Joseph	1		3		
Brown, Jonathan	1	3	3		
Brown, Charles, ye 3d	1	4	2		
Hall, Abigail		2	2		
Cecil, Rodman	1	3	4	4	
Barber, Ezeikel	2	1	3		
Hoxie, Elijah	1	4	5		
Spencer, Samuel	1	2	4		
Albro, Henry	2	4	3		
Chace, Daniel	1		2		
Brown, Samuel, Jun	1	3	2		
Button, Lodowick	1	1	1		
Tillinghast, Philip (of Pardon)	1	1	2		
Bently, Mary	1		2		
Holmes, Toby				2	
Clerk, James	3	2	3		
Case, Nathan	1		4		
Rhodes, John	1	1	3		1
Reynolds, Robert	1	1		1	
Reynolds, Robert, Jun	2	2	4		
Bently, Benjamin	2	2	6		
Corey, Gideon	1	1	2		
Wait, Benjamin	2	2	5		
Case, Thomas	1	2	2		
Button, John	4		1		
Button, Samuel	4		1		
Barker, Patience		1	1		
Albro, John, Jun	1	2	6		
Lawton, Benjamin	4	1	5		
Gardner, Nicholas (of Ezeikel)	1	2	6	1	
Shaw, Anthony	2	3	6		
Smith, William	1		1		
Hill, Davis	1		2		
Albro, Thomas	2	1	2		
Josylin, John, Jun	1	4	2		
Josylin, Clerk	1	1	4		
Josylin, John	2	1	5		1
Dawly, Daniel	1	1	3		
Cobb, John	1	2	3		
Tabor, Benjamin	2	2	3		
Huskins, Joseph	1	2	3		
Hill, Barnes	1		6	1	
Rathbun, George	1	1	1		
Josylin, Sylvester	1	1	2		
Rathbun, Joseph	1	1	4		
Rathbun, Joseph (negro)				3	
Benjamin, David	1	3	2		
Davis, William	1	1	2		
Benjamin, Jonathan	1		3		
Smith (Widow)	1		3		
Targee, Peter	1	1			
Pendleton, Jeremiah	1	1	3		
Tillinghast, Stephen	1		2		
Sweet, George	1		2		
Sweet, Jarvis	1	4	4		
Herrington, David	2	1	9		
Arnold, Caleb, Jun	1	4	3		
Arnold, Gideon	1		3		
Arnold, Peleg	1	1	3		
Cottrell, John	2	1	1		
Northup, Benjamin, Jun	1		2		
Benjamin, Thomas	1		2		
Tanner, Thomas	1		3	1	
Smith, Samuel	1		1		
Tillinghast, Stukely	4	2	9		
Tillinghast, Steven	1	2	1		
Allen, Joseph	2	4	2		
Davis, Benajah	1	3	2	2	
Dawly, Michael	1	4	4		
Austin, Ezeikel	1	3	4		
James, Steven	2	2	2		
Reynolds, Henry	1	3	6		
Phillips, Samuel	1	3	2		
Babcock, James	1		3		
Whitman, George	1		1		
Bissel, Samuel	1	1	1		
Bissel, David	1	2	2		
McGuire, John	1	1	3		
Gardner, John, Jun	1	1	6		
Reynolds, Benjamin	2	1	2		
Gardner, Abel	3		3		
Champlin, Nathaniel	1	1	1		
Weeden, Thomas	1	1	2		
Clerk, Benjamin	1	1	2		
Pilsbury, Tobias	2		3		
Allen, Pardon	2	3	3		
Brown, Beriah, 2d	1	1	5		
Potter, Benjamin	1		2		
Whitford, Amos	3	3	3		
Freeborn, Gideon	1	1	1		
Guinidore, Louis	1	1	2		
Arnold, Josias	3	4	3		
Josylin, Henry	1	2	3		
Vaughn, Sylva				3	
Carr, John	1	3	4		
Austin, Thomas	1				
Whitford, John	2	2	5		1
Grinnel, Jonathan	2	5	3		
Nile, Nathaniel (of Jeremiah)	1		2		
Trip, Peleg	1		2		
Lewis, Sylvester	3		3		
Lewis, Caleb	1	2	1		
Boone, Richard	2	3	6		
Corey, Sheffield	1	1	2		
Lewis, Stephen	1	3	6		
Wilcox, Mary (widow)			3		
Gorten, Samuel	3	4	5		
Barber, William	1	2	2		
Reynolds, Demas (negro)				1	
Sheldon, Roger	1	3	3		
Bates, Morey	1	4	2		
Terry, William	1	3	4		
Phillips, Freeman	1	1	3		
Lillibridge, John	2	1	4		
Wilcox, Isaac	2	5	5		2
Allen, Samuel	1	3	3		
Wilcox, Abraham	3	2	3		2
Robinson, John (negro)				5	
Pulman, Mary			2		1
Lewis, Jonathan	1		1		
Lewis, Jonathan, Jun	1	4	5		
Lewis, Benjamin	1	4	3		
Lewis, Solomon	2		3		
Wilcox, Ebenezer	1	4	6		
Watson, Nicholas	1		1		
Baker, Joseph	3	1	4		
Perkins, Paul	1	1	4		
Perkins, Ebenezer	4	1	3		
Perkins, Newman	1		1		
Perkins, Uriah	2	3	1		
Hazard, Jeofry	1	1	4		
Young, Elias	1	1	4		
Rathbun, John	3	1	2		
Rathbun, Daniel	1	1	4		
Gates, Caleb	1	1	4		
Rathbun, John, Jun	1	3	4		
Rathbun, Gideon	3	3	2		
Rathbun, Green	1		1		
Ireby, John	1	1	4		
Rathbun, Simeon	2	2	7		
Lewis, Jacob	1				
Lewis, Asa	1	1	1		
Lewis, Obadiah	1				
Lewis, Elizabeth		1	4		
Matthewson, Joseph	1	2	5		
Rathbun, Elias	1	1	4		
Bouroughs, Joseph	1	1	4		
Rous, Elias	1	1	2		
Allen, Benjamin	1		1		
Wilbore, John	1	2	3		
Rathbun, Joshua	1	2			
Reynolds, James	3		3		
Codner, George	1	1	2		
Tanner, Gideon	1	2	1		
Merris, John	1	1	3		
Rathbun, Rowland	1				
Rathbun, Parish	1	2	5		
Merris, William	1		3		
Bates, John	1	1	1		
Rathbun, Nathan	1	1	2		
Crandal, Joseph	1	1	4		
Cottrell, Samuel	2	1	2		
Church, Benedict	2	2	2		
Cottrell, Samuel, Jun	1	1	2		
Reynolds, Gardner	2	1	2		
Cottrell, David	2	1	5		
Weaver, Peter	2		1		
Champlin, Benjamin	2		1		1
Champlin, Daniel	1	1	1		
Browning, Isaac	4	1	3		
Fish, Joseph	2	3	1		
Sherman, Cuff (Negro)				7	
Potter, Pero				6	
Tisdale, Joseph	1	2	5		
Browning, Daniel	1	1	1		
Southwick, Jonathan	1		1		
Southwick, Aaron	1	1	1		
Holloway, William	4	1	2		
Belcher, Joseph	1	2	2		
Whitford, David	1	1	4		
King, Earl	3	2	2		
Reynolds, John	1		3		
Sherman, Robert	1	6	3		
Sherman, Cuff				5	
Champlin, Jeofry	2	1	2		
Champlin, William	1	2	3		
Champlin, Benjamin, Jun	2	1	2		1
Champlin, Daniel	1				
Sherman, Benajah	3	3	4		
Fish, Benjamin	1	2	4		
Cottrell, David	2	1	5		
Weaver, Peter	1		1		
Carpenter, Thomas	2	3	1		
Foster, Anthony	1		2		
Townsend, George	1		3		
Lock, Joseph	1	2	3		
Wilcox, Noah	1	4	2		
Wilcox, Elijah	1	2	6		
James, William	2	2	3		
James, Stephen	1	2	2		
Bently, Caleb	1	2	3		
Moor, David	1		1		
Lawton, Timothy	1	2	4		
Wilcox, Susanna			2		
Wilcox, Robert	1	3	1		
Sherman, Ebez	1	3	4		
Brown, Sherman	1	2	2		
Sprague, Docter Solomon	4	2	7		
Rogers, Jonathan	1	1	1		
Reynolds, Joseph	2	3	3		
Lewis, James	1	4	8		
Lewis, Joseph	1	3	4		
Wilcox, George	1	2	2		
Greene, Joseph	1	1	1		
Jaques, Wilson	1	3	1		
Palmer, Ezra	1	2	2		
Palmer, Amos	1	3	4		
Kinyon, Phineas	2	1	2		
Morgan, Wheeler	1	1	5		
Onion, Ceasar				1	
Sherman, Reynolds	1	2	2		
Barber, Josias	1	2	3		
Money, Joseph	3	1	5		
Money, Samuel	1	3	3		
Hymes, William	1	2	1		
Hymes, James	1	1	3		
Bates, John	1	6	3		
Crandal, Mary (widow)	2	1	4		
Pettis, Nash	2	4	4		
Crandal, John	1	2	5		
Kinyon, John	1	2	5		
Palmer, Amos, Jun	1	3	4		
Richmond, Edward	1				
Watson, Stephen		2	2		
Richmond, Stephen	1	5	3		
Wilcox, Thurston	1		5		
Richmond, John	1	2	2		
Barber, Jonathan	1	2	4		1
Barber, Asa	1	3	2		
Barber, Daniel	2		2		
Barber, Daniel, Jun	3	4	3		
Wilcox, Capt Job	4	4	6		
Bates, Samuel	1		1		
Barber, Moses	1	4	2		
Lawton, Josias, Jun	1	4	2		
Lawton, Josias	2		2		
Lawton, Thomas	1	3	1		
Mowry, Amos	1		4		
Mowry, Robert	1		3		
Terry, Silas	1		3		
Northup, Benjamin	1	3	4		
Codner, Ephraim	1	3	4		
Bates, John	1	1	3		
Strange, William	1	1	3		
Barber, Benjamin	1	1	3		2
Nigh, John	1	1	2		
Nigh, Isaac	1		4		
Terry, Elnathan	2		4		
Terry, Seth	2	1	4		
Lewis, John	1		3		
Lewis, Samuel	2		3		
Lewis, Abigail			3		

WASHINGTON COUNTY—Continued.

Name of head of family.	Free white males of 16 years and upward, including heads of families.	Free white males under 16 years.	Free white females, including heads of families.	All other free persons.	Slaves.
EXETER TOWN—con.					
Barber, Lillibridge	4	2	3		
Sherdon, Joseph	1	3	4		
Spink, Oliver	2	1	4		
Barber, Nathaniel	3	1	4	1	
Browning, John	1	4	5	1	
Lewis, Elisha	1	3	4		
Reynolds, Stephen	1	5	5		
Tift, Nathan	1		4		
Tift, Sprague	1	1	1		
Lewis, Benoni	1				
Moone, Sandford	2		2		
Moone, Ebenezer	1	3	3		
James, Joseph	1	2	4		
Hoxie, John	2	3	5		
Hoxie, John, Jun	1	3	3	1	
Wilcox, John	1	3	1		
HOPKINTON TOWN.					
Barber, Josias	1	2	3		
Phillips, John	4	2	3		
Goodbit, Samuel	1	1	1		
Griffin, James	3	3	5		
Hoxie, William	1	2	3		
Kinyon, Stanton	2	3	2		
Kinyon, Benjamin, yᵉ 2d	2	1	3		
Kinyon, Steven	1	2	3		
Bilgood, John	1	4	3		
Burdick, Jesse	1	1			
Merris, Phelix	1	3	3		
Merris, Samuel	1		2		
Maxin, George	2	3	4		
Crandal, Luke	1	2	3		
Merris, Henry	1	4	6		
Larkin, David	1	2	4		
Larkin, John	1	1	2		
Saunders, William	2		1		
Saunders, Joshua	2		2		
Saunders, Uriah	2	1	5		
Maxin, Zackeus	1	1	5		
Saunders, Henry	1	1	4		
Tanner, William	1	2	4		
Wells, John	1	1	2		
West, Henry	1		2		
Maxin, Benjamin	1		1		
Crandal, Benjamin	1	1	3	2	
Burdick, Stephen	4	6	2		
Burdick, Luke	1	4	2		
High, Benjamin	1		1		
Brigs, Jacob	1		1		
Burdick, Perry	1		3		
Maxin, Daniel	1		1		
Granger, Molly		1	3		
Crandal, Rowland	1	1	1		
Clerk, Jesse	1	2	2		
Crandal, Samuel	1	1	3		
Peckham, Stephen	1	2	2		
Clerk, Daniel	1		2		
Lamphere, Ebenezer	1	2	3		
Maxin, Nathan	6		2		
Burdick, William	1	6	3		
Burdick, Peter	1		1		
Burdick, Elnathan	1	3	1		
Wright, John	2	3	2		
Barber, William	1	1	3		
Dyre, Jonathan	1	2	1		
Clerk, David	1	4	3		
Griffin, Joshua	1	4	3		
Brown, John	4	4	9		
Brown, James	1	1	2		
Brown, John, Jun	1	1	2		
Leynard, Elijah	1	1	3		
Popple, William	1	1	4		
Church, Joshua	1	2	3		
Pendleton, Zebedy	1	1	3		
Cheesbrook, James	1		1		
Hyde, John	1	6	4		
Hall, Elijah	1	1	1		
Larkin, Gideon	1		1		
Church, Lodowick	1		3		
Carpenter, Hezekiah	1	1	3		
Davis, Aaron	1	1	5		
Clerk, Pardon	1	3	4		
Barber, Reynolds	3	4	4		
Essex, David	1	3	3		
Barber, Moses	1	2	3		
Barber, Nathan	1	3	4		
Barber, Benjamin	1	4	5		
Foster, Gideon	1	2	4		
Potter, Jonathan	2	4	4		
High, Caleb	3		3		
Kinyon, Samuel	1				
Mowry, Hazard	1	1	1	1	
Crandal, James	1	2	2		
Coone, Joshua	1		6	2	

Name of head of family.	Free white males of 16 years and upward, including heads of families.	Free white males under 16 years.	Free white females, including heads of families.	All other free persons.	Slaves.
HOPKINTON TOWN—con.					
Coone, Joshua, Jun	1		1		
Styles, Izrail	1		2		
Winter, Josiah	2		6		
Champlin, Samuel	1	1	1		
Tanner, Abel	1	3	7		
Kinyon, Peter	1	1	2		
Kinyon, Mary (widow)		1	2		
Patterson, Amos	1		4		
Davis, Aaron	1	3	2		
Coone, Abraham	1	3	2		
Taylor, Benjamin	2		2		
Cottrell, William	1	1	3		
Wilbore, Clerk	1	1	4		
Hill, Josiah	1		2		
Champlin, Jeofry	1	6	2		
Thurston, Gardner	1	2	1		
Palmeter, Joseph	1	4	2		
Wells, Thomson	2		10		
Wells, Thomas	1	2	4		
Clerk, Nathan	1		2		
Utter, Abraham	2	3	4		
Lewis, Izrail	1	4	6		
Burdick, Joshua	1		2		
Lewis, March	2		2		
Peckham, Robert	1		2		
Basset, William	1	3	3		
Peckham, Daniel	1	3	4		
Wells, Matthew	1	4	3		
Wilbore, Thomas	3	2	4		
Wilbore, William	1	1	1		
Slocum, Samuel	1	6	6		
Mowry, Gideon	1	1	5		
Collins, John	2	4	2		
Button, Josiah	3	1	3		
Button, George	1		1		
Coone, Ross	1		1		
Lewis, Paul	1	2	4		
Lewis, Greene	1	1	2		
Lewis, Eleanor	1	1	2		
Button, Syrus	1		1		
Langworthy, Amos	3	1	6		
Crum, Daniel	1	4	3		
Crandal, Benajah	1	1	1		
Stanbury, James	1	3	3		
Carey, Crandal	1	3	2		
Collins, Hezekiah	2	1	3		
Robinson, Ann (widow)			1		
Burdick (Elder)	2	2	2		
Burdick, Phineas	1		3		
Burdick, Phineas, Jun	1	6	2		
Button, Joseph	3	1	1		
Burdick, Jesse, Jun	1	2	3		
Crandal, Samuel	3	1	3		
Dyre, Jonathan	1	2	3		
Button, Daniel	1	1	3		
Odel, Joseph	1		1		
Burdick, Joseph, Jun	1	2	3		
Coone, Asa	3	3	4		
Coone, David	1	4	4		
Button, Rufus	1		3		
Button, Abel	1		3		
Sheffield, Samuel	1	4	4		
Burdick, John	3	1	2		
Burdick, John, Jun	1	2	3		
Clerk, David	1	3	3		
Burdick, Ebenezer	1	5	2		
Vincent, Nicholas	1	2	7		
Bently, Norman	1		1		
Saunders, Caleb	1		1		
Coone, Benjamin	1	5	3		
Verner, Bowen	1		1		
Carpenter, Daniel	1	2	3		
Barber, Levy	1	2	3		
Venner, John	1	3	3		
Bromly, Rowland	2	2	1	1	
Saunders, George	1	1	1		
Button, Joseph	1	1	1		
Button, Daniel, Jun	1	1	3		
Maxin, Abel	1	2	2		
Burdick, Joel	1	2	3		
Davis, Oliver	1	4	5		
Healy, Joseph	1	3	1		
Lawton, Joseph	1		4		
Dye, Michael	1	2	5		
Lewis, Elias	1		5		
Lewis, Daniel	1	2	3		
Wells, Jonathan	1		5		
Wells, Elnathan	2	1	6		
Wilbore, Woodman	1	1	2		
Wilbore, Gideon	1		5		
White, Godfrey	1	3	3		
Studson, Thomas	1	1	1		
Crandal, Joseph	1	2	4		
Gardner, Stephen (Indian)				10	

Name of head of family.	Free white males of 16 years and upward, including heads of families.	Free white males under 16 years.	Free white females, including heads of families.	All other free persons.	Slaves.
HOPKINTON TOWN—con.					
Tim, Sarah (Indian)				4	
Palmer, John	1	1	1		
Popple, George	1	2	2		
Potter, Caleb	1	3	4		
Champlin, Samuel	1		3		
Winter, Josias	1	2	5		
Thurston, Joseph	3	5	2		
Thurston, William	4	2	6		
Weaver, Zebulon	1	3	5		
Winter, Samuel	1	3	4		
Winter, John	1		1		
Edwards, Perry	1		4		
Winter, Joseph	1		1		
Winter, Joseph, Jun	1		1		
Winter, William	1	3	7		
Crandal, James	1	1	4		1
Coone, William, Jun	1	1	3		
Davis, Niles	1	4	2		
Babcock, Paul	1	1	4		
Crandal, Christopher	1	3	5		
Collins, Joseph	3	2	5		
Palmer, Nathan	1	3	3		
Holloway, Joseph	1	4	2		
Hull, John	1	1	1		
Kinyon, George	4	2	6		
Hall, Jonathan, Jun	1	1	4		
Larkins, Timothy	3	3	5		
Collins, Jabez	2	2	5		
Collins, Samuel	1	1	1		
Palmer, Laten	1		3		
Sheldon, William	1	1	1		
Peirce, Nanny		1	2		
Sheldon, Potter	1		2		
Potter, Judith			2		
Hoxie, Stephen	1		1		
Collins, Joseph, Jun	1	2	2		
Babcock, Hezekiah	3	2	7	4	
Will, Exchange				6	
Merrit, Felix	1	4	4		
Merrit, Henry	1	4	6		
Palmer, Nathaniel	1	3	2		1
Holloway, Joseph	1	3	4		
Kinyon, George	2	2	3		
Perry, Simeon, Jun	1	3	5		
Babcock, James	1		2		
Wells, James	2	1	6	5	
Gardner, Samuel (Deacon)	4	1	8		
Clerk, Thomas	2	10	8		
Babcock, Samuel	2	3	4	2	1
Congdon, John	1		1		
Lewis, Jesse	3		4		
Wall, Henry	1		4		
Barber, Thomas	5	2	4	5	
Barber, Zebulon	1	1	3		
Gardner, Potter	1	1	5		
Hall, Ephraim	1	1	1		
Brown, Samuel	1		1		
Davis, Mary			3		
Varon, Joseph	1	2	1		
Coone, Elias	2	2	6		
Coone, William	2	2	5		
Coone, Samuel	1	2	4		
Coone, Stephen	1	1	1		
White, Godfrey	2	3	5		
Wilbore, Woodman	1	1	2		
Wilbore, Gideon	1		2		
Coone, John	1		2		
Saunders, Thomas	1	2	4		
Kinyon, Wells	1	2	3		
Babcock, Lucas	1	2	1		
Langworthy, Samuel	1	5	6		
Lamphere, Pardon	1	1	1		
Burdick, Robert	1	3	4		
Burdick, Clerk, Jun	1	1	1		
Coone, Peleg	1		4		
White, Daniel	1		5		
Clerk, Josias	1	1	3	3	
Babcock, Oliver	3		1		1
Maxin, Samuel, Jun	2	3	3		
Wells, Joshua	3	3	4		
Aldridge, Doctor John	1	1	4		
Wells, Rebecca (widow)	1	2	2		1
Wilbore, Woodman	1	1	4		
Wilbore, Gideon	1		4		
Cheap, Nanny (Indian)				3	
Maxin, Amos	1		1		
Babcock, Simeon	2	1	2		
Maxin, John	1	1	4		
Maxin, John, Jun	1	2	3		
White, Roger	1		1		
White, Oliver	1		3		
Maxin, Elisha	1	1	2		
Maxin, Samuel, Sen	1	1	4		
Maxin, Joseph	1		2		

WASHINGTON COUNTY—Continued.

NAME OF HEAD OF FAMILY.	Free white males of 16 years and upward, including heads of families.	Free white males under 16 years.	Free white females, including heads of families.	All other free persons.	Slaves.
HOPKINTON TOWN—con.					
Wells, Clerk	1	1	2		
Maxin, Sylvanus	3	2	4	1	
Babcock, Daniel	4	2	4		
Crandal, Amherst	1	2	1		
Kinyon, Benjamin	3	1	3		
Langworthy, Joseph	1	3	4		
Wells, Samuel	1	1	2	2	
Wells, Randall	1	4		3	
Wells, Edward	1		2	1	
Champlin, George	1	3	3		
Burdick, Elias	1	1	1		
Hiscock, Simeon	1	11	5		
Wells, Thomas (Elder)	1	1	2		
Wells, Amos	1	1	2		
Clossen, Nathan	1	3	3		
Wells, Joshua, Sen	1	1	3		
Grinman, Silas	1		2		
Burdick, Henry	1	3	2		
Babcock, Sarah (Indian)				5	
Kinyon, James	1		1		
Maxin, Coll. Jesse	3	2	4	1	
Peckham, Avis			3		
Maxin, Isaiah	1	1	2		
Maxin, Clerk	1	4	3		
Maxin, Paul	1		3		
Clerk, Nathan	2	2	3		
Maxin, Perry	1	2	4		
Langworthy, Thomas	3	1	6		
Cole, Joseph	2	1	1	1	
Thurston, Coll. George	3	1	5		
Lewis, Mary		1	2	3	
Maxin, William	1	1	4		
Maxin, William, Jun	2	2	8	1	
Reynolds, Zackeus	1	1	7	1	
Palmer, Jones	1		3		
Reynolds, Clerk	1	3	3	1	
Crandal, James	1	2	4		
Clerk, Joshua (Elder)	1		1		
Clerk, Job	1	1	3	1	
Cheesbrook, Christopher	1	1	2		
Cheesbrook, James	1		1		
Pendleton, Zebulon	1	1	3		
Rogers, Amos	1	2	1		
Coone, Benjamin	1	5	3		
Burdick, Phineas	1	5	4		
Burdick, John	1				
Lewis, Greene	1	1	2		
Lewis, Paul	1	1	5		
Allen, Pearceful	2		1		
Kinyon, Samuel	2		2		
Carpenter, Daniel	1	3	5		
Kinyon, Nathaniel	1		1		
Kinyon, Nathaniel, Jun	1	1	2		
Harvey, James	2		2		
Saunders, William	1		3		
Saunders, Henry	1	1	4		
Tanner, William	1	2	4		
Tanner, Joshua	1	7	1		
Larkin (Widow)	1		2		
Lamphire, Joshua	1	2	6		
Burdick, Joseph	3	4	5		
Bromby, Thomas	1	1	2		
Stillman, Elisha	1	2	4		
Brightman, Thomas	1	1	6		
Kinyon, Thomas	1	1	1		
Brightman, Joseph	1	2	2		
Cheesbrook, Harris	1	1	1		
Champlin, Parish	1		1		
Bramin, John	1		2		
Brown, Chris	2		2		
Brightman, Henry	1	3	5		
Sheffield, Samuel	1	4	4		
Church, Caleb, Sen	1	2	6		
Larkin, Tabathy			4		
Church, Caleb (of Joshua)	1	4	2		
Popple, John	1	4	1		
Hall, Asil	1	1	1		
Hall, Moses	1		4		
Hoxie, Steven	1		4		
Brown, Zepheniah	3	6	5		
Coone, David	1	3	6		
Wells, Matthew, Jun	1		2		
Barber, Levy	1	2	3		
Sheffield, Samuel	2	3	3		
Foster, David	1		4		
Edwards, Phineas	3	1	5		
Rogers, Anthony	1	3	3		
Brown, Molly (widow)		1	3		
Clerk, Jesse	1	2	5		
Crandal, James	1	4	3		
Palmer, Amos	1	1	4		
Clerk, Ephraim	1		2		
Saunders, Caleb	1				

NAME OF HEAD OF FAMILY.	Free white males of 16 years and upward, including heads of families.	Free white males under 16 years.	Free white females, including heads of families.	All other free persons.	Slaves.
HOPKINTON TOWN—con.					
Burdick, Joseph	2	1	1		
Clerk, Daniel	1		4		
Burdick, Elnathan	1	2	4		
Burdick, Peter	1		2		
Burdick, Rebecca			3		
Merriott, Samuel	3	4	5		
Saunders, George	1		2		
Crandal, Benjamin	1	2	3		
Maxin, Daniel	1		4		
Maxin, Martha		1	5		
Maxin, Nathan	1	3	3		
Burdick, Willis	2	2	3		
Burdick, Amos	1		2		
Kinyon, Elizabeth	2	2	2		
Griffin, James	1	2	3		
Burdick, Perry	1	2	1		
Josylin (Elder)	1	2	2		
Maxin, Zackeus	1	2	5		
Burdick, Luke	1	4	3		
Burdick, Steven	1	4	2		
Burdick, Abel	1	4	4		
Palmer, Amos, Jun	1	3	4		
Larkin, Nathan	1	1	4		
High, Benjamin	1		1		
Briggs, Jacob	1	8	5		
Wells, John	1		3		
Saunders, William	1	1	3		
Saunders, Joshua	4		1		
West, Henry	1	3	1		
Saunders, Henry	1	4	4		
Lamphire, Ebenezer	1	5	4		
Gardner, John (Elder)	4	4	1		
Gardner, John, Jun	1	3	3		
Saunders, Thomas	1	2	3		
Potter, Caleb	2	3	5		
Kinyon, Wells	1		4		
Herrick, Benjamin	2		1		
Nichols, David	1	3	2		
Hall, William	4	3	3		
Davis (Widow)			2	3	
Lewis, Elias, Jun	1	2	2		
White, Mary (Widow)		4	2		
Burdick, Robert, Jun	1	3	4		
Burdick, Charles	4		2		
Larkin, Timothy	3	3			2
NORTH KINGSTOWN TOWN.					
Gardner, William	1	6	3	1	
Tenant, George	2	1	7		
Brenton, Samᵘ	4		3	3	
Dayton, Benedict	2	5	3		
Cooper, James	2	1	2		
Case, Imanuel	2		3		
Cooper, Edmund	1		1		
Cooper, Gilbert	2		3		
Hyams, George	1	3			
Brown, Wait (Widow)			1		
Eldridge, Robert	2		2		
Reynolds, Abel	1	1	2		
Williams, Israil	1		2		
Healy, James	1				
Tallman, James	1		2		
Gould, James	1		2		
Baily, Ely	2	4	4		
Updike, Richard	2		1		
Updike, Daniel	1	1	1		
Reynolds, William	2	5	2	1	
Thomas, Samuel	1	2	3		
Baker, Elisha	1	5	1		
Cozzens, John	2	2	3		
Fowler, Benjamin	1	2	2		
Carter, Thankfull (widow)	1	3	3		
Parish, Docter William	1	2	2	1	
Smith, William	2		2		
Cooper, Updike	1	1	2		
Henly, Matthew	1	1	1		
Cooper, Cresy & Nancy			2		
Whitford, Elizabeth			2		
Cutter, Thomas		1	8		
Bates, Jonathan	2	3	2		
Wall, Daniel	1	2	3		
Corey, Job	1	3	4		
Peckham, Benjamin	1	3	4		
Cole, Thomas	1	3	2	1	
Herrington, Eben	1		5		
Phillips, Peter	2		2		
Taylor, Spencer	1	2			
Bally, Samuel	1		5		
Gates, Asa	1	1	3		
Northup, Stephen	1	2	4		

NAME OF HEAD OF FAMILY.	Free white males of 16 years and upward, including heads of families.	Free white males under 16 years.	Free white females, including heads of families.	All other free persons.	Slaves.
NORTH KINGSTOWN TOWN—continued.					
Reynolds, Mary			2		
Northup, Francis (widow)			3		
Updike, James (Negro)				7	
Whitman, John	1	2	2		1
Fowler, George	1		2		
Bissel, John	1	1	5		
Baker, Benjamin	2	4	3	2	
Reynolds, Benjamin	2	2	3		
Reynolds, Tanner	1	2	1		
Peirce, Mary (Widow)			3		
Peirce, Joseph	1	1	3	1	
Peirce, John	1		2		
Peirce, David	1	1	1		
Tenant, Benajah	1		1		
Reynolds, Jonathan	1	3	3		
Barber, Edmund	1	1	1		
Phillips, Richard	3	1	3		
Brown, Benjamin	1		3		
Weathers, Thomas	1		1		
Manny & Robert (Negro)				4	
Weathers, Abel			3		
Updike, Lodowick	4	3	6	4	3
Hall, Slocum	2	4	3		1
Hall, William	1		1		3
Whitman, James	1	4	4		
Smith, Ephraim	2	1	2		
Rathbun, Roger	2	4	4		
Coggeshall, Joseph	1		2		1
Bently, Akus	1	1	1		
Boone, Mary	3	2	3		
Peckham, Benedict	2	1	5		
Thomas, George, Esqʳ	2	1	4		2
Thomas, George, Junʳ	1	3	1		
Onion, Nathaniel (Indian)				7	
Allen, William	1		2		
Cranston, Thomas (of Thomas)	2		3		
Phillips, Samuel (of Thomas)	2	2	3		3
Lawton, Job	1	2	5		
Eldridge, Joseph	2	2	7	1	
Whitehorn, Samuel	1		4		
Card, Bowen	1	5	2		
Carr, Samuel	2	2	4		
Phillips, Elizabeth (widow)		2	5		
Westcoat, John	2		4		1
Corey, Ruth		2	4		
Eldridge, Henry	1	3	2		
Brown, Scipeo				6	
Alsbro, Robert	1	2	2		
Wait, Beriah	3	5	3		1
Taylor, Nathaniel	1	2	3		
Congdon, James, Esqʳ	2	1	3		
Sweet, Stephen	1	3	4		
Sandford, Isbon	2	1	2		
Dyre, Collᵒ Charles	2	2	4		2
Bissel, Thomas	1		1		2
Bissel, John, Sen	1		2		
Bissel, George	1		2		
Bissel, Samuel	1	2	3		
Northup, Nicholas	1	1	4	1	
Place, John	1	1	1		
Cranston, Thomas (of John)	1	1	5		
Place, Sarah (Widow)			4		
Northup, Capᵗ Henry	1	3	4		5
Cole, William	1	2	4		
Cole, John	2	1			
Northup, Joseph	2	2	3		
Munro, Nathan	1	5	3		
Piggin, Robert (Indian)				1	
Douglass, Barzilla	2	4	4		
Congdon, Stephen	1		4	2	
Congdon, Ann (widow)			2		
Sherman, John (Widow)			2		
Taylor, Collᵒ Joseph	1	1	3		1
Northup, Ceasar				4	
Austin, Polopus	1	2	4		
Rome, Tuba (Negro)				9	
Greene, David			2		3
Greene, David, Jun	1	3	3	1	
Greene, Jonathan	1	1	2		
Allen, Capᵗ Matthew	2		2		2
Reynolds, James	3	3	5		
Douglass, James	1	1	1		
Congdon, James	3	4	6		
Gardner, Maj. Sylvester	3		2	2	
Gardner, Capᵗ James	4	1	3	1	
Gardner, Chris	3	1	3	4	

WASHINGTON COUNTY—Continued.

NORTH KINGSTOWN TOWN—con.

NAME OF HEAD OF FAMILY.	Free white males of 16 years and upward, including heads of families.	Free white males under 16 years.	Free white females, including heads of families.	All other free persons.	Slaves.
Lawton, George	1	1	1		
Davis, Jeoffry	1	1	4		
Davis, Benjamin	1	1	3		
Bradford, Sarah (widow)	1		2	1	
Phillips, Major Samuel	2	2	5		3
Dyre, Thomas	1	2	4	1	
Vaughn, John	3	1	3		
Whitman, Paul	2	1	8		
Hall, William, Esqr	2		4	3	
Congdon, Stukely	1	1	1		
Carr, Oliver	1	2	3		
Reynolds, John	2		5		
Carpenter, Joshua	1	1	2		
Slocum, Ebenezer	1		2		
Sweet, Ezra	1	1	1		
Carpenter, Daniel	1	2	2		
Dyre, Charles, Junr	1	1	2		
Ellis, Gideon	1	4	10		
Chadsey, Jabez	1	2	5		
Peirce, Sylvester	1	3	5		
Jones, Josias	1	2	2		
Cottrell, John	2	6	2		2
Peirce, Joshua	2	1	4		4
Helme, Rous	1		1		
Mowry, Robert	3		4		
Tillinghast, John	2	1	5		
Lawton, Edward	2	5	4		
Dyre, Samuel	4	1	6		
Clerk, Thomas	2	4	6		1
Peirce, John	1	4	3		
Dyre, Esther			6		
James, Silas	2	2	4		
Hamilton, Frederick	2	5	4		
Clerk, Gardner	1		3		
Bently, Caleb	1	5	3		
Corey, Capt William	3	4	5		
Spink, John	1	5	4		
Spink, Ishmail	3	2	3		
Greene, John	3	1	4		
Spink, Nicholas	3	4	6		
Briggs, Sweet	1	5	2		
Allen, Christopher	3	1	4		
Spencer, Peleg	1	1	3		
Aylsworth, Arthur	3	1	5		
Aylsworth, Jeremiah	2	4	3		
Whitman, Holmes	2	2	2		
Spink, Josiah	1		2		
Allen, Jonathan	2		2		
Allen, Samuel	2	1	6		
Whitman, George	1	3	4		
Reynolds, George	2	3	5		
Spencer, William	1	1	2		1
Remington, William	3	2	5		
Allen, John	3	3	4		
Reynolds, Jabez	1	1	2		
Tenant, Havens	1	3	4		
George, Joshua (Indian)				3	
Studson, Judiah	1	1	2		
Hill, Caleb	1		4	1	
Hill, Caleb, Jun	1	2	2	1	
Briggs, Ebenezer	1		2		
Tibbits, Darkus (widow)	1	2	4		
Hill, Stukely	1	2	4		
Tanner, Benjamin	2	2	7		
Tanner, Palmer	1		2		
Dixon, Robert	2	1	2		
Whitford, Benjamin, Jun	1		4		
Whitford, Benjamin	1		1		
Targey, Peter	1		1		
Streight, Jonathan	1	1	1		
Hall, Newport (Indian)				5	
Austin, Henery	1		2		
Hunt, Jeremiah	3	2	8		
Essex, Corps	1	3	2		
Austin, James	1	3	5		
Hunt, William	1	2	3		
Hunt, Adam	1	1	6		
Hunt, George	1	1	2		
Hunt, Ezeikel	1		2		
Hunt, Bartholomew	1		2		
Hunt, Charles	4		5		
Hunt, Samuel	4		3		
Hunt, Hazleton	1	1	4		
Reynolds, Francis (of John)	1	3	5		
Reynolds, Henry (of John)	1	1	3		
Slocum, William	5		5		
Sweet, James	1	2	3		
Chadsey, Jabez	4		3		
Vaughn, Royal	2	1	2		
Warner, Samuel	2	2	6		
Jenkins, Philip	2		5		
Bowls, John	2		3		
Corey, Peleg	1	1	7		
Reynolds, John	1		1		
Reynolds, Benjamin	3	3	7		
Wall, William	1	1	1		
Campbell, Joseph	1	1	1		
Johnson, Sylvester	1	2	3		
Cooper, Steven	1	3	2		
Havens, Sylvester	2		1		
Havens, William	1	2	3		
Slocum, Peleg	1	3	5		
Gardner, Samuel	1	1	2		
Dixon, Charles	1	5	3		
Davis, Joshua	2	3	6	1	
Targee, John	1	1	3		
Maxfeild, Joseph	2	1	3		
Whitford, Thomas	1	5	4		
Scranton, Stafford	1	3	2		
Fones, William	1				
Tenant, John	1	4	5		
Fones, Joseph	2		6		
Card, Peleg	1	1	9		
Dawly, Daniel	1	6	5		
Helme, William	1	4	3		
Peirce, John (Quidneset)	1	4	4		
Carr, Caleb	1		1		
Fowler, John	1		3		
Bliss, Ephraim (Indian)				9	
Havens, Nathaniel	1	1	3		
Sweet, James	1	1	3		
Diamond, Elizabeth (widow)	1		4		
Briggs, Amos	1	1	5		
Spencer, William	1	5	5		
Nichols, Thomas	3		3		
Mitchell, Thomas	1	2	3		
Mitchel, Ephraim	3	1	4		
Nichols, George	1		2		
Briggs, William	2	1	3		
Spink, Nicholas	1	2	1		
Brown, Samuel	1		3		
Cleavland, John	1	1	3		
McKensie, Catharine	1	2	4		
Smith, Thomas	1		2		
Congdon, George, Jun	1		1		
Rathbun, Thomas	1	2	1		
Northup, James	2	4	1		
Congdon, Elizabeth		1	1		
Spencer, Patience (widow)	1	3	1		
Brown, William	4	2	4		
Rathbun, Anthony	1	3	4		
Rathbun, John	1	2	3		
Hymes, James	1	1	1		
Northup, Samuel	1	3	2		
Northup, Stephen (Swamptown)	1	2	3		
Arnold, Edmund (Enterd)					
Thomas, George (Swamptown)	1	2	5		
Vaughn, Daniel	2	1	4	1	
Hymes, Sylvester	4		4	5	
Congdon, George	2	3	8		
Congdon, John	1	3	4		
Congdon, Jonathan	2	4	3		
Northup, James	1	1	5		
Gardner, Pero (Negro)					5
Kingsly, Samuel	1	2	3		
Case, Joseph	5	2	5	1	4
Brown, Beriah	2		1		5
Huling, Alexander	2	1	4		
Wilkie, John	2	1	2		
Brown, Benedict	1	2	4		
Brown, Jack (Negro)					6
Wilkie, Jeremiah	1		1		
Austin, John	1	2	3		
Brown, John	1		1		
Brown, John, Jun	1		1		
Northup, Zebulon	1	1	3		
Brown, Charles	1	4	6		
Brown, Stukely	1	2	4		
Brown, Charles, Jun	3	3	3		
Brown, Joshua	1	2	3		
Congdon, Henry	2	1	2		
Allen, Nathan	1	1	3		
Vaughn, Joshua	1	1	2		
Northup, Libius	2		4		
Eldred, Daniel, Jun	1	3	4		
Arnold, Edmund	1		2		
Greene, Abraham	3	2	3		
Browning, John	1	3	5		
Kingsly, Judiah	1	1	5	1	1
Smith, Fones	1	1	3		
Northup, William (Elder)	1	1	2		
Cole, Benjamin	2	2	4		
Eldred, James	1	3	7	1	
Eldred, Daniel (Enterd)					
Kingsly, Saywell	1	2	2		
Kingsly, Jonathan	1	3	5		
Smith, Benjamin	2	3	3		
Carr, Samel	1		3		
Congdon, Stephen (Butcher)	1	2	3		
Brown, Beriah, Jun	1	3	3	3	
Watson, Doctor Samuel	1		2		1
Hill, John	1	1	3		
Phillips, Susa		1	1		
Dyre, Pheby		1	1		
Cottrell, Thomas	2	2	5	1	
Fowler, George	1		2		
Hill, Elder	1	2	3		
Havens, George	1		1		
Northup, John	1		5		
Brown, Nathan	1	2	5		
Essex, James	2	1	2		
Fenner, John	1	3	3		
Brown, Kingsly	1	2	6		
Havens, Patince (Negro)				11	
Spencer, Nicholas	1		5		
Huling, Andrew	1	1	2		
Brown, Benidict	1	2	5		
Havens, John	1	3	2		
Gardner, Patience (widow)			1	2	
Gardner, Gideon		2	3		
Jefferson, Benjamin	3	2	5		
Wells, Joshua	3	1	1		
Gardner, Jeremiah	2	2	4		3
Gardner, Huling	1	2	6	1	
Reynolds, Henry	1	3	4		
Mowry, William	1	1	3		
Browning, Samuel	1		2		
Reynolds, John	1		2		
Cole, Joseph	1	3	4		
Sweet, Mary (Widow)	1		2		1
Alsbro, Benoni	1		3		
Douglass, Charles	1	1	3		
Reynolds, Joseph (of Oliver)	1	1	4	1	3
Austin, Pikus	1	1	5		
Targee, Thomas	1	1	2		
Watson, Robert	1	2	4		
Champlin, Stephen	1	3	1		
Sherman, Nathaniel (of Silas)	1	2	2	1	
Sherman, Robert	1	2	2		
Rose, James	1	1	3		
Gardner, Philip (Negro)				7	
Sherman, William	2		5		
Rose, Rufus	1	1	1		
Sherman, John (of Henry)	1	2	2		1
Sherman, John, Jun	2	2	2		
Sherman, Eber (of John)	2		5		
Sherman, Remington	1	2	1		
Gardner, Fredrick	1	3	5		
Spink, Isaac	1	3	2		
Hazard, Jonathan (of Thoms)	1	3	3		
Sherman, Henry, Jun	1	2	3		
Sherman, Henry	1	1	1		
Potter, Ceaser				2	
Gardner, Ezekiel	2	1	2		5
Watson, Jeofry	3		3	3	1
Arnold, Samuel	1	1	4		
Watson, Steven	1	3	2		
Sherman, Margaret			4		
Sherman, Silas	2	2	2		
Peirce, Langworthy	1	3	5		
Smith, Jeremiah	1	2	4		
Card, Job	2	1	3		
Smith, Charles	1	1	1		
Phillips, Richard	1	1	1		
Arnold, Peleg	1	4	2	1	
Sweet, Mary (widow)			2		1
Phillips, William	1	1	6		
Austin, Peirce	1	4	1		
Davis, Steven	2	1	5		
Sweet, Stephen	1	4	3		
Hitt, Thomas	2	2	4		
Onion, Darkus (Indian)				5	
Phillips, Jack (Negro)				7	
Stanton, Sarah (Negro)				3	
Gardner, Samson (Negro)				8	
Hazard, Gideon	2		3		
Sheffield, Amos	1		1		
Hazard, Freeborn	1	2	3		
Austin, Mary (Widow)			1	2	
Hazard, Ephraim	1	1	2	2	
Reed, Martin	3	2	5		

WASHINGTON COUNTY—Continued.

NORTH KINGSTOWN TOWN—con.

NAME OF HEAD OF FAMILY.	Free white males of 16 years and upward, including heads of families.	Free white males under 16 years.	Free white females, including heads of families.	All other free persons.	Slaves.
Fry, Windson (negro)				7	
Northup, David	1	1	2		
Gardner, Ezeikel, Esqr	3	5	6		
Gardner, George	1	2	2		
Burlingham, Nehemiah	1	3	2		
Douglass, George	3	1	4		
Northup, Robert	2	1	1		
Mowry, John	2	1	2		
Douglass, William	1	2	2		
Northup, Stukely	2	1	3		
Manchester, John	2	3	3		
Burlingham, Peter	2	2	5	4	
Peirce, Joseph	1	2	3		
Hazard, John	1	4	4	7	
Austin, Prismus	1	3	2		
Rose, Oliver	1	1	2		
Peirce, Giles	1	1	2		
Allen, Hanah (widow)			2		
Douglass, John	2	2	3		
Carr, Oliver	1	2	3		
Allen, Jeofry	1	1			
Northup, Stephen (fisherman)	1			2	
Gardner, Pero				4	
Watson, Benjamin	2	2	6		
Watson, Benjamin, Jun	1		4		
Watson, Stephen	3	1	2		
Watson, Caleb	2	3	2	1	
Stanton, Joseph (Negro)				3	
Gardner, Bristol				3	
Hazard, Experience (Negro)				1	
Warmsly, Zebedy (Negro)				6	
Hazard, Isaac (Negro)				3	
Watson, Daniel (Indian)				1	
Congdon, Dinah (Indian)				3	
Spooner, George	1	1	3		
Potter, Ceasar (Negro)				2	
Browning, Primus (Negro)				3	
Davis, Steven	2		8		
Knowls, Reynolds	7	4	12		
Browning, William	1	2	3		3
Northup, William (fisherman)	1	2	3		
Northup, Gideon	5	1	3		
Cranston, Caleb	3	1	2		
Hazard, Jeremiah	3		6		1
Congdon, John, Esqr	1	1	9		3
Casey, Silas	1	1	7		
Hammond, William, Esq	1	1	5		7
Smith, Benajah	1	2	5		
Bignall, Jeptha	1	2	3		
Carpenter, Esther (widow)	1	1	7		
Dixinson, Thomas	1	4	4		
Boone, Peggy	1		3		
Congdon, George, Junr	1	1	4		
Hiams, George (Swamptown)	1	3	2		
Brown, Shearman	1	2	2		
Sweet, Samuel	1	3	4		

RICHMOND TOWN.

NAME OF HEAD OF FAMILY.	Free white males of 16 years and upward, including heads of families.	Free white males under 16 years.	Free white females, including heads of families.	All other free persons.	Slaves.
Clerk, Joshua	4	5	1		
Clerk, James	4		4		
Clerk, Remington	1	1	6		
Clerk, Peter	1	2	4		
Clerk, Weeden	1	4	2	1	
Knowls, John, Jun	2	3	4	1	
Potter, James	1	2	3		
Babcock, Elisha	2	1	5		
Babcock, Jesse	1	2	6	1	
Saunders, Luke	2	3	2		
Austin, Joseph	1	2	2		
Nichols, Joseph	1		7		
Nichols, David	1		2		
Clerk, Joshua (Lawyer)	3	2	5		
Clerk, Samuel	1	1	2	4	
Mallard, Henry	1	1	3		
Stanton, Robert	1	2	4		
Stanton, John	1	1	3		
Wilbore, William	1		3		
Potter, Jonathan	1	3	2	3	
Kinyon, John	1	3	2		
Kinyon, Thomas, Jun	1	2	1		
Kinyon, Thomas (of John)	1	2	1		
Goodbit, John	1	3	2		

RICHMOND TOWN—con.

NAME OF HEAD OF FAMILY.	Free white males of 16 years and upward, including heads of families.	Free white males under 16 years.	Free white females, including heads of families.	All other free persons.	Slaves.
Lock, Joseph	1	3	3		
Maxin, Jonathan, Jun	1		1		
Griffin, John	1	4	3		
Lock, Ellis	1	1	3		
Lock, Benjamin	1		2		
Wilbore, William	1	1	2		
Champlin, William	1	1	1		
Hoxie, Barney	1	2	2		
Hoxie, Stephen	1		1		
Hoxie, John	1	2	3		
Hoxie, Peter	2	2	4		
Worden, John	1	2	3		
Babcock, Ezeikel	1	1	2		
Tift, Thomas, Esqr	1	4	5		
Tift, Clerk, Esqr	1		7		
Bates, David	1	1	1		
Tift, Jeremiah	1	3	4	1	
Heffernon, William	1		1		
Boss, Jonathan	2	2	3		
Boss, Peter	3	3	4		
Tift, Samuel	2	6	6		
Larkin, David	1				
Tift, Joseph	2		3		
Herrington, William	1	6	3	2	
Watson, Perry	1	2	2		
Knowls, John, Jun	1	4	5	1	
Web, George, Jun	1	3	2		
Enos, Benjamin	1		1		
Enos, Park	1	1	1		
Austin, Joseph	1	2	4		
Rogers, Wait	2	1	3		
Pettis, Robert	1	3	2		
Crandal, Oliver	2	3	2		
Nichols, David	1		2		
Rogers, Thomas	1	3	4	1	
Clerk, Perry	3	1	3		
Clerk, Steven	1	4	5		
Kinyon, Jonathan	1	3	2		
Kinyon, John	1		1	2	
Kinyon, Jarvis	1	1	3		
Foster, John	2	2	6		
Johnson, Ezeikel	1		4		
Kinyon, Jonathan, Jun	1	1	1		
Boss, Gideon	1	1	1		
Austin, George	1	3	2		
Kinyon, Thomas W	1	1	5		
Wilbore, Jesse	1	2	3	1	
Cagwin, Amos	1	2	3		
Johnson, Latham	1	2	3		
Sheldon, William	2	2	2		
Enos, Paul	1	4	5		
Lewis, Jesse	1	1	3		
Larkin, Samuel	3	2	4		
Bags, John	2	1	2		
Larkin, Jesse	1	1	2		
Enos, Benjamin	1	1			
Maxin, Coll. Jonathan	1	3	5		
Bags, Nathan	1	1	1		
Burdick, Edmund	1	1	2		
Bill, Dick (Indian)					5
Champlin, William	1	1	1		
Lillibridge, Champlin	1	1	3		
Eldridge, Humphry	1	3	1		
Woodmansey, Joseph	1	3	1		
Brand, Samuel	1	1	3		
Brand, Rosswell	1	2	2	1	
Davis, Nicholas	1		4		
Wilcox, Job	1	3	1		
Card, Benjamin	1	3	1		
Foster, Caleb	1	2	2		
Carpenter, Daniel	1	6	4		
Griffin, Philip	1	2	5		
Griffin, John	2		5		
Kinyon, Thomas, Sen	2	2	3	3	
Kinyon, Clerk	1	1	3		
Tift, Hezekiah	1	1	3		
Foster, John, Sen	2		1	1	
Kinyon, Oliver	2	3	3		
Larkin, David	1	3	4	3	
Lewis, Nathan	1	3	3		
Lillibridge, Edward	2	4	5		
Lillibridge, Thomas	2	1	4		
Lillibridge, John	2	1	3		
Tift, Samuel, Jun	1		2		
Lillibridge, Edward, Jun	1	2	2		
Perry, Benjamin	1		4		
Baker, James	1	1	1	1	
Phillips, Joseph	1	1	4		
Lock, Alexander	1		3		
Woodmansy, John	1	4	5		
Lillibridge, Edward (of Thomas)	2	1	2		
Web, George	2	1	4		
Hall, Ebenezer	2	1	2		
Hall, Ebenezer, Jun	1	2			

RICHMOND TOWN—con.

NAME OF HEAD OF FAMILY.	Free white males of 16 years and upward, including heads of families.	Free white males under 16 years.	Free white females, including heads of families.	All other free persons.	Slaves.
Moshier, Hanah		1	3		
Little, William	1		4		
Wilbore, John	1		2	1	1
Web, Joseph	1	2	3		
Tift, Joseph (of Robert)	1	3	2	1	
Sprague, Simeon	1	1	5		
Babcock, Elisha (of Elizabeth)	1	1	1		
Babcock, Benjamin	1		2		
Holloway, George	1		3		
Holloway (Widow)			2		
Mumford, Peleg	1	1	3		
Codner, Samuel (alias Justin)	1	1	3		
Rogers, William	2	2	3		
Potter, William	2		2		
Potter, Income	2	4	3		
Kinyon, Jonathan	1	2	4		
Phillips, Joseph	1	3	2		
Potter, Daniel	4	1	3		
Alsworth, Ayswell	1	2	1	1	
Baily, Smith	1		2		
Records, John	1	2	3		
James, Robert	2	4	5		
Tanner, Thomas	1	1	5		
Barber, Benjamin, Jun	1	1	4		
Records, Comfort	1	1	2		
James, Thomas	2	3	3	1	
Clerk, Simeon	1				
Clerk, Simon, Jun	2	3	5		
Potter, Smiten	2	3	4		
Wilcox, Peleg	1	6	3		
Wilcox, Edward	1				
Wilcox, Henry	1	1	2		
Sheldon, James, Esq	2	1	7		
Sheldon, Augustus	2	1	4		
Sheldon, Henry	1		5		
Hoxie, Presbury	1		1		
Foster, Gideon	1	1	1		
Leonard, Silas	1	4	3		
Colegrove, Oliver	5	5	5		
Kinyon, Green	1	1	2		
Wilbore, Benjamin	1	3	3		
Larkin, Nicholas	2	2	2		
Larkin, Nicholas, Jun	1		1		
Larkin, Edward	1	2	1		
Champlin, Thomas	1	2	3		
Larkin, David	4	2	3	2	
Josylin, Rufus	1	1	3		
Boss, Jonathan	2	3	2		
Trude, John	1	2	4		
Clerk, Samuel	1	1	2	4	
Lock, Joseph	1	3	3		
Mallard, Henry	1	2	2		
Austin, Joseph	1	6	5		
Clerk, Weeden	1	4	4	1	
Potter, James	2	2	2		
Hoxie, John	1	3	6	1	
Hoxie, Stephen	1		2		
Hoxie, Barnabas	3	2	5		
Hoxie, Peter	3	1	4	1	
Brown, Andrew	1	4	1		
Worden, John	1	4	4		
Tift, Clerk	1		6		
Hall, John	1	4	5		
Tift, Thomas	2	4	5		
Wilcox, Oliver	1		2		
Bently, Ezeikel	1		2		
Lillibridge, Champlin	1		3		
Tift, Ezeikel	2		3		
Tift, Ezeikel, Jun	1	2	3		
Tift, Joseph	1	1	3		
Clerk, Moses	1	3	5		
Clerk, Thomas	1		1		
Barber, Caleb	2	1	3	1	
Barber, Caleb, Jun	1	2	3		
Boss, Jeremiah	1	3	2		
Barber, Samuel	1	3	2		
Rogers, Thomas	1	6	1	1	
Clerk, Arnold	1	2	3		
Tift, Benjamin	2	2	4		
Lock, Benjamin	1	1	1		
Potter, Robert	1	2	7		
Dye, Samuel	1	2	2		
Dye, Richard	1	2	2		
Dye, John	1	2	4		
Dye, Daniel	1	4	2		
Sheldon, James	1	1	6		
Kinyon, George	1	1	2		
Valet, John	1	1	2		
Phillips, Ellery	1	1	2		
Potter, Daniel	1		2		
Card, Joseph	1	2	1		
Allen, James	1	1	2	1	
James, Thomas	1	2	4		

WASHINGTON COUNTY—Continued.

NAME OF HEAD OF FAMILY.	Free white males of 16 years and upward, including heads of families.	Free white males under 16 years.	Free white females, including heads of families.	All other free persons.	Slaves.
RICHMOND TOWN—continued.					
Lillibridge, Josias	1		1		
Reynolds, Robert	1	2	3	1	
Reynolds, William	1	1	2	1	
Reynolds, Jesse	1	1	3		
Hoxie, Joseph	3		2		
Hoxie, Benjamin	1	5	3		
Hoxie, Matthew	1	1	1		
Wilcox, Noah	1		2		
Reynolds, Gideon	1	1	1		
Wilcox, Steven	1	1	2		
Hoxie, Elijah	1	4	4	1	
Barber, Ezeikel, Jun	1	2	3		
Young, Caleb	1	2	4		
Cecil, Rodman	1	2	3		
Potter, David	1	2	3		
Moor, George	1	7	1		
Moor, Robert	1		6		
Moor, Silas	1	1	5		
Moor, John	1	3	2		
James, George	1	3	5		
James, Mary		1	2		
Moshier, Gideon	1	3	3		
James, James	1	1	1		
Babcock, Ezeikel	1	1	1		
Tindale, Jonathan				6	
Lillibridge, Benjamin	2	1	2		
Barber, Ezeikel	2	1	3	2	
James, Jonathan	1		3		
Clerk, Thomas	1		1		
Clerk, Moses	1	3	5		
Tift, Joseph, Jun	1		3		
Corey, Samuel	1		3		
Brown, Prince				3	
Wilcox, Steven	1	2	3		
Wilcox, Stephen, Jun	1	2	6		
Wait, Payne	1	4	1		
Sheldon, Augustus	1	2	2		
Sheldon, Henry	1	2	3		
Tanner, Hazard	1		4		
Barber, Ezekel, ye 3d	1	1	1		
Barber, Benjamin (of Ezeikel)	3	2	3		
Hall, John	1				
Knowls, John, Jun	1	1	1		
Webster, John	1	1	1		
Webster, John, Jun	1	1	2		
Webster, Thomas	2		2		
Webster, Moshier	1		2		
Woodmansey, James	1	4	5		
Gardner, William	3	1	7		
Peterson, Ichabod	2		4		
Dunn, John	1	1	4		
Knowls, Robert	1		1		
Wilcox, Robert	1	4	4		
Knowls, John	2	2	4	3	
Tift, Robert	1	1	2		
Lillibridge, Lester	1	1	2		
Kinyon, Benidick	2	4	3		
Wilcox, Philip	2	6	3		
Wilcox, Steven	1	3	2		
James, John	1	1	3		
Perry, Simeon	1	3	5		
Crandal, Christopher	1	3	3	1	
Babcock, Paul	2	4	3	2	
Carpenter, Daniel	1	3			
Peterson, Ichabod	2		4	1	
Peterson, Nathan	2		3		
Watson, Perry	1	2	2		
Brown, Andrew	1	4	4		
James, William (of John)	1	1	1		
James, William (of James)	1	3	3		
James, Ezeikel	1		5	2	1
Champlin, William	1	1	1		
Sweet, Elizabeth (Widow)			4	3	
Hall, Jeremiah	1	1	2		
Lewis, Nathan	2	1	4		
Barber, Benjamin (of Ben)	1	1	3		
Potter, William	1	2			
James, Thomas	1	2	3	2	
Reynolds, Gideon	1	2	1		
SOUTH KINGSTOWN TOWN.					
Robinson, Rowland	1				6
Arnold, Oliver	1	1	6	1	1
Scott, George	1		1	1	
Robinson, John	1		1		
Sambo (Negro)				2	
Sweet, Benoni	1	1	1		
Franklin, John			3		7
SOUTH KINGSTOWN TOWN—con.					
Gardner, James (of Amos)	1	5	2	1	1
Castle, Philip	1		4		
Sherman, Thomas	1	3	5		1
Curtis, Mary (Widow)		1	3		
Hazard, Robert (of Richard)	3	1	7		
Barber, Thomas	1	1	2		
Gardner, Dick (Negro)				9	
Douglass, George	2	1	6		
Cole, John (at the Glebe)	2	3	6	1	
Gardner, Samuel	3		4	2	
Gardner, Silas	1	2	3		
Gardner, Lowry	1		5		
Stafford, Daniel	1	1	1		
Gardner, Chris., Jun	1	2	4		
Mays, William	1	1	2		
Mays, Elijah	1	1	4		
Smith, Amos	1	3	1	2	
Gardner, Amos	2	1	2	1	
Franklin, John	3	3	1	5	
Gardner, Coll. John	4	2	4		7
Gardner, John (fisherman)	1	2	2		
Gardner, Thomas	1	1	3		
Carpenter, Jeremiah, Jun	1	2	4		
Chapel, William	1	3	3		
Chapel, John	1		4		
Capwell, Philip	1	1	3		
Browning, Gardner	1	1	2	1	
Brown, Rowland	2	3	3	3	4
Brown, Adam (Negro)				8	
Greene, Coggeshall	1	2	4		
Robinson, John (Indian)				6	
Sweet, Joshua	1	1	3		
Oatly, Benedict	2		3		
Helme, Samuel	1				
Hull, Joseph	2	3	3		
Sherman, Philip	1	2	1		
Robinson, Benjamin	1		1		
underwood, Anna (widow)	2		1		
Nichols, Andrew	3		1		
Gardner, Jeofry	1		4	1	
Northup, Nicholas	3	1	2	1	
Watson, Jeofry, Jun	1		3	2	
Corey, Richard	1	2	1		
Gardner, Amos	1	2	3	1	
Smith, Benjamin	1	2	4		
Brown, George	1	2	6	2	7
Brown, Newbury	1		3		
Hazard, Robert	1		7	7	
Wanton, Thomas				6	
Gardner, Peleg	1		4		
Sherman, Daniel (of Philip)	1	3	4		
Sweet, ...	1		1		
Tew, Cuff (Negro)				6	
Gardner, Jeofry	1		3	3	
Sherman, Henry (of Henry)	1	2	3		
Gardner, John (of William)	1		1	3	
Smith, John	1		3		
Gardner, Stephen	1		1		
Sherman, Thomas	1	4	6	1	
Hazard, Enoch	1	1	4		
Brown, Jeremiah	1	2	2		
Watson, John	1		2		
Watson, John, Jun	3	2	3		
Peckham, Peleg	2	1	2		
Perry, Samuel	3	3	4		6
Helme, Samuel	2		1		
Hull, Joseph	1	4	3		
Northup, Nicholas	2	1	2		
Sherman, Philip	1	2	1		
Watson, Job	1	2	3	2	
Dyre, William	4	1	8	2	
Oatly, Abigail (widow)	1	3	3		1
Allen, Christopher	1	4	6		
Hazard, Thomas	1	1	2	3	
Hazard, Robert	3	4	3		
Gould, Thomas (Negro)				4	
Sherman, John	1	1	2	1	
Mumford, Nathaniel, Pt T	3	1	5	2	4
Robinson, Sylvester	2		1		
Robinson, John	3		2	5	
Robinson, Christopher	5		2		6
Gardner, John, Sen	2	2	7		1
Hazard, Caleb	2		4		
Hazard, Green	1	2	1	1	
Knowls, Joseph	2	2	6		
Champlin, Robert	2	2	4	1	
SOUTH KINGSTOWN TOWN—con.					
Northup, Henry	1	1	3	1	
Jaques, Joseph	1	1	8		
Niles, Henry (Negro)				4	
Sweet, Rufus	2		2		1
Hazard, Benjamin	3	1	3		3
Hazard, Sylvester	1	1	3		3
Hazard, Robert (of Joseph)	3	1	5		4
Hazard, Steven	2	1	5		2
Jaques, Nathan	1	2	2		1
Collins, Nathan	3		1		
Knowles, John	1	1	1	4	
Knowls, William	2	3	3	1	
Harvey, Thomas	1	1	4		
Kinyon, Gardner	3	1	2	1	
Luther, Jabez	1	3	2		
Kinyon, Green	1	1	3		
Armstrong, Thomas	3	4	6		
Perry, Edward	2	2	5	1	
Eldred, Daniel	1		4		
Congdon, Joseph	1	3	4	1	
Hazard, Carder	9	1	4	3	
Harvey, Edward	2	2	1		
Robinson, Cuff (Negro)				4	
Gardner, Jeofrey	1	3	4	1	
Hazard, Robert	2	2	3	2	
Bramin, Thomas, Jun	1	5	2		
Hazard, Caleb	2	2	5		
Weeden, Jesper (Negro)				4	
Northup, Henry (enter'd)					
Perry, Joseph	1	3	5		
Congdon, Samuel	1	3	4	1	3
Niles, Quash (Negro)				4	
Potter, Sambo (Negro)				4	
Sweet, Rufus	2		2		1
Babcock, Robert Hazard	2		3		
Potter, Elisha	1	3	4		2
Hazard, Sylvester	1	2	3		3
Champlin, Prince				8	
Carter, William	1	1	4		
Monk, Cuddy (Negro)				5	
Champlin, Robert	2	2	3		
Potter, Robert	2	2	3		5
Potter, Gov. Samuel	1	2	5	5	
Grinman, John	2		3		
Congdon, Samuel	1	3	3		3
Lock, Jonathan	1	3	4		
Watson, Ned (Negro)				7	
Dyre, Prince (Negro)				5	
Brown, Adam (Negro)				6	
Williams, Joshua	1	5	5		
Torey, Doctor Joseph	1	1	2		
Cooke, William	1		2		
Stedman, Thomas	2		4		
Sweet, Job	3		3	1	
Babcock, Benedict	1		1	1	
Gavit, Samuel	2	4	6		
Gardner, James	2	2	3		
Tift, Stephen	1		2		
Stedman, Job	1	2	2		
Stedman, James	2	1	3		
Stedman, Enoch	1	2	2		
Stedman, John	2		1		
Williams, Coone	4	4	3		
Williams, Henry	1	1	1		
Stedman, Daniel, Jun	1	1	5		
Grinman, Gideon	1	1	2		
Allen, Samuel	1	3	2		
Grinman, Silas	1	1	1		
Fowler, Sarah & Molly			2		
Grinman, John	2		1		
Hooper, Henry	2		1		
Hooper, Henry, Jun	1		2		
Stedman, William	2	5	5		
Stedman, Thomas, Jun	1	1	1		
Hawkins, Thomas	1		4		
Torey, Cuff (Negro)				4	
Champlin, Thomas	2	2	6		2
Jaques, Nathan	1	1	1		1
Gardner, Allen	1	3	2		
Targe, Philip	1	3	3		
Tift, Caleb	3		4		
Chapel, Holey	1	1	3		
Wilbore, Samuel	1	2	2		
Hazard, Hull	1	1	1		
Watson, Jack (Negro)				4	
Babcock, Esther (widow)		2		3	
Smith, Ebenezer	2		6		
Northup, Sylvester	1	1	4		
Northup, Stephen	1	4	3		
Watson, Jeofry	5	1	4	1	6
Sherman, James	3		5	1	7

33830—08——4

WASHINGTON COUNTY—Continued.

SOUTH KINGSTOWN TOWN—con.

NAME OF HEAD OF FAMILY.	Free white males of 16 years and upward, including heads of families.	Free white males under 16 years.	Free white females, including heads of families.	All other free persons.	Slaves.
Case, Henry	1		2		1
Robinson, Amos (Negro)				3	
Champlin, John (Negro)				5	
Tenant, Oliver	1	2	4		
Champlin, Stephen	1	2	7		1
Knowls, Jeremiah	1	2	1		
Champlin, Jeofrey	2	5	3		1
Hazard, Jonathan, Esq	2	1	3		
Sherman, Lodowick	1	3	4		1
Champlin, Thomas	4	1	4		
Bramin, Joseph	1	2	4		
Card, Stephen			2		
Bently, Ebenezer	1	1	2		
Armstrong, Hanah		1	2		
Davis, Samuel	1	1	2		
Tift, Ebenezer	1	2	3		
Potter, William, Esq	4	3	7	13	
Perry, Jonathan	1				
Gardner, Henry, Esq	1		1		9
Gardner, Nathan	3		1	2	3
Gardner, Nathan, Jun	1	2	4	9	3
Peirce, Laurence L	4		7	1	
Taylor, William	2		5	1	
Sweet, Ruth		1	2	1	
Gardner, Nicholas	1	2	3		1
Watson, Basheba (widow)	3	4	4		5
Watson, John			6		2
Champlin, William	1	1	5		
Pettis, Robert	1	1		1	
Gardner, Gideon	1	2	2		
Gardner, William	1		1		
Gardner, Richard	2	7	2		1
Alsbro, Samuel	1		1		
Rose, John	1	6	5		
Hazard, Thomas C	1		3		1
Dyre, George	1	2	5		
Whaley, Joseph	1	2	4		
Bramin, Daniel	1	2	2		
Gardner, Caleb	3		4	4	7
Boss, Peter	1		1	2	
Knowls, Daniel	1	3	5		2
Peckham, Benjamin	2		1		4
Peckham, Josephus	1	4	1		4
Potter, Thomas	2		4	3	
Barker, Charles	1	4	3	1	
Helme, James	1	4	3	2	
Champlin, Hannah (Widow)			2		1
Gardner, Sarah (Widow)			2		
Gardner, Elisha	1		3		
Lunt, William	2	1	3		
Peckham, George	1	5	3		
Nichols, John	1	5			
Clark, William Case	1	3	3		
Cottrell, Abe	1	4	4		
Potter, Elisha (Lawyer)	2	1	2	1	
Tift, George	2	1	6		
Reynolds, Henry	1	2	2		1
Reynolds, Elisha	1				4
Peckham, Timothy	3		2	1	
Wait, John	2	2	3		
Weeden, John	1	3	4		
Sands, Robert G	1	3	2		1
Polock, William Wilson	3	4	2	1	
Potter, William	1	2	3		
Potter, Cole Robert } Sherman, Docter }	2	4	4		5
Douglass, David	1	5	4		
Totten, John L	1	1	1		
Stanton, Joseph	1	1	4	2	
Cross, West (Negro)				4	
Larkin, John	1		4		
Kinyon, Solomon	1	1	2		
Kinyon, Thomas	1	3	2		
Brown, Robert	6		2	1	1
Cooke, Silas	1		2		
Brown, Deptford				5	
Brown, James			3	3	
Wilcox, William	3		1		6
Allen, William	1	1	2		
Jaques, James	1	2	5		
Wilcox, Sylvester	1	2	3		
Browning, Ephraim	6	1	2		
Sweet, William	1	1	2		
Carpenter, Thomas	1	3	1		
Shearman, David	1	2	3		
Little, John	1	2	5		
Bently, Ezekiel	1	6	5		
Larkin, Steven	1	1	2		
Underwood, Samuel	3	5	4	4	
Niles, Mingo				4	
Sheffield, Jeremiah	1	1	4		
Perkins, Sands	1		4		
Ervin (Widow)			1	5	
Trude, John	1	2	5		

SOUTH KINGSTOWN TOWN—con.

NAME OF HEAD OF FAMILY.	Free white males of 16 years and upward, including heads of families.	Free white males under 16 years.	Free white females, including heads of families.	All other free persons.	Slaves.
Wilcox, Whitman	1	2	4		
Larkin, Abigail		1	2		
Clarke, Gideon	4		2		
Clarke, Silas	1	2	1		
Babcock, Joseph	3	2	7		
Babcock, Gideon	1	4	3		
Haywood, Joseph	1		2		
Card, Stephen	1		2		
Bently, Ebenezer	1	1	3		
Armstrong, Hannah		1	2		
Davis, Samuel	1	1	1		
Sylvester, Peleg	1	3	4		
Eldridge, Thomas	1	1	3		
Eldridge, Henry	1	3	4		
Eldridge, Mercy	2		1	4	
Champlin, Thomas					
Champlin, Thomas, Junr }	4	1	4		
Babcock, Judge Samuel	1	2	2		
Babcock, John	1	2	1		
Charles, Sarah (Indian)				9	
Robinson, Matthew	1		2	8	
Billington, Thomas	1	3	3		
Potter, Benjamin	1	1	2		
Potter, Benjamin, Junr	1	1	1		
Sweet, Thadeus	1	2	3		
James, Edward	1		2		
Waistcoat, Caleb	1	3	4		
Alsbro, Mary	1		2		
Cottrell, Stephen	2	1	2		
Peckham, Barber	2		5	3	3
Mumford, Gardner	1	5	4		
Hopkins, John	1		3		
Tanner, Isaac	2	5	5		
Tanner, Josias	1	2	5		
Bramin, Thomas	1	3	4		
Tanner, Francis	1	1	1		
Watson, William	1		1		
Sheldon, Isaac	2	5	6		
Downing, Marshall	1	2	3		
Johnson, Michail	1	5	10		
Smith, Ephraim	1		1		
Boss, Philip	2		2		
Albro, John	1	3	2		
Hoxie, Samuel	1	2	3	1	
Hopkins, Clerk	1	3	2		
Sheldon, John	1		3		
Smith, James	1	3	3		
Sherman, Daniel	5	3	6		
Frasier, John	3	2	1		
Cottrell, Samuel	1	3	2		
Cottrell, Sarah (widow)	1	2	3		
Arvin, Samuel	1	1	1		
Peckham, Timothy, Senior	2	1	3		
Peterson, Nathan	2				
Hopkins, Hanah & Sarah			2		
Hammond, Joseph	1		6		
Southwick, Elijah	1		1		
Hopkins, Thomas	4	7	5		
Barber, Moses	1	2	5		
Barber, James	3	3	6		
West, James	1	3	2		
Robins, Thomas	1	5	5		
Murphy, Edward	1	1	2		
Draper, Amos	1	10	2		
Knowls, Robert	1	2	3		
Whaley, John	1	2	6		
Whaley, Thomas	1	3	3		
Hubbard, Henry Clerk	1		1		
Whaley, Samuel	3		6		
Whaley, Samuel, Jun	1	1	3		
Hopkins, Thomas	1	11	6		
Robinson, Stepeny (Negro)				8	
Wait, Benjamin	1	2	3		
Hammond, Joseph, Sen	1		4		
Eldridge, Mercy		1	4		
Potter, Elisha	1	1	4		
Powers, Samuel	3	2	4		
Tucker (Widow)			2		
Brownell, Joseph	2	1	4	2	
Brownell, Stephen	1	2	4	1	
Brownell, William	1		3	4	
Brownell, Christopher		1	2		
Potter, Ichabod	1	1	4		
Congdon, James	1	1	2		
Potter, James	1		2		
Hazard, Jonathan (Green Hill)	1	1	4		
Enos, Jesse	1	1	3		
Babcock, Hezekiah	1		3		
Babcock, Caleb	1	2	3	1	
Hull, William	1	3	4		
Knowls, William	1	4	3		
Perry, John	1	3	2		

SOUTH KINGSTOWN TOWN—con.

NAME OF HEAD OF FAMILY.	Free white males of 16 years and upward, including heads of families.	Free white males under 16 years.	Free white females, including heads of families.	All other free persons.	Slaves.
Johnson, Jonathan (Enterd)					
Card (Widow)	1	4	2		
Card, Christopher	1	3	4		
Card, Silas	1	4	2		
Robinson, Philip	1	3	2		
Hull, Edward	1	4	7	1	
Hull, Sylvester	1	3	3		
Hazard, George (Blacksmith)	1	1	4	1	5
Browning, Atkinson	1	4	1		5
Healy, Thomas	1	1	6		
Arnold, Tift	1	1	1		3
Hazard, Henry	1	3	3		
Potter, Mingo (Negro)				10	
Potter, William	3	5	3		
Gardner, Benjamin	4	1	2	1	
Baker, Amos	1	4	5		
Knowls, Ebenezer	1	3	3		
Clerk, James	1		2		
Hazard, Robinson	1		2		
Wilbore, Joshua	1		1		
Granger, Asamy	1	1	2		
Whitehorn, James	3	1	4		
Tift, Tenant	1	1	2		
Tift, Tenant, Jun	1	2	1		
Tift, Gardner	1	3	5		
Castle, John	1		1		
Tift, Ebenezer	1	2	2		1
Fowler, Gideon	1		3		
Congdon, Robert	1	2	4		
Tift, Daniel	1				
Tift, Daniel, Junr, ye 3d	1	1	5		
Wells, Joseph	1	2	2		1
Larkin, John	1		4		
Littlebridge, Gideon	2	4	3		1
Helme, Robert	3	3	5		
Gardner, Paris	2		4		
Albro, Jeremiah	1		1		
Albro, Stephen	1		2		
Fowler, Samuel	1	1	1		
Nash, Nathan	1	1	4		
Watson, Guy (Negro)				6	
Helme, Abigail (Indian)				4	
Gardner, Nathaniel	1		2		
Holloway, Ezeikel	1		1		
Helme, Niles	1	2	2		
Holloway, Peter	2	1	2		
Babcock, Ephraim	1		3	2	
Hazard, Christopher	1	4	1		
Carpenter, Joseph	1	5	6		
Curtis, Samuel	1	3	5		1
Babcock, Abijah	2	4	6	1	4
Kant, Philip (Negro)				4	1
Stanton, Samuel	2	2	5		1
Gavit, Samuel	3	3	6		
Targee, William	1	3	4		
Babcock, Benedict, Jun	1	1	1		
Oakly, William	1	4	6		
Dewey, Elias	1	1	4		
Carpenter, Stephen	1	2	4		
Perry, Doctor Joshua	4	7	1		
Carpenter, Jonathan	1	4	4		
Rodman, Robert	1	3	2		
Rodman, Benjamin	1	4	3		
Gould, Adam			3		5
Congdon, Stukely	1	1	2		
Watson, Jeofry, Jun	1	1	2		
Stedman, Enoch	1	2	3		
Gould, John	1	1	6		
Stedman, Job	1	2	4		
Gould, Nicholas	1		4		
Grinman, Silas	1		1		
Grinman, John	1		2		
Stedman, James	1	1	5		
Williams, Joshua	1	6	3		
Holland, Henry Hooper	1	3	2		
Potter, Henry (Tavern Keeper)	4	3	13	4	
Whaley, Jeremiah	3		3		
Babcock, George	1	4	2		3
Segus, Samuel	1	5	3		1
Potter, George	1	2	5		
Champlin, Joseph	1		1		3
Fones, Stephen	3		3		
Segus, John	1		3		
Champlin, Elijah	1	1	4		
Holloway, Hanah			2		
Browning, Hazard	1		3		
Browning, Robert	1	2	2		
Young, Saphick			2		
Grinnell, Pricilla			3		
Gould, Joseph	1	2	3		
Carpenter, Benjamin	1		3		
Rock, Samuel	1	1	1	3	1
Potter, Elias	1	2	3		1
Segus, Mary (widow)	3		2	1	

WASHINGTON COUNTY—Continued.

SOUTH KINGSTOWN TOWN—con.

NAME OF HEAD OF FAMILY.	Free white males of 16 years and upward, including heads of families.	Free white males under 16 years.	Free white females, including heads of families.	All other free persons.	Slaves.
Segus, Thomas	1	1	2		
Segus, William	2		3		
Card, James	1	1	3		
Johnson, Jonathan	1	2	3		
Hoxie, Joseph, Jun	2	1	3		
Champlin, Michael	1		3		
Card, Christopher	1	1	1		
Reed, Thomas	1	1	1		
Card, Silas	1	1	1		
Champlin, Jeofry	1	3	4		
Card, Jonathan	5	2	8		
Hoxie, Joseph, Sen	1		3	1	
Perry, John	1	2	3		
Card, Samuel	1	1	1		
Perry, Samuel	1	2	1	1	
Card, Hazard	1	1	2	1	
Hull, William	1		2	1	
Knowls, William	4	1			
Card, Joseph	1	1	2		
Babcock, Peleg	1	4	7		
Segus, Joseph	1	4	5		
Powers, Samuel	1	2	3		
Hamas, John (Indian)				10	
Champlin, Jonathan	1	2	4		
Perry, Benjamin	1	1	1		
Johnson, Kinyon	1	1	1		
Hazard, Quash (Negro)				2	
Babcock, Southwick (Negro)				4	
Babcock, Ceasar (Negro)				8	
Cross, West (Negro)				6	
Perry, Quash (Negro)				7	
Murphy, Martin	1	3	4		
Cottrell, Stephen, Jun	1	3	3		
Babcock, John	1	2	2		
Perry, Henry (Negro)				6	
Perry, Daniel	1	1	2		
Perry, Phillis (Negro)				5	
Watson, Ceasar (Negro)				5	
Peckham, Phillis (Negro)				3	
Chapel, Stephen	1	2	2		
Cupidore (Negro)				6	
Murphy, Edward	1	1	2		
Jaques, Jonathan	1	4	3		
Bacon, Uriah	1	2	2		
Stanton, Robert	1	1	1		
White, Jonathan	1	1	2		
Babcock, Thomas	1	1	1		
Webster, Thomas	1	2	2		
Babcock, Gideon	2	7	3	3	
Ely, Thomas	1	1	7		
Babcock, Job	2	2	4		
Grinnell, Thomas	1	4	5		
Holloway, Stephen	1		3		
Gavit, Edward	1	5	5		
Hazard, George	1	2	3	1	
Gardner, Daniel	1	5	5		
Congdon, Hanah			3		
Tucker, Joshua	2	2	4	7	
Babcock, James	1	1	4		
Babcock, Benedict	1	3	5		
Congdon, James, Jun	1	1	2		
Potter, Ichabod	1	2	4		
Champlin, Elihu	3	4	3	2	
Crandal, Eldridge	1	1	3		
Potter, Stephen	1	4	4		
Babcock, Augustus	1		1		
Diskill, John	1	2	4		
Hoxie, Gideon	1	2	2	4	
Ward, Dick	1	4	5		
Cheah, William (Indian)				5	
Peckham, Benjamin	5	4	1	2	
Hazard, Thomas	1	1	3		
Peckham, William	1	2	5	2	
Hill, Henry	1	2	3		
Greene, Maxin	1	1	1		
Holloway, Benjamin	1	3	1		
Potter, Samuel, Jun	1		4		
Champlin, William	1	1	2		
Perry, Freeman	1	1	3		
Peckham, Peter (Negro)				5	
Nash, Ann			1		
Eldridge, Mary (widow)	2		4	1	
Harvy, William	1	3	5		
Hazard, Jack (Negro)				9	
Hazard, Elizabeth (widow)	2		8	2	
Sheffield, Nathan	5		4		
Cross, John	4	2	5		
Douglass, Thomas	1	3	1		
Lock, Edward	3	2	5		
Congdon, William	1	1	6	1	
Peckham, Timothy	2	1	4	1	
Congdon, John	2		4	1	
Hull, Charles	3	1	4		

SOUTH KINGSTOWN TOWN—con.

NAME OF HEAD OF FAMILY.	Free white males of 16 years and upward, including heads of families.	Free white males under 16 years.	Free white females, including heads of families.	All other free persons.	Slaves.
Peirce, Langworthy	1	3	4		
Helme, Benedict	1	1	1		
Lillibridge, Gideon	1	6	4		
Dockray, John	1	2	6	3	
Champlin, Prince (Negro)				9	
Peirce, Samuel	1	2	5		
Stillman, Daniel	2	2	5		
Williams, Daniel	1	7	2		
Whaley, John P	1	4	1	1	
Oakly, Joseph	1	1	5		
Hazard, Stephen	1	1	1		
Holland, Henry, Jun	1		2		
Niles, Jeremiah	1	1	1	8	
Carpenter, Ephraim	1	4	5		
Champlin, Thomas	1	2	6		
Hazard, Simeon	1	1	1		
Smith, Simon	1	1	1		
Lewis, Enoch	1	5	1		
Robinson, Jesse	1	1	2	2	
Dewy, Christopher	1	1	2		
Boss, Job	1	2	5		
Williams, Coone	2	6	2		
Williams, Henry	3		3		
Fowler, Sarah			3		
Allen, Samuel	1	2	4		
Eck, John (Indian)				3	
Rodman, Jack (Indian)				3	
Chapel, Caleb	1	2	3		
Watson, Elisha	1	6	7		
Carpenter, James	1	3	3		
Barber, Gideon	1	1	1	1	
Pollock, William	1	2	1		
Babcock, Esther (widow)			3		
Mitchell (Widow)	2		4		
Rodman, Celia (Negro)				3	
Taylor, Jacob (Negro)				2	
Smith, Ebenezer	1		6		
Grinman, Gideon	1	1	5		
Stedman, William	1	4	4		
Congdon, Robert	1	1	3		
Gardner, Nathaniel, Esq.	1		2		
Rodman, Philip (Negro)				7	
Holloway, Ezeikel	1		1		
Hull, Charles Higginsbottom	1	1	1		
Hawkins, Thomas	1	1	5		
Kant, Philip (Negro)				7	
Remington, Holden	1	2	5		
Babcock, Thomas	1	3	1		
Holloway, John	1	2	4		
Chapel, Frederick	1	1	1		
Robins, Thomas (Negro)				6	
Perry, Daniel (Negro)				4	
Clerk, Joshua	1				
Hill, Henry	1	2	5		
Stedman, Thomas	1	1	3		
Sweet, Job	1	3	3	1	
Tony, Cuff (Negro)				6	
Babcock, Ceasar, ye 2d				2	
Tift, Stephen	1		1		
Helme, Benedict	1				
Carpenter, Joseph	1	5	6		
Tift, Daniel, Senior	1	4	5		
James, Randal	1	3	3		
Reynolds, Thomas	1	2	1		
Clerk, Peleg	1	3	3	1	
Nichols, John	4	3	2	3	
Clerk, William Case	1	4	3		
Carpenter, Jeremiah	2	6	3		
Carpenter, Jeremiah, Jun	1	3	2		
Hull, Edward	1	2	5		
Hull, Sylvester	1	3	3		
Robinson, Rowland	1				6
Arnold, Oliver	1	1	6	1	1
Scott, George	1		1	1	
Robinson, John	1		1		
Lambo (Negro)				2	
Sweet, Benoni	1	1	1		
Franklin, Capt John	2		3	7	
Castle, Philip	1		4		
Sherman, Thomas	1	3	5	1	
Curtis, Mary (widow)	1				
Hazard, Robert (of Richard)	3	1	7		
Barber, Thomas	1	1	2		
Gardner, Dick				9	
Douglass, George	2	1	8		
Sweet, Sylvester	1	2	2		
Wilson, John	4		4		
Clerk, Samuel	2	1	6		
Cottrell, Stephen, Jun, ye 3d	1		3		
Knowls, James	2	1	3		

SOUTH KINGSTOWN TOWN—con.

NAME OF HEAD OF FAMILY.	Free white males of 16 years and upward, including heads of families.	Free white males under 16 years.	Free white females, including heads of families.	All other free persons.	Slaves.
Potter, Rous	1	1	6		
Chapel, Thomas	1	1	5		
Champlin, Jonathan	2	2	4		
Austin (Widow)			1		
Browning, Stephen, Sen	1	1	2	1	
Barber, Gideon	1	1	3		
Card, Christopher	1	1	1		
Browning, Joseph	1	1	2		
Sheldon Jonathan	1	2	4		

WESTERLY TOWN.

NAME OF HEAD OF FAMILY.	Free white males of 16 years and upward, including heads of families.	Free white males under 16 years.	Free white females, including heads of families.	All other free persons.	Slaves.
Saunders, Augustus	1	3	2		
Vars, Isaac	3	2	4		1
Saunders, Edward	2	2	3		
Burdick, Jonathan	1	2	1		
Burdick, Simeon, Junr	1	2	1		
Louis, David	1	2	6		
Larkin, Abel	3	2	3		
Hull, Hannah			4		
Wight, Walter	1	1	3		1
Peckham, Peleg	1	2	1		
Saunders, Charles	1	3	8		
Studson, Cornelius	1	3	4		
Lovis, David, Junr	1		3		
Sisson, Oliver	1		3		
Peckham, Abel	2		3	2	
Cross, Susa (Widow)		1	1		
Bowen, Susanna			1		
Hall, Isaac	1	1	3		
Babcock, Christopher, Esqr	1	3	4		
Babcock, Christopher	1	2	2		
Allen, Lemuel	1		6		
Saunders, Stephen	1	4	6		
Saunders, James	1	1	2		
Saunders, James, Junr	1	3	5		
Maxin, Joseph	1	2	2		
Perkins, Silas	1		2		
Hitchcock, Clerk	1	1	3		
Hitchcock, Joseph	1	1	2		
Louis, Joseph	1	1		2	
Clark, George	1		3		
Saunders, Hezekiah	1	6	3		
Davis, Peter	1		1		
Clark, Ichabod	1		1		
Clark, Ichabod, Junr	1		3		
Brown, John	1	2	3		
Saunders, Joseph	1		3		
Saunders, Joseph, Junr	1	1	3		
Bleven, Samuel	1	4	4		
Bleven, Samuel, Junr	1	1	1		
Peckham, Benjamin	1	2	2		
Boss, Peleg	1	2	2		
Crandal, James	1	1	1		
Crandal, Benedict	1	1	6		
Crandal, Clark	1	5	2		
Crandal, Paul	1	1	1		
Rogers, Jesse	1		1		
Bleven, Daniel	1	2	5		
Burdick, Robert	1		1		
Bleven, Theodate	1	1	1		
Bleven, John	1		1		
Rathbun, Ebenezer	2		2		
Crandal, Joshua	1	2	1		
Crandal, Peter	1	3	1		
Crandal, Clement	1	3	1		
Greene, Capt William	1	6	5		
Crandal, Joshua, Esqr	1	3	4		
Crandal, Phineas	1	4	2		
Taylor, Thomas	1	2	3		
Taylor, Humphrey	1	1	1		
Crandal, Henry	1	3	5		
Crandal, Stenet	1		2		
Peckham, James	1	1	2		
Rathbun, James	1	1	2	1	
Peckham, William Sweet	1	1	6		
Hall, Peer Data	1	3	4		
Clerk, Edward	1	6	3		
Burdick, James	1	3	4		
Babcock, Christopher	1	3	4		
Ross, Bennet	1		2	1	
Hall, Isaac	1		2		
Davis, James	1	2	6		
Sisson, John	1		3		
Sisson, Mary	1		3		
Burdick, Amy (Widow)		1	3		
Crandal, Paul	1	1	3		
Sisson, Jonathan	1		3		
Sisson, Thomas	2	3	5		
Rathbun, Thomas	3		2		
Blevin, William	1	5	5		
Davis (Widow)			2	1	
Crandal, Barney	1	2	2		
Blevin, George	2	1	3		
Greene, Pardon	1		3		
Blevin, Arnold	2	1	6	4	

WASHINGTON COUNTY—Continued.

WESTERLY TOWN—con.

NAME OF HEAD OF FAMILY.	Free white males of 16 years and upward, including heads of families.	Free white males under 16 years.	Free white females, including heads of families.	All other free persons.	Slaves.
Noyce, Colo Joseph	6	1	4		7
Bent, Prince				4	
Dodge, Oliver	3		5	1	
Burdick, Libeus	1	3	5		
Noyce, Thomas	1	4	2	2	
Sisson, Joseph	1		2		
Burlingham, Samuel	2	1	6	2	
Allen, Samuel	1	2	5		
Noyce, Mary (Widow)			1		
Champlin, Samuel	1		3	1	
Champlin, Oliver	1	1	2		
Slatery, Thomas	1	2	2		
Champlin, Samuel, Junr	1	2	3		
Taylor, Samuel	1	3	2		
Taylor, Jude	1	2	3		
Frasier, Gideon	1	4	4		
Gavis, Joseph	1		4		
Gavis, Sandford	1	2	2		
Gavis, Oliver	1	3	3		
Gavis, Hezekiah	1	2	2		
Lumber, William	1		1		
Ross, John, Junr	2	6	1		
Ross, James	1	1	6		
Gorten (Widow)			3		
Gorten, Joshua	1	1			
Harvey, John			1		
Diskill, William	1	1	6		
Babcock, William	1	2	4		
Clerk, Christopher	1	3	4		
Wilcocks, Valentine	1	3	3		
Wilcocks, John	1	1	4		
Wilcocks, Isaiah (Elder)	4	3	6		
Wilcocks, Nathan	1				
Wilcocks, Prudence			1		
Sisson, Peleg	4		1		
Sisson, Peleg, Junr	1	4	4		
West, Simeon	1	1	2		
Babcock, Joseph	3	8	4		
Pendleton, Simeon	1	3	7		
Babcock, Christopher (Sea Side)	1	5	2		
Barber, Capt Nathan	2	4	6		
Barber, John	1	1	1		
West, Timothy	1	3	1		
Wilbore, Joseph	4	1	7		
Wilbore, John	1	2	6		
Babcock, Nathan	3	4	6		
Babcock, Silas	2	2	1	2	
Babcock, Jerard	1	1	2		
Pendleton, Nathan	2	3	9	2	1
Gavit, Stephen (post road)	1	1	2		
Gavit, George	1	5	3		
Blevin, Nathan	1	3	5		
Blevin, John	2	1	5		
Segars, Christopher	1	1	4		
Brown, James	1	1	1		
Sims, William	1	2	2	3	
Babcock, Jesse	1	1	2		
Babcock, Henry	1	4	2		
Babcock, Isaac	1	1	2		
Babcock, Daniel (in the Wood)	1	2	3		
Babcock (Widow)		1	2		
Sims, Samuel, Junr	1				
Ross, Jesse	1	1	1		
Gavit, Sylvester	1	1	1	1	
Foster, George	1		4		
Babcock, Samuel	1	3	7		
Rathbun, Stephen	1	1	2		
Chester, Christopher	1	2	2		
Lewis, Charles	1				
Lewis, Nathaniel	1	2	3		
Crandal, John	1	3	4		
Allen, Samuel	1	2	5		
Gavit, Oliver	1	3	4		
Crandal, Arnold	1	1	6		
Ray, Thomas (Indian)				5	
Ward, Cudgo				4	
Bent, Prince				3	
Hedan, Mary (Indian)				6	
Wilcox, Volentine	3		1		
Wilcox, John	1	1	4		
Hardy, William	1	3	4		
Thomson, William	1	2	10		
West, John	1	1	5		
Quash, Mary				4	
McCurdy, James	1	2	4		
Foster, George (watch Hill)	1	3	4		
Wilcox, Hezekiah	4		2		
Dixon, Trustram	1	3	3		
Wilcox, Peleg	1	4	2		
Hall, Bradick	1	1	2		
Barns, Nathaniel	1	2	4		

WESTERLY TOWN—con.

NAME OF HEAD OF FAMILY.	Free white males of 16 years and upward, including heads of families.	Free white males under 16 years.	Free white females, including heads of families.	All other free persons.	Slaves.
Pendleton, Benjamin	1	5	2		
Burdick, Oliver	1	1	2		
Burdick, Roger	1	1	2		
Nash, Jonathan	1	4	5		
Thompson, Joshua	1	1	2		
Dunbar, Thomas	1		4		
Wilcox, Asa	1	1	4		
West, Arnold	1		1		
Dodge, Joseph	1	3	5		
Wilbore, John	1	2	1		
Hall, Stephen	1		1		
Murphey, Smith	1	3	3		
Hall (Widow)	1	2	12		
Pendleton, Amos	4	6	2		
Pendleton, Benjamin, Junr	1	3	2		
Cheesborough, William	1	4	4		
Saunders, Peleg, 2d	1	3	2		
Pendleton, John	1	4	4		
Ross, Isaac	1	2	5		
Babcock, Johanne (Enterd)					
Wilbore, Joseph, Junr	1	1	1		
Sheffield, James	1	1	4		
Sheffield, William	1	1	2		
Brown, James	1	1	4		
Babcock, Henry	1	4	4		
Lamphere, Elias	1	1	1		
Thomson, Samuel	6	2	3		
Townsend, Robert	1	2	1		
West, William	1	4	3		
Lewis, Jeptha	2	1	2		
Barber, Joseph	1	3	4		
Thompson, Mary (Widow)			3		
Thomson, John	2	4	5		
Crandal, Lewis	2	2	3		
Lewis, Hezekiah	1	6	3		
Kinyon, George, Junr	1				
Kinyon, Arnold	1		5		
Babcock, Anna (Widow)	1	1	5		
Wells, Edward Sheffield	1	1	1		
Chapman, Timothy	1	2	4		
Townsend, Thomas	5	2	2		
Rhodes, James	1	2	1	1	
Lewis, Maxin	2		5		
Lee, Doctor Daniel	1	1	4	1	
Crandal, Christopher	1	3	2		
Crandal, Joseph	1	2	1		
Kinyon, Augustus	1	2	2		
Brown, Samuel	2	4	4		
Clark, Phineas	1	3	5		
Clark, Benjamin	1		2	1	
Rhodes, William	3	4	4	1	
Brand, Walter	1	3			
Brown, Caleb			6		
Clerk, Paul	2		1		
Burrington, Alephales	4	3	1		
Brand, Nathan	1	1	1		
Parks, Asa	1	1	3		
Wells, Henry	2		5		
Champlin, Nathan	2	1	3		
Lewis, Simeon	3	3	1	1	
Lewis, John	2	1	3		
Lewis, William	2	1	3		
Congdon, Joseph	1	1	1	1	
Maxin, Paul	2	3	2		
Lewis, Elias	1	1	2		
Dee, Christopher	1				
Saunders, Luke	1	2	3		
Stillman, George, 2d	1	1	6		
Edwards, Clerk	1	2	3		
Lamphere, Champlin	3	2	3		
Kinyon, George			2		
Chace, Frederick	1		2		
Thomson, Thomas	5	5	2		
Vincent, Docter	1	1	5		
Chapman, Matthew	1	1	2		
Burdick, John	1	2	5		
Clerk, Benjamin	1		2	1	
Babcock, William, Junr	2	5	2		
Brown, Capt David	1				
Vincent, Joshua	1	1	3		
Clerk, Capt. Samuel	2	5	4		
Berry, Samuel	2	2	7		
Brand, Samuel	1	5	2		
Babcock, William, 2d	1	5	2		
Babcock, William	1	1	2		
Babcock, John	2				
Hall, David	1	2	3		
Saunders, Joshua	3	3	4		
Clark, Joshua	1	4	2		
Crum, Sylvester	1		2		
Crandal, Elias	1	3	8		
Crum, Joseph	1	4	6		
Stillman, Clerk	1		3		

WESTERLY TOWN—con.

NAME OF HEAD OF FAMILY.	Free white males of 16 years and upward, including heads of families.	Free white males under 16 years.	Free white females, including heads of families.	All other free persons.	Slaves.
Wilbore, David	1	4	4		
Pendleton, Samuel	1	2	4		
Davis, Joseph	1	1	3		
Edwards, Thomas	1	4	4		
Bromly, Elizabeth (Widow)	1		1		
Lamphere, Daniel	1	2	4		
Lamphere, David	1	4	4		
Lamphere, Daniel, Junr	1	3	4		
Clark, Elisha	1	2	3		
Pendleton, Joseph	1	2	8		
Pendleton, Simeon	1	4	2		
Pendleton, James	2	1	6		
Crum, William	1		2		
West, Robert	1	1	2		
Champlin, Asa	1	3			
Stillman, George, 1st	1	5	6		
Stillman, John	2		9		
Stillman, Joseph (Deacon)	2	6	6		
Crum, Simeon	1	1	5		
Crandal, Joseph, Senr	1		1		
Cottrell, John	1	1	4		
Burdick, Arnold	1	1	4		
Potter, George	1		4		
Potter, George, Junr	2	3	3		
Barber, Amos	1	1	2		
Potter, Joseph	3	3	1		
Maxin, Martha (Widow)	1	1	2		
Maxin, Amos	1		2		
Cottrell, Daniel	1				
Saunders, Peleg	1	3	4		
Chambers, William	1		1		
Maxin, Asa	1	2	4		
Maxin (Widow)	1		2		
Hitchcock, Nathan	1	2	4		
Hitchcock, Epharim	1	1	2		
Stillman, Nathan	1	3	2		
Lamphere, Abraham	1	1	5		
Lamphere, Nathan	1	3	4		
Lamphere, Nathan, Junr	1	5	4		
Hiscox, Epharim	1		2		
Thayer, Capt. David	1				
Gavit, Isaiah	1	1	6		
Hiscox, Elizabeth (widow)		1	2		
Burdick, Kinyon			2		
Chapman, Sumner	2	5	2	1	
Clark, William	2	2	7		
Cottrell, Elias	1	3	4		
Chapman, William	1		1	1	
Chapman, William, Junr	1	4	2		
Clark, Nicholas	1	5	2		
Chapman, Plum	2	1	3		
Crandal, Paul	1	3	2		
Crandal, John	1	5	2		
Davis, Sarah (Widow)	1		5		
Hiscox, Epharim, Junr	1	4	4		
Pendleton, Major Joseph	2	1	7	3	
Minor, Phenias	2				
Voss, Joshua	1	2			
Tift, John	1	5	5		
Babcock, Elkana	1	5	7		
Gavit, Stephen	1	3			
White, James	1	3	1		
Berry, Peleg	1	5	3		
Davis, Johnson	1	2	2		
Allen, John	1				
Babcock, Sylvia (Widow)	1	4	1		
Love, Roswell	1		1		
Burdick, Maxin	1	1	2		
Chace, Frederick	3	1	2		
Lewis, Oliver	1	2	2		
Chester, Christopher	1				
Gavit, Ezekiel	1		1		
Gavit, Ezekiel, Junr	1	1	8		
Gavit, George	1	1	3		
Larkin, Abel	1	4	3		
Babcock, Daniel	2	3	3		
Hitchcock, Thomas	2	1	8		
Thomson, Robert	1	2	4		
Thomson, William	1	3	8		
Sims, Samuel	2	1	4		
Babcock, Rous	2	1	6	2	
Babcock, Amos	1		2		
Babcock, Juda					
Babcock, Joshua					
Burdick, Simeon	1				
Hitchcock, Edward	1	4	4	2	
Berry, Elijah	4	5	5	1	
Stillman, Joseph, Junr	5	3	5		
Clark, Joseph, Esqr	1	4	5	2	1
Swan, John	1		4		
Saunders, David	1	4	5		

[1] No attempt has been made in this publication to correct mistakes in spelling made by the deputy marshals, but the names have been reproduced as they appear upon the census schedules.

O